Still Having Fun

A Portrait of

The Military Marriage of

Rex and Bettie George

1941-2007

Candace George Thompson

PUBLISHED BY WESTVIEW, INC. KINGSTON SPRINGS, TENNESSEE

PUBLISHED BY WESTVIEW, INC.
P.O. Box 605
Kingston Springs, TN 37082
www.publishedbywestview.com

ISBN 978-1-937763-62-6

First edition, August 2012

Printed in the United States of America on acid free paper.

Still Having Fun

Prologue

Rex and Bettie George, my parents, pursued their life adventure with energy and enthusiasm. The path wasn't always smooth. Along the way their marriage was tested by the death of a child, a murder, a family suicide, a betrayal of trust and several personal and family health crises. They chose to approach adversity as a challenge. They would learn what they could from it and move on.

They found joy in the simplest pleasures – conversations, a ride to the beach, poker for pennies, making new friends. Their love and faith were a constant source of strength to each other, and an inspiration for those who had the good fortune to know them.

Rex enlisted in the Army Air Corps a little over a year after he and Bettie married. His first mission in World War II was as a B-24 navigator on D-Day, June 6, 1944. He stayed in the Air Force for 30 years, retiring as a Lt. Colonel.

My father was a neat, precise, deliberate man who could fix just about anything. He had a talent for making friends and for helping people in need. He offered good counsel to many and mentored friends and family. He was especially successful with young people.

Bettie was blessed with a perpetually cheerful outlook, intellect and a great sense of humor. She followed Rex from post to post and endured many periods of separation during his Air Force career. She was known for her wit, her poetry repertoire, her prolific correspondence, hostess skills and her incredible bent for winning contests and sweepstakes. Mother decided to go to college in her mid-30s. She graduated with honors four years later.

Even after Rex retired they continued to travel. Some years later, Alzheimer's disease began to steal Bettie's independence and Rex became her sole caretaker. He shopped, cooked, cleaned and did the laundry. He dressed her, fixed her hair and applied her make-up. When concerned family and friends asked how he was holding up, Rex's answer was always, "We're still having fun."

Rex and Bettie were known by family and close friends as Fath and Moth (Moth pronounced as in "mother.") and collectively were referred to as "the Pares." They amassed a collection of interesting, often humorous stories. Their adventures and recollections inspired and were an unending source of entertainment for friends and family. It is my hope that their story will entertain, educate and inspire readers to live life as they did - to the fullest.

Part One:
The Early Years, 1941 – 1946

Chapter 1

A Wink to Build a Dream On

"Don't you think those details should be private?" my father said with mock modesty as he eyed my tape recorder. It was the eve of my parents' sixty-second anniversary and I had just asked him about their courtship.

"In high school your mother and I dated each other when it was convenient, for a dance or an event. And I had been attending Easter service with her and sending Easter corsages since 1939.

"Bettie always dated other people until we committed to each other. In fact, she dated as many as three boys at a time - that I'm aware of." He raised his eyebrows at Mother across the dinner table; she smiled demurely.

"We continued dating occasionally after I graduated. Our dates were almost always on Sundays. I would pick her up from church and we would go to the park or a movie. At some point later in the afternoon I would learn that she had another date and needed to be home by 5:00 to get ready for another guy at 6:00."

"That didn't bother you?" I asked.

"Well," he shrugged, "that's the way it was. I took her home and there would be Mrs. Gibson and Ralph or Roy waiting on the porch. Bettie would disappear into the house to change clothes. I would sit down and talk with Mrs. Gibson and Ralph or Roy. Bettie would come back out and take off with her next date. If I wanted a Sunday evening date, I had to make that very clear; she wasn't going to waste an hour of her Sunday dating time.

"Yes," he chuckled, shooting a sly glance at Mother, "You were a hot number, Bettie."

"Moth," as we called her (short for Mother and pronounced the same way), may have been a hot number, but she wasn't easy to get. According to Fath, "Her modus operandi to keep the guys from bothering her, was to talk non-stop. She was always reciting poetry or singing. You couldn't kiss her because she was constantly talking.

"One cold winter night," he recalled, "I made her stop talking because my car – a '36 green Olds I'd bought jointly with my dad - didn't have a heater, the defroster was ineffective and the windshield was frosting over."

"Well," I mused, "you must have had something going for you."

"Mrs. Gibson liked me," he explained, as his chest puffed and he sat straighter in his chair, "and I had a good job at the Great Atlantic and Pacific Tea Company. I had been transferred from a smaller A & P store in Louisville to New Albany, Indiana to help open a new "super" market, with four checkout lanes and a big parking lot. Most stores didn't have their own lots back then.

"Anyway," he went on, "I had been so busy with the new store that I hadn't seen Bettie for some time. Rumor had it she was waiting tables at the coffee shop in the Clark Hotel in Jeffersonville. I knew the new A&P would have better paying jobs and thought Bettie, with her energetic personality, would be a good candidate, so I drove by the coffee shop to tell her. She met with the store manager the next day and he hired her on the spot.

"She started working at the bakery counter and in about three weeks was promoted from bakery to the dairy department. She didn't know anything about different types of cheese," Fath recalled. "Everybody in the store helped teach her. 'This tastes like…, this tastes sharp, this is soft, mellow.' In a matter of hours she knew more about cheese than anybody in the store.

"I was in charge of ordering merchandise and stocking the shelves. I would start stocking at the opposite side of the store, working my way around to the coffee section where I could watch Bettie. One day she caught me sneaking a glance at her and gave me a flirtatious wink.

"Bettie would wink at me," he grinned as he remembered. "I'm putting up Maxwell House Coffee and she'd wink at me. I couldn't wink back. I didn't know how to wink. Well, she taught me how to wink right there. Little by little I learned and things started to heat up.

"Bettie was engaged to Ralph at the time," Fath revealed. "Ralph had tickets for a Valentine dance but couldn't go. He asked me if I'd be willing to take Bettie to the dance. I tried not to sound too eager when I agreed to his plan.

"On the day prior to the dance, Ralph broke off his other commitment, so he proposed to pick up Bettie and me and drive us to the dance. He promised he'd stay out of our way. Well, Ralph never had a chance or a dance with Bettie that night. I had them all," Fath crowed. "We completely ignored him. On her next date with Ralph, Bettie gave him his ring back."

"Hmmm," I broke in, "the story I remember Moth telling had a bit more drama. I recall her saying she threw the ring out the window of Ralph's car."

"Well, at any rate," he replied, ignoring my interruption, "Ralph was devastated for weeks, but it was for the best. I always thought Ralph drank way too much.

"About Easter of the same year – this would be 1941 - Bettie and I were getting pretty close but neither of us had made a commitment. We had a Saturday night and all day Sunday date to go to the Easter Sunrise service in a big amphitheater at Cherokee Park in Louisville.

"Easter morning dawned cold and we got our shoes good and wet in the dew. During the course of the day, I asked Bettie to marry me.

"When I went home and told Mom I had something to tell her, she said, 'You and Bettie are getting married' before I could say more. Bettie wrote our news to her mother who had moved back to Covington, Kentucky when she and Bettie's father separated."

"About when did they separate?" I asked.

"I don't know exactly. I had only met him once – on Valentine Day. Probably would have been '39. I think Bettie was a junior in high school.

"After her family moved away," he continued, "she lived at Jean Weber's house, sharing a bed with Jean. Upon hearing our news, Jean's mother told Bettie, 'You'll never feather your nest with Rex.' I lost some respect for Mrs. Weber about that.

"Well, I proposed on Easter and we married in June. We consulted the pastor of Bettie's Lutheran Church, Reverend W. Franklin Lahr, telling him we wanted to marry as soon as possible but that we had almost no money. Everything I owned you could have put in your pocket almost. The pastor suggested a Sunday because flowers would already be in the sanctuary and the organist could stay after the service and play for us.

"We sat down and looked at a calendar. It was then I realized my birthday was on a Sunday that year, so we chose June 8, 1941. I had to take my parents with me when we went for our marriage license because boys had to be 21 to be able to marry on their own; I wasn't quite 20. Girls only had to be 18, so Bettie didn't need her parents' permission."

At twelve o'clock noon on a Sunday in June, Bettie Jane Gibson and Rex Hall George got married. It was a hot, river-valley humid day. Inside St. Luke's Lutheran Church the air was cool and the organist played softly.

The Jeffersonville newspaper reported that the bride wore a navy blue marquisette street-length dress, a wide-brimmed navy straw hat and a corsage of red rosebuds. Rex looked dapper in a new blue Easter suit and brown and white cap-toe leather shoes. Their attendants were Jean Weber, dressed in pink crepe, with a corsage of pink rosebuds, and Robert McCormick, one of Rex's childhood friends.

"After the ceremony," Fath recalled, "we rode around town for a few minutes in a car borrowed from a friend's mortuary before we went to our reception at the Weber house. Mrs. Weber served ice cream, lemonade and a homemade cake decorated with a celluloid bride and groom.

"A friend took a snapshot of us standing on Jean's front porch looking into each other's eyes, me with my arm around Moth's waist, looking very eager; she looks a bit mischievous."

A friend took a snapshot.

The happy honeymooners headed for Nashville in a rented car, Mother wearing the $49 ring set for which Fath was making $1/week payments.

"We spent our first night at Wigwam Village in a concrete, teepee-shaped cabin near Mammoth Cave in Kentucky," Fath continued. "The main building was also a big teepee with a small restaurant. That night I was still excited and not hungry so I had chicken noodle soup. I was sick all night.

Honeymoon, first night at WigWam Village.

"The next morning we had planned to visit Mammoth Cave, but left for Nashville instead. We didn't have any reservations and stopped at the first tourist court inside the city limits. We had our wedding dinner at the Blue Boar Cafeteria. Had to park a block away and got caught in the rain on the way to the restaurant. Bettie's big blue straw hat was ruined."

"We mailed a postcard to ourselves; I wrote, 'Hello you nice people. We're down here in the deep, deep South and having a swell time. Wish you were here. See you soon, Rex & Bettie.'

Day two, on the road to Nashville.

We had about used up our time and decided to head back to Mammoth Cave," Fath recalled. "We counted our money and realized we didn't have enough to pay for the car and the cave. We drove right on by it.

"I took Bettie to the little apartment where she'd been living, returned the car to Louisville where I had rented it, and rode the streetcar back. I had to work the next day. I had empty pockets with a week to go 'til I got paid. I borrowed ten dollars from Dad and paid him back on payday.

"That was the last time I ever borrowed money from my parents," Fath proclaimed.

"I remember Moth telling stories about her tiny apartment," I prompted.

"Bettie's apartment, which I moved into, was too small to really be called an apartment. Although the United States wasn't in the war yet, Southern Indiana had dozens of factories making munitions, powder, and shell casings. Draftees were drilling using broomsticks for guns. All this activity had created an instant need for accommodations.

"Mom had rented out the bedroom my brother Max and I used; I'd been sleeping on the couch. Mrs. Weber rented Jean's room where Bettie had stayed. Jean ended up sleeping on a day bed and Bettie moved to the tiny apartment."

"How tiny was it?" I teased.

"Her place at the Getz Apartments in New Albany was one third of a room in a big old home that had been divided to take advantage of the boom in the local economy. Her teeny closet had one end of the fireplace mantel in it. The ceilings were about the height of two men. Soot build-up from coal-burning heat blackened the papered walls. The walls were customarily cleaned once a year, but only as high as a person could reach, leaving the top half and the ceiling dark with soot.

"The apartment was furnished with a three-quarter bed, a broken-down bamboo loveseat and a little table. There was a small wooden ice box. The kitchen was a little closet with no door. In it were a very small wash basin, a two-burner gas flame, a Coleman baker to put on top of the burner for baking and a fold-up cardboard cupboard. The shared bathroom with toilet and tub was down the hall."

"Do you remember what Moth paid for it?"

"Indeed I do. Five dollars a week, and they didn't raise it when I moved in. After two months we moved to the adjacent apartment which was larger and had a real kitchen. That cost us $8/week."

One of the treasures I found as I explored the contents of the boxes I shipped from my parents' home after their deaths was a LIFE magazine they'd picked up for 10 cents while on their honeymoon. It described the government's increasing concerns about the war in Europe and the measures that were already being taken in the United States to deal with shortages and defense preparation.

Thirteen days before their wedding, President Roosevelt addressed representatives of Canada and South American countries. The radio audience - an estimated 85,000 people – was the largest ever.

Under the headline "President Commits U.S. to Far-Ranging Action in National Emergency", LIFE quoted Roosevelt, "The immediate issue ... is whether, in the present crisis, Americans shall act with whole-souled vigor and conviction or whether they shall continue to be plagued by what Hitler has named as his weapons - 'mental confusion, contradiction of feeling, indecisiveness, and panic.'"

Roosevelt ended his speech by proclaiming "a state of unlimited national emergency."

Another LIFE article reported that the German press, "with a scorn that was almost too insistent, has dismissed America as 'an automobile, radio, jazz-band, 5-&-10-cent-store civilization.'"

In England, 37% of the civilian food supply had been diverted to defense operations. The British food minister appealed to Americans to cut their own consumption in order to send more supplies to Britain.

In the U.S. there were gas shortages on the east coast. On May 28 Roosevelt announced that the country's steel shortage was 1,400,000 tons, and was anticipated to be 6,400,000 tons by

1942. On May 30, 1941 the government launched experimental campaigns to collect old aluminum to build bombers.

Other articles in LIFE ranged from a report of Nazi airborne troops conquering Crete to stories about the Joe Louis/Buddy Baer fight, advice from Gene Krupa on how to play drums, and a piece about Bushman, the Chicago Lincoln Park Zoo's gorilla celebrating his 14th birthday.

Ads touting new products were plentiful: "Cellophane – the best wrap for keeping cigarettes fresh!" "The new Bendix fully automatic washer – rinses your clothes three times!"

Studebaker prices started at $695 for a Champion Business Coupe. A cartoon drawing by Dr. Seuss, Theodore Seuss Geisel, advertised FLIT insecticide bomb."

Pan American Airways' full-page color spread boasted "13 years of over-ocean flying … we fly to 55 countries with a 98.62% on-schedule record." A flight from California to Hong Kong "only takes seven days – eleven days faster than by boat."

This was the world in which Rex and Bettie began their marriage. Little did they know how much their lives would change in just a few short months.

Chapter 2

Childhood

Bettie Jane Gibson was born in 1923 in Covington, Kentucky of Howard Daniel Gibson, a sometimes meat cutter, and Lona Rosemary Belleman Gibson. Bettie's five-foot, fair-skinned, blond mother graduated from junior high school and attended Curtis Business School in Covington. She worked at Kroger's Grocery until World War One when her family moved to Dayton, Ohio. There the teen-aged Lona worked at the Wright Airplane Company where she sewed fabric on airplane wings.

As her daughter would do some 20 years later, Lona fell in love in a grocery store when she came back from Dayton and returned to work at Kroger's. There she met tall, dark-haired, handsome Howard. She said she was weighing lard during the Christmas season when Howard kissed her under the mistletoe.

Howard, wasting no time in his pursuit of Lona, brought her home to meet his parents that very night. He soon discouraged another suitor by chasing him down the street while brandishing a butcher knife. Howard and Lona married 6 months later.

(During a 1980 visit to Chicago – a year before she died – Grandma Lona told me she believed she had no choice but to marry Howard. He had raped her, she confided, and she feared she would become pregnant.)

My mother was the second of Lona and Howard's six children and the only girl. Young Bettie looked forward to spending time in the peaceful home of her maternal grandparents where she didn't have to keep watch on her younger brothers. During summer visits, her grandmother Cecilia Belleman made her new dresses for the next school year.

Howard James (Jimmy) Gibson, Bettie's older brother and Bettie Jane Gibson
@1924-1925

Bettie loved to listen to her Grandfather Herbert read and recite poetry. His animated declamations launched Bettie's lifelong passion for anything that rhymed. One of his favorite poems was the humorous "I Had But Fifty Cents." In short order Bettie had memorized all 52 lines.

Bettie was also interested in geography. She devoured books about other countries, dreaming of a world beyond the sooty Ohio River Valley.

Her hot-tempered father Howard had a hard time keeping a job, necessitating frequent moves around Ohio, Kentucky and Indiana. He worked as a meat cutter, a manager at a grocery and as an automobile tire salesman.

Bettie was the first and only one in her family to graduate from high school. At Jeffersonville High Bettie joined the broadcasting and dramatics clubs and performed in a three-act comedy. She also won a county-wide patriotic essay and oratory contest.

According to the Jeffersonville newspaper, the purpose of the contest was to "create interest in and respect for the basic principles of our form of government. All orations will have as a basic theme the Constitution of the United States." In addition to a ten minute prepared speech, each contestant had to deliver a five minute extemporaneous address on some phase of the Bill of Rights without notes or reference books. (The article, titled "Betty Gibson Advances in Oratory Test," spelled her first name wrong, as would happen frequently throughout her life.)

Rex Hall George, Bettie's future husband, was born in 1921 in Calloway County, Kentucky. He was the oldest of three children. Rex's mother, Susan Edith Workman, was an elegant, proper woman who always wore gloves and a hat when she went to town. She tended a kitchen garden and was known to feed an out-of-work neighborhood black man on the back stoop during the depression.

Known as Edith, she was an only child. Her mother died when Edith was two. Four years later her father was killed playing sandlot baseball when an errant ball hit him in the temple. Edith, now a six-year-old orphan, was raised by her maternal grandparents, John and Susie Stewart.

Rex's father, Hall George, was the second of ten children of a Kentucky tobacco farmer. Hall's stories about flying in World War One inspired Rex's fascination with airplanes and photography. Hall was a gunner and aerial photographer in the 248th Aero Squadron of the U.S. Army Signal Corps. On one flight over France, his plane crashed in the countryside, killing the pilot. A French farmer found Hall, with a pierced lung, lying unconscious against a stone fence.

Rex was five when his father took him to an air show in Louisville where he first saw an airplane and a blimp. The blimp dropped Baby Ruth candy bars, each floating down from the sky on a tiny parachute. His father caught several for Rex who spent hours playing with the chutes.

Rex liked playing with Lincoln Logs and erector sets. "Dad was a machinist employed in an iron works company," Fath told me. "He brought home floor sweepings, out of which I salvaged bolts, the most desired parts of erector sets. Dad also came home with his pockets full of defective ball bearings that kept me supplied with ammo for my BB gun."

Rex was equally enamored of reading and won a spelling bee in second grade. "I was better by far than all the rest," he bragged. "My prize was a book, 'Brownies in the Coal Bin,' the second book I ever owned. As I got older I read every book I could find about flying."

1923 George family, Edith & Hall George, Max on left, Rex @ 3 yrs old.

When the 1932 World War One Veterans' March on Washington finally brought the long-awaited war bonus, Rex's father used the money to open his own shop. George's Appliance Store carried Zenith radios, Kelvinator refrigerators, washers and ironers. His first sale was a radio for $175.

"I took a radio class at the YMCA," Fath told me. "I would buy Zenith Arial kits from Dad for $25, charge $50 to install the antennas on the roofs of customers' homes, then I'd split the $25 profit with Dad."

Young Rex liked being self-sufficient. He claimed he "invented" apple sauce pie at age 15. "My pie crust was so good that from then on I was the family's pie crust maker. I taught myself to sew and embroider, too, and once I altered a new pair of trousers to wear on a date with Bettie."

One of Rex's most vivid memories of his teenage years was the 1937 Ohio River Flood[1] when he was almost sixteen. Residents of Jeffersonville and Clarksville were evacuated by train to points farther north where they stayed for about a week. Always looking for opportunities to earn money, Rex got a job with Western Union delivering back-logged telegrams after the flood waters subsided.

As a young teenager Rex dreamed of becoming a physician or a pilot, but by the time he and Bettie married, the A&P job looked pretty good.

Chapter 3

Newly Wed

After they married, Rex and Bettie's combined income from their jobs at A&P was $45 a week. They anticipated Fath would become a store manager for the rapidly expanding grocery chain within a couple years. Mother, the budgeter, started saving for a larger apartment.

Within days after the Japanese attack on Pearl Harbor on December 11, 1941, Moth learned she was pregnant. Shortly afterward, Fath found higher paying work as a lab technician at a BF Goodrich plant in Louisville, Kentucky, that was gearing up for war production. They moved across the Ohio River and Moth parlayed her grocery store experience into a cashier position at Stewart Dry Goods.

Stewart's used a pneumatic tube system to transport cash and receipts to and from various departments to a centrally located cashier office on a higher floor. Like magic, bronze cylindrical containers were sucked into a tube and whisked between sales clerks and the centralized cashiers. The cash carrier system allowed pregnant Bettie to work seated, but she missed face-to-face contact with customers.

The newly-weds bought solid maple furniture at Huff Furniture Company – dining table, four chairs, bed, vanity, chest of drawers, bench, and a Spring Air mattress and springs. The total cost was $163.58. They paid $25 cash up front and made monthly payments for the next three years. They still owned several of these pieces when they died in 2007.

Bettie and Rex looked forward to becoming parents and spent many evenings discussing their upcoming roles. On Valentine Day 1942, Moth gave Fath a card mentioning his soon-to-be "Daddy" status. For his 21ˢᵗ birthday in June she gave him a homemade card from herself and their unborn child. Moth hoped their child would never hear the yelling and screaming she'd grown up with. Never disagreeing in front of their children topped Fath's list.

By the time Moth was ready to deliver, they had spent hours talking about how they would raise their child. They were ready to be parents. On July 31, 1942 at 3:40 AM, their first daughter, Susan Cecilia, was stillborn at St. Edward's Hospital in Jeffersonville.

Before sunrise that morning the doctor advised Fath not to allow Moth to see the infant. Susan was buried at Walnut Ridge Cemetery in a little $17 casket the very same day while Moth was still hospitalized.[1]

Mother mourned their loss and grieved for never having held her daughter. She clipped a poem from the newspaper about a baby boy who had died in infancy, hand-copied it - changing the pronouns from "he" to "she" - memorized it and kept it in her Bible for the rest of her life.

Now childless, 21-year-old Rex's draft status changed. He learned he would be conscripted into the Army within weeks. Fortunately, the Army Air Corps had changed its enlistment requirements shortly after the attack on Pearl Harbor. Enlistees no longer had to be single, nor did they need two years of college as previously required. Just days after Susan's burial, Fath presented himself at his local draft board to volunteer for the Army Air Corps.

His high school education with courses in Algebra and Trigonometry, World History and French, along with his electrical experience and work on Boy Scout merit badges in aviation, electricity, radio and marksmanship served him well. He passed the written qualifying exam easily. On September 1, 1942, he was officially enrolled in the Air Cadet program although he wasn't called to active duty until January, 1943.

Fath's timing couldn't have been better. After January 1943, men could no longer enlist nor choose their branch of service; they had to wait until they were drafted.[2]

In January – about the same time Army Air Corps bombers made their first raid against Germany - Fath left for basic training. Bettie moved in with her mother and three younger brothers in Covington. Fath wrote his first letters to her from a troop train bound for Texas.

1-28-43, En Route to Columbus, Ohio

Dearest Bettie,

I love you, dear. It's 1 o'clock now & I get in to Columbus at 2:10 A.M. Miss you terribly. The train is so rough I can hardly write. I've tried sleeping and it won't work. This coach is full of soldiers on furlough. Most of them are from Penn. & N.Y.

I hope you are feeling OK, Honey. Is Mother [Bettie's] working yet or is she still home? I hope she's at home so you won't be quite as lonesome.

Bettie, I can't begin to tell you how much I love you - not by writing. Just ask your heart how much and you'll know. We'll be together again before you know it.

This is the first letter I have ever written to my wife. Did you know that? By the way if you see Bettie tell her I'm with her always in my heart. When I get to the hotel I'll look at your picture and realize what a wonderful girl I married.

The train's getting the best of me, dear. I'll quit now and try sleeping again. They just turned the lights out. Good nite Bettie. I love you, Rex

1-29-43, Fort Hayes [near Columbus]

Dearest Bettie, I love you.

We're about to start to move. This morning at 6:15 we got up and marched to the Fort. Had roll call and parked our bags in Barracks 6, Company C. Before daylite we had breakfast. Pancakes (12" in diameter with brown sugar syrup), cornflakes & milk, grapefruit, coffee. After breakfast we were free till 10 o'clock, when we went to the recreation hall and saw a U.S.O. show. From there we went to mess. For dinner[3] we had fish, potatoes (boiled in jackets), green beans, slaw, whole wheat rolls, coffee, ice cream & cookies.

After dinner we were told to be ready to move about 3:30 P.M. It's about 12:15 now. I love you, Bettie, and soon we'll be down in Texas together. Don't forget to write every day. Send me all the letters after I get an address.

I hope you enjoy your vacation a whole lot. Go out with your girl friends but no men are allowed. (You know what I mean.)

See that you don't work too hard, honey. I don't want you to hurt yourself.

All the fellows here are writing letters now. They are all a pretty nice bunch. I think I'll like it fine after I get placed permanently.

Well, dear, I had better get washed and shaved now because it will be rather hard to shave on the train. I'll probably look like the old man of the mountain when I get to Texas.

I love you, dear, keep your chin up and a smile on that pretty face of yours. I'm waiting for that hour that I can hold you & kiss you again.

So long for now, dear. I'll be loving you always, Your Rex (Leiutenant Lieutenant) Maybe I should learn how to spell it.

1-30-43, En Route Texas; Railroad Yards, St. Louis

Dearest Bettie, I love you,

Well, dear, here we are in the R.R. yards at St. Louis. We just finished breakfast. At Columbus we had supper and a final roll call about 5:00 P.M. yesterday. At 8:00 we pulled out, 15 cars of us. Ah! These cars are really fine. Vintage 1850 (Ha!) They are old day coaches. Last nite we took the coach apart and made a rough kind of a bed. I got about 5 hours sleep.

Really, Bettie, I've enjoyed every bit of it so far. (Except I miss my little girl.) The food is very good, only we have very little time to eat.

You should see this gang. Whiskers, dirt, mussed clothes and everything. There are no washing accommodations at all. Last nite and this morning we washed our teeth, hands & face at the drinking fountain.

From all indications we should arrive at Sheppard Field about daylite tomorrow morning. We'll be a rough bunch when we crawl out.

I wrote Mom & Ann [Rex's younger sister, age ten] and the lab crew at B.F.Goodrich.

Honey, we are about ready to roll so I'll have to quit for now. Be a good girl and remember to pray each nite and don't forget that I love you. I'll write later. Bye. Always yours, Rex

P.S. I'll be looking for a letter real soon. Bye, Rex XXX

1-31-43, 8:30 PM

Hello, Bettie,

Have you been waiting for this long? I haven't had time to write since yesterday afternoon.

Finally I'm in Texas. We arrived at Sheppard Field about 6:30 this morning. I never saw such a place! New barracks and mess halls as far as one can see in either direction.

For dinner we had chicken & ice cream among other things. Very good food.

I've been separated from the Kentucky fellows I met in Columbus but I'm with a good bunch of guys. Quite a few married too. I was assigned bedding and am in Barracks 610.

No one seems to know how many days or weeks we'll be here. Since last Wednesday 4,500 men have come in. More coming all the time.

Lights out in 10 minutes (9:00). We'll be up tomorrow at 4:30 A.M. Shots & exams all day I guess.

This bed sure feels swell after 2 days in a day coach. I'm going to have to quit in a couple of minutes now, honey. You'll be a good girl for me, won't you? I love you more than I ever realized before. Your picture is here beside me in my bag. I haven't put it out yet.

The lights are out now. I love you dear. Think of me in your prayers. Loads of love, Rex

Chapter 4

Air Cadet and Camp-Follower

Time Magazine, August 30, 1943, "Army and Navy – Wither Thou Goest..."

"No one knows how many women have packed up and moved to be near camps, naval stations or training bases, nor how many are traveling at any one time. No agency has coordinated information on them. But several agencies can testify that the total is very large – such agencies as the Travelers Aid, U.S.O., Red Cross, and Army & Naval Relief organizations. Special war travel gave Travelers Aid 885,000 cases to handle last year [1942]. That was about six times the total for 1941. This year the total climbed to 1,250,000 in the first six months, is still climbing. Agencies come into contact only with women who have run into difficulties in their journeys and need help. They have no estimate of the many thousands who are luckier, or have greater means."

Soon Bettie was one of those million plus women following her man. Living accommodations near Army bases were hard to come by but Mother always managed to find a room and a job.

Her quick smile, gregarious nature and keen interest in learning served her well as she followed her cadet around the country. First stop, Alva, Oklahoma where Rex was in the College Training Program at Northwest State College. Alighting from the train in March, 1943, Bettie met Norma Kepets, an attractive

Jewish girl from Cleveland, also following her recently enlisted husband, Sidney (Sid).

Norma Kepets & Bettie, Alva, OK, 1943.

Moth and Norma decided to pool their resources and went in search of a place to live. The best they could do was a small shared room in the home of an older woman. Moth quickly found a job at a Safeway grocery store.

One day Norma came home and found Moth packing their bags, insisting they move out immediately. In response to Norma's perplexed look, Bettie revealed she'd heard their landlady make anti-Semitic remarks. Moth was open-minded and easy going until her values were violated. The two young women lugged their suitcases out to the sidewalk and started a new search for lodging.

On another occasion in Alva, Moth boarded a crowded bus and sat down in the only available seat – next to a black woman. As she did so, several white men jumped up to offer her a seat. Quietly defiant, she replied, "I'm just fine, thank you," and remained in her seat.[1]

I've often wondered how my parents came to be so open and accepting of people of different races, nationalities and religions. How I regret never asking them. I can only surmise that their beliefs were built from a combination of strong, independent personalities and their religious convictions. They both had a keen sense of fairness and were guided by the Golden Rule.

They always seemed to have a place in their hearts for the outcast and the underdog. Both had inquisitive minds and were curious about people whose backgrounds differed from theirs.

Mother's participation in the American Legion's oratory contest on the U.S. Constitution and Bill of Rights, makes me think that she would have been familiar with the Declaration of Independence also. I have no doubt that she would have believed that "all men are created equal" and would have interpreted "men" to include "women."

Another possible influence on the Pares' values might have been the Ku Klux Klan. This theory is strictly speculation, but the following facts aren't. Starting in 1920, the year before my father was born, the Indiana Ku Klux Klan held considerable power. The Klan was against Roman Catholics, foreign-born, Blacks, Jews and labor unions. They had infiltrated state and local politics and established a foothold in some Protestant churches. By the mid-1920's thirty percent of the state's white males were KKK members and the Klan held a majority in the Indiana state legislature.[2]

The Indiana Klan went into decline in the 1930s after Pulitzer Prize winning articles in the Indianapolis Times exposed KKK scandals and corruption. Considering the omnipresence of the Klan in Indiana, it seems quite possible that, as high school students, Rex and Bettie were well aware of its pervasive influence. Perhaps my parents' progressive, democratic values were, to some extent, a result of their rejection of the KKK.

I would also be willing to bet they heard the 1939 radio broadcast of African-American contralto Marian Anderson singing from the Lincoln Memorial to a crowd of 75,000 on Easter Sunday. Ms. Anderson's concert had shown a spotlight on racial discrimination when she was denied permission by the Daughters of the American Revolution to perform in Constitution Hall. The concert was subsequently championed by the First Lady herself, Eleanor Roosevelt, who sponsored the free Easter recital.

When Rex and Sid finished the College Training Program in Alva, they were sent to San Antonio Aviation Cadet Center for flight classification and pre-flight school. Bettie and Norma followed. They found the housing situation even tighter and ended up sharing not only a room, but a bed. They soon discovered their room had additional occupants – "roaches almost as big as mice," Norma recalled.

One night as they were in the bathroom down the hall preparing for bed, they saw one of the giant roaches spread its wings and fly. Terrified, they both jumped into the bathtub. Moth reached out, grabbed the big flat-iron used as a door stop and dropped it on the roach. From that night on, the roommates always carried the flat-iron when they went into the bathroom.

Moth landed a cashier job at the Base Exchange (BX) where her duties included cashing checks for cadets and selling condoms.

In August of 1943, Fath and Sid were sent to different flying schools for "Primary" training. Moth followed Fath to Curtis Field in Brady, the geographic center of Texas, and Norma accompanied Sid to Chickasha, Oklahoma. Like most of the training sites, the Brady Flight School was civilian owned and operated. Fath and 239 other cadet pilot trainees were assigned to class 44B.

The cadets were told that, although the school's policy was to graduate as many students as possible, "...past experience has shown that a few will fall by the wayside... A cadet who has been eliminated should not feel that he is inferior in any way... A man who cannot sing is not at fault because he has no voice. Each of you has your place and job to do in the war. We are merely trying to place you where you are best suited...

"The policy of the Air Forces is not to spend years teaching a boy to operate a low-powered trainer [aircraft] without mishap, but to rush thousands of combat crews at the throats of our enemies."[3]

Cadets received $75 a month base pay, $1/day for rations and $1/day for their living quarters. The Brady Aviation School charged each cadet $1/day for meals and $1.15/day for their quarters.

Rex put his sewing skills to work, saving money by altering his own uniform and earning a little extra when fellow cadets paid him 50 cents to sew new insignia on their uniforms. With his earnings from sewing he purchased Bettie's first "real" jewelry at the BX – a pair of gold bow-shaped earrings.

It was customary for each training group to publish a class book with photos of all the cadets. These were intended to be sent home to the men's parents. Never shy about expressing her opinion, Bettie wrote notes beside many of the cadets' pictures before she sent the book on to Rex's parents in Jeffersonville.

"Longest legs you ever saw. Looks like a duckling." "Hot pilot. He's a scream when drunk. Otherwise very quiet." "His wife won the title of locker queen." "He plays the piano in the recreation hall and we all sing." "Best friend. Washed out." "Engaged to a nurse. We like him a lot." "Studying for Baptist Ministry." "Swell little fellow." "Married here. We stood up with him and Beth." "Always has a cigar." "Former show producer." "Just a kid who was afraid to fly, but got by." "A born comedian and kind fellow." "First washout. Didn't solo." "Was an actor on Broadway." "He married a Texas girl and wonders if she'll like Nebraska." "Phoney." "A screwball and a wolf." "Proud he's a yankee." "Everyone knows his dad's a Lt. Colonel."

Under Rex's photograph she penned, "My cadet."

Rex, cadet headshot, 1943

Of the 240 cadet pilots training on PT19A aircraft in Class 44B while Rex was there, three cadets died in crashes. One hundred and four men - including Rex – were assigned to other crew positions before completing the pilot program. This reassignment was commonly referred to as "eliminated" or "washed out," although it was often due to "needs of the Service." Rex was moved to navigation school.

Before he shipped out for Navigation School[4] at San Marcos Army Air Field in San Marcos, Texas, Rex bought himself a $20 wedding band at a drug store in Brady.

Bettie followed him to San Marcos, which was rumored to have an even tighter housing situation. On the bus to San Marcos she met some cadets who took her to a local women's college where she managed to talk her way into a basement room.

She lasted two days, sharing her room with a horde of crickets, before she found a motel room in Austin. There she soon came to the attention of the proprietor, a state senator who owned many of the hotels in town. Impressed with her spunk, he told the Postmaster to hire her. Just like that, Bettie had a job.

After four months of navigator training, Rex and the other newly-commissioned officers in his group received their Navigator's Certificates, Navigation Wings and Celestial Navigation Kits. They were congratulated and told, "Your country is facing the greatest crisis any country has faced in the history of civilization. You have chosen to step forward and to protect your country and its ideals. You have shown by your effort here that you are capable of doing so. May every success be with you.[5]"

Bettie, San Antonio, 1943

Rex traveled to Tucson, Arizona for Combat Crew Training School in early April, 1944. Bettie arrived two weeks later on the Saturday night of the annual rodeo, only to learn there was no room at the inn.

She spent the night in a hotel lobby and the next morning went in search of a motel room. Five dollars a night was expensive, but the price included a daily newspaper. For the first time since she had been following Rex, Bettie couldn't find a job and returned to Covington.

Rex's original crew was broken up and he was reassigned to fill a hole in Crew 74 right before they left for Topeka, Kansas where they would test their brand new B-24 Liberator heavy bomber. He had only a few days to get to know a new crew and a new plane.

The crew needed to make a few shakedown flights with their new aircraft before heading overseas. On one of those flights they flew to Montevideo, Minnesota where pilot Leroy (Lee) Connor's fiancée lived.

In his journal, Lee reported, "… even though the cloud ceiling was quite low we managed to get underneath and 'buzzed' the farm. In the process, we flew over a country school and were low enough to cause some concern. All the students came running out of the building to wave and see the plane."

The crew had been told they would be flying this plane on their European Theatre missions, so they decided to name it DO-BUNNY after Connor's fiancée, Doris, whose nickname was Bunny. Lee drew a sketch of a sexy rabbit with a fencing epee on a sheet of stationary from the Officers' Mess, and had the picture painted on the nose of the plane.

Bettie arrived in Topeka the day after the crew did and stayed for the next two weeks until they left for Great Britain.

On April 29, 1944, the crew began their trip to Ireland where they would go through initial European Theatre training. First stop was Grenier Field in Manchester, New Hampshire. Fath, always the detail man, described the landscape, weather, food and facilities in his journal. At Grenier all the navigators received their maps, charts and secret radio information for the next leg of the trip.

Due to "a few bugs" in their aircraft (Lee's journal says, "fuel leaks in the bomb bay ... tanks were replaced."), the crew was held up for a week at Grenier with nothing to do but explore the New England countryside and streams which, Fath wrote, "ran rampant over the rocks and were alive with speckled trout – an outdoor man's paradise."

The men caught "about 14 beauties" which were cooked for them at the Post Exchange restaurant. They fired their new 45 caliber pistols on the practice range. Fath also tried his hand at skeet shooting, pronouncing himself "not too bad a shot." Somewhere, he and a couple other guys came up with plastic flutes and had fun "nearly driving the rest of the post crazy" with their tootling.

They took off for Goose Bay at 0700 AM on May 6, 1944 with 2,200 gallons of gas and loaded with over 63,000 pounds of luggage and freight. After crossing the U.S. border, Lee handed out their secret orders: Crew 74 was to be attached to the Eighth Air Force in Great Britain.

"Soon after crossing the St. Lawrence River," Fath wrote, "we got beyond the range of the radio stations and were flying by metro D.R. [dead reckoning] over a solid overcast. The metro [weather data] turned out to be lousy and I found myself in uncharted Labrador. By working backwards, reading drift with that damned B-5 [drift meter] and doing a lot of sweating, I figured an approximate position and altered course for Goose.

"So far I hadn't told the crew about our predicament, no use worrying them about it. So we came within range of Ford radio at Goose and two minutes after my E.T.A. [estimated time of arrival] was up we sighted the base. I breathed a sigh of relief as the DO-BUNNY and her 10 men settled to the long runway. There's snow piled up all along the runway here.

"We were met by a big car and taken to base operation. My ears are plugged solid now by our quick let-down, so I went to see the Flight Surgeon, Captain Bigler. He opened them and said come back in the morning, Sunday at 0900.

"Goose Bay is a pretty place, very isolated and bleak. Everything must be flown in except for about a month and a half in the late summer when the bay thaws out and a few boats can make their way in.

"Well, Sunday morning my ears were worse and the captain decided I'd be better off in the hospital for a few days. I went down and gave them my master watch and billfold to put in the safe for me and signed in. I had a private room in the ward with quite a few other fellows who got stuck.

"I was afraid they'd send the crew and ship [airplane] on over without me. The hospital is very nice and the nurses swell. I don't think I'd have the nerve of these girls. Only about 15 of them up here with all these men.

"The rest of the crew went to briefing at 3:30 P.M. (So far they didn't know I was in the hospital.) and there they got the news. The next 6 days I spent taking it easy while the rest of the fellows fished through the ice in the bay, bowled and slept. Finally on May 12th I talked my way out and we briefed for the Goose Bay to Meeks Field, Iceland leg."

Reminiscing in a 1991 letter congratulating the Pares on their 50th anniversary, Lee Connor recalled the flight from Goose Bay to Meeks Field at Reykjavik, Iceland:

"Our departure from Goose Bay was made in very inclement weather and the forecast called for poor weather all the way to Meeks Field, with light to severe icing in the clouds. There were no navigation facilities between Goose Bay and Iceland and our briefing stressed the unworthiness of the facility at Meeks.

"The entire flight was in solid clouds with light to moderate icing and presented no opportunity for 'star shots' nor were there any navigational facilities to check our course. All navigation was done by 'dead reckoning' – airspeed, time and distance. As I recall, the flight was in the neighborhood of 8 hours flying time. When the ETA Rex had given me had run out and we let down through the clouds, we were within one minute and one-half mile of Meeks Field. I knew then that I had a real navigator.

"Throughout our missions together Rex did an outstanding job. He kept the crew advised of our approximate location and when the lead crew made a bad bomb drop he could just about pinpoint their error and tell us just how far we missed. Our Crew 74 was a very good crew but we had the 'best damn navigator' in the ETO [European Theatre of Operation]. I'm glad Rex was on my crew and am proud to call him my friend."

The men quickly judged Meeks Field "a desolate place with nothing to entice us to stay there any longer than necessary." Crew 74 departed the next morning, May 14, at 3:45 A.M., arriving at Mailey, Wales at 0930. There they learned the DO-BUNNY would be taken from them.

"We were very disappointed and voiced our displeasure" wrote Lee. "We had cared for the plane as though it was a baby. Checked it and cleaned it with thorough care, since we had been advised it was to be ours to fly our missions. We were all downhearted but our protests were to no avail."[6]

The crew moved on to Ireland where they were given additional instruction on aircraft recognition, ditching procedures, flight control and intelligence.

Chapter 5

D-Day[1] and Distinguished Flying Cross

Crew 74 finally arrived late afternoon June 4, 1944 at Seething Airfield, the war-time home of the 448th Bomb Group[2], 2nd Air Division of the 8th American Air Force. Seething, located in East Anglia, is about nine miles southeast of Norwich, England.

"Just after midnight on June 5 (early AM of June 6)," Fath told me in 2002 on his 81st birthday, "I was awakened and assigned to fill a hole in another crew. My entire crew was split up and used in this way. We got up and went to breakfast."

I was curious: "What did they feed you for breakfast?"

"I don't remember for sure. Probably toast with ground beef and gravy," he recalled. "We called it SOS – not a very nice name – but if you put enough salt and pepper on it, it was good. It always lacked salt."

I smiled a secret smile. Except for the occasional "hell" or "damn," I'd never heard my father swear. I thought that maybe, talking about the war, he would translate SOS for me. No chance. Even though he had heard me say s..t on occasion, he wouldn't say it.

"From the mess," he continued, "we went to the locker area where we suited up in all our gear and headed to the briefing room. We didn't know what our mission was or anything else."

Suiting up was no small matter. Planes were not heated or pressurized. They didn't come close to being airtight, even before the bomb bay and the two large waist gunner "windows" midway down the body of the aircraft were opened. Cold air rushed through the fuselage. Early in the war there were many casualties due to frostbite or hypothermia.

By the time Fath arrived in the ETO, airmen wore woolen long-johns and electrically heated suits they would plug into a charger at their station. On top of those were sheepskin-lined coveralls and a flak vest similar to a knight's suit of mail. A life jacket came next, and finally a parachute.

The flyers also wore electrically heated gloves, a wool cap, a helmet and an oxygen mask. They needed headsets to communicate with crew members over the noise of the engines and the wind roaring through the open plane "In the briefing room," Fath explained, "they called us to attention, then our group commander, Col. Jerry Mason, said we were going to be part of the invasion of Europe that we had all been waiting for - what we now know as D-Day. He went through a few more details and turned it over to the briefing officer.

"We took off and headed out over the English Channel toward the coast of France and when it got light enough to see, we looked down and the sea was filled with boats and ships of all sizes and kinds, all headed for the beach-head at Normandy.

"We went inland perhaps 50-60 miles, broke into squadron formation, made a big right turn and headed west to our target, a choke point in a railroad marshalling yard near Coutances.

"We dropped our bombs and we wiped the whole railroad yard out – and probably some of the town - but, uh, that's what we did… We had no opposition of any sort…. The next day we all flew together as a crew.

"That was the gist of it," he wrapped up. "I had no idea how many people were involved or when the landing actually started. We didn't find out those things till we got news over the radio and read Stars & Stripes later that day.

"Our mission, like most missions of the heavies [large bombers] was to knock out all railroads, bridges, all communication and travel connections we could identify, and any large defense establishments – and there were a lot of them. We flew as often as the law and the weather allowed."

Not long after D-Day, Fath learned that Mother was pregnant, due to deliver in January, 1945. Back on the home front, Norma and Sid Kepets visited Moth while Sid was at a transition flight base near Louisville prior to going overseas to Burma. Norma reported she was the first person to hug me, snug in Mother's womb.[3]

Now that I had my father talking about the War – the first time I had ever heard him do so, I wasn't about to let him off with just D-Day. "What was your most memorable mission?" I asked.

He hesitated only a moment. "That would probably be July 29, 1944. It was over Germany near Bremen - the nearest we came to going down. The target was a heavily defended oil storage center. We were hit with three bursts of flak just before we dropped our bombs. We lost control of everything. The aileron cable was severed. The plane dropped about 6,000 feet. We couldn't get air speed to catch up with the formation or climb back up to them.

"Our crew of ten had talked months before," he recalled, "and had agreed, by unanimous vote, that if it was doubtful we could make it back to base, we would attempt to crash land or bail out over land, rather than risk certain death if we were forced to ditch in the frigid North Sea.

"I salvoed the bombs. I hit two switches and dropped them all. I have no idea what they hit. I didn't care. I couldn't see the ground.

"There was no good reason to think we could get back. We didn't have navigation; we didn't know if we had lost fuel. We were not air-worthy. I already had my parachute ready to go.

"Almost all at the same time, I heard the rest of the men say, 'Let's go home.'"

[At this point in his taped narration, Fath began to sob. I stopped the tape until he had composed himself.]

"With that", he continued, "I settled down. I couldn't talk to the rest of the crew because the communication system was down. I was standing on the ammo can with one foot on either side and a hand on the astrodome for celestial observation.

"I could reach the pilot and co-pilot's feet with a yardstick to get their attention. I pointed to communicate direction and give them a change of course.

"We headed for what I thought was the closest way to the nearest ocean. I was just guessing. None of the four compasses were pointing in the same direction. England was some 300 miles away across the North Sea. The plane was listing to one side.

"When we got back to base we bailed out all but three of the crew and managed to make it to Woodbridge, an auxiliary field with a long, wide runway where we somehow made a safe landing. One of our guys counted over 200 holes in the plane.

"And for that I was awarded the Distinguished Flying Cross."[4] [He got choked up again.]

I doubt Fath had ever talked about his war experience in such detail as he did that day. I don't believe Moth had ever heard him describe his most harrowing missions. My brother Christopher recalls being eleven, caught rummaging in a footlocker where Fath stored his WW II memorabilia. Chris expected to get into trouble, but remembers that Fath took the opportunity to talk about some of his war experiences.

"He made it seem sort of matter-of-fact," Chris said at our parents' memorial service. "He was doing his job, and it was difficult being separated from Mother when Candy was born. He did tell me about one mission where the plane was damaged and difficult to navigate, but he didn't make it seem heroic. The medal - the Distinguished Flying Cross - stayed in the footlocker for the rest of his life."

This is the citation:

"29 September 1944, Award of Distinguished Flying Cross to Rex H. George, 1st Lt, 448th Bombardment Group. Citation: For extraordinary achievement, while serving as Navigator of a B-24 airplane on many bombardment missions over enemy occupied Continental Europe. Displaying superior navigational ability, this Officer has materially aided in the successful completion of each of those missions. The courage, coolness and exceptional skill displayed by this Officer on all these occasions reflect the highest credit upon himself and the Armed Forces of the United States."[5]

Chapter 6

Rex Writes Home

Rex writes home,
Seething Air Base, UK,
summer 1944

In the following letters Fath refers to "infantile paralysis" and "polio." In the United States the polio "season" was summer and early fall when the weather was warmer. Because the virus is highly contagious, parents kept their children out of public swimming pools and other places where they might ingest contaminated food or water. Pregnancy is one of several factors that increase susceptibility to infection.[1]

Only a week after the trauma of the Bremen flight, Fath wrote a light, chatty letter to his sister Annetta, about to turn twelve.

Saturday Night, August 5, 1944

Dear Ann,

How are you tonight, Sis? Do you still have to stay home because of the infantile paralysis? Thanks a lot for writing me. How about some more? I didn't answer right away because I've been pretty busy.

In this letter you'll find a card with seven English coins on it. I've marked them all so you'll know how much they're worth. Leave them on the card so you won't lose them. They're not worth anything in the U.S., so you can't spend them.

How's the canary? And what about Cynthia [the cat]? What did you do with all the kittens? Did you keep any of them? You should see all of our pets here. Just outside my barracks there's a bee hive full of pet bees. Next door are two little cocker spaniel pups, also one of the boys bought a baby parrot and a monkey in London last week.

Are you still taking music lessons, Sis? How about getting the music for "I'll Walk Alone" and learn it so you can play it for me when I come home. I'm going to be there real soon, I hope, 'cause I've finished 23 of my 30 missions already.

Now I'd better write Dad and Mom a letter. They'll wonder what's happened to me if I don't. Be good and wait for me 'cause I'm practically there now. Save a big kiss for me too. Good night now, Ann. Remember all of us in your prayers. God bless you always. Love & Kisses, Rex

On August 10, due to the trauma of the Bremen mission, Rex and the rest of the crew were assigned a week of rest and relaxation (R & R) at Roke Manor in the village of Ramsey in Hants.

Rex wrote to his mother about a month after the Bremen flight. In his letter he mentions Bettie's next younger brother Mickey who had enlisted in the army in February, 1942. Mick was wounded in Germany in 1943. He met Mary Cooper, a nurse in the Women's Royal Naval Service (WRENS) while he was hospitalized in England. They married before he was shipped home to the U.S.

Mary gave birth to their daughter, Rosemary Ann Gibson, about 5 weeks after D-Day. Fath got a three-day pass and, in uniform and posing as the father, he was allowed onto the maternity ward to visit Mary. He continued to visit these new family members as often as he could, often bringing them scarce food and other "luxury" items.

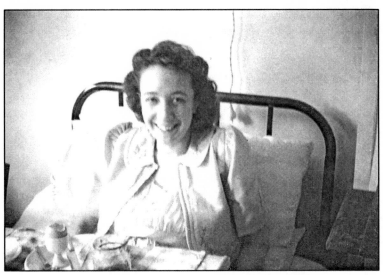

Mary Cooper Gibson, post partum, July, 1944.

Rex with Rosemary Ann Gibson, July 1944

Thursday Nite, August 31, 1944

Dear Mom,

I've had two swell letters from you this week, Mom, one on the 24th and one yesterday. Gosh, but it's swell to hear from you. I'm sorry the mail has been so slow. I know I don't write often, but it's pretty messed up sometimes. Bettie says she hasn't had a letter from me for over a week and the poor kid's worried. I guess she has a right to be but there's no reason in the world for the mail not to come. I write her every night. Can't figure what's wrong.

I haven't heard from Dad or Max since I wrote you last.[2] Today's Dad's 50th birthday. I hope he's home for it. Maybe next year we'll all be home for it. I pray each night it soon will be over. I've only been at war a short time compared to some boys but I've already had my fill of it. I'm ready to stop it any time now.

I'm afraid, Mom, I'll never tell you all I've seen and done either. Dad's very right in never having talked about it much

[World War One]. Lots you do and see in war are much better forgotten. I'd rather just let it die in the back of my mind. Lots I've seen is very beautiful and inspiring and I'll be very proud to tell you all about it but please never question me or ask me to tell anything unless I do it of my own accord. It'll be better that way.

Guess it's still hot as ever there. August and early Sept. usually is. Tonight I'm pretty chilly. Again we have a fire and I'm wearing my sweater. They really feel good. Last night the moon was very pretty. It was only a half moon but it was silver and it's the same one that shines on home. Gosh, I wish I were there now.

I'm due another pass pretty soon. Think I'll spend it with Mickey's family.

We've developed a few pictures this week, Mom. The work is pretty lousy so they aren't much good. We only had enough paper at the time for one of each.[3] I've sent them to Bettie and asked her to send them on to you so you can see them. If we can get any more paper I'll send you some of them. We'll have lots more once I get back to the States.

I hope the polio [season] is gone by now and you and Ann can visit Bettie before school starts again. She'll love to have you. Before long it won't be a good idea for her to do much traveling.

Well, Mom, I'm about out of stuff to write about. So I'd better quit while I still have time tonight to write Dad. Write again, Mom, soon. Your letters are wonderful. God bless you always. Goodnight and sweet dreams to the swellest mother in the whole world.

All my love,

Rex

When I first read this letter, I assumed Fath was referring to his July 29 Bremen flight when he wrote "I'll never tell you all I've seen and done ... Lots you do and see in war are much better forgotten." Now, having studied his flight log, I wonder if he might also have been thinking of his 19th mission, the July 25 flight to Saint Lo - Operation Cobra.

Operation Cobra was conceived by General Omar Bradley to enable our ground troops on the north side of the St. Lo-Periers Road to break through the German concentration on the south side of the road.[4] Bradley's plan called for U.S. airmen to carpet bomb the German troops ahead of the advance of our ground troops.

General Bradley wanted the American bombers to fly parallel to the road to avoid flying over their own troops on the bombing approach, but, due to misunderstandings or, as Bradley believed, "Air Force brass simply lied...," American airmen were instructed to fly perpendicular to the road. On July 24 some of our bombers, as they flew over American troops on approach, accidentally dropped their loads behind their own lines, killing 25 Americans on the ground and wounding 131.

On the following day, July 25, 2,430 American aircraft, including the B-24 heavy bomber Fath was navigating, dropped 4,000 tons of bombs and napalm at St. Lo. Once again, some of the planes prematurely released their bombs over friendly lines.

Fath's flight log shows his aircraft was carrying forty 100-pound bombs.[5] At 10:08 A.M. he logged "Bombs away on briefed target." In the same column, he wrote, "Flak at 2 o'clock" and "10:07 – 448th ship hit. Blew up." At 10:23 he noted, "Enemy Coast as Briefed." They were headed back over the English Channel.

One hundred and eleven American troops were killed and 490 wounded by friendly fire on that second day. Despite heavy casualties, General Bradley considered Operation Cobra a great success. He declared that it "would go down in history as the 'St. Lo Breakout.' It was, in fact, a total and smashing breakin, breakthrough and breakout, a major turning point in the war."[6]

There were, no doubt, many things Fath and other airman would have liked to forget about the war. Witnessing one of your squadron's B-24's explode beside you in mid-air would have been horrific enough. Could Rex's Crew #74 have been among those who inadvertently dropped their bombs short of the target at St. Lo.?

Sometimes bomb drops landed on innocent civilians. Crew #74's mission to Politz on June 20, 1944 involved bombing a synthetic fuel facility manned by concentration camp slave labor. It's no wonder Fath, like many other returning veterans, didn't want to talk about his war experiences.

Fath did, however, describe the crew's September 18, 1944 mission while I had the tape recorder on. This was Operation Market Garden, when his crew, minus the bombardier and forward gunner, dropped supplies to the 82nd airborne paratroopers encircled by German troops near Groesbeek, Holland.[7] "The bomb bay was loaded with bundles of supplies," Fath told me. "The plane was flying at windmill and church steeple level and I could see Dutch children and women waving at the planes. Just over a hedgerow, the aircraft was hit by rifles and machine gun fire.

"One of the shots shattered a window in the nose, spraying it with powdered glass. I felt a stinging sensation in my left foot and buttocks.

"When word came that two men in the bomb bay had been hit, I went back to check their injuries. I gave two shots of morphine each to the tail gunner and the nose gunner and bandaged them up.

"When the crew got back to the base, I peeled off my flying suit to discover my thigh and buttocks covered with red spots that looked like measles. Lee and other crew members carefully felt for glass and removed many tiny glass shards from my skin."

Rather than be grounded, Fath chose not to report this incident, thereby forgoing an almost certain Purple Heart decoration.

Thursday Afternoon, Sept. 21, 1944

Dear Mom,

Our mail has been pretty scarce for about two weeks. Don't know where it's being held up.

Today I'm sitting in our hut in front of a nice warm fire. Kinda cold outside. Haven't seen the sun for over a week now. Wonder what it looks like. Is it cool enough there for a fire yet? Bet the trees are getting pretty now. Wish I could be there to see them. Maybe by next fall this will all be over and we'll all be home. Hope so.

Did you and Ann enjoy your visit in Covington? How's Bettie looking now? I have a new picture of her. You should see it. Sure is good. She's so pretty, Mom. Guess I'm about the luckiest guy in the world to have such a swell family and wife as I have.

Now, Mom, as you can see, there's nothing to tell from over here. Guess I'll have to stop for this time. Please take good care of you and Ann. And write me again soon. Bye for now. God bless you always, Mom. All my love, Rex

P.S. Hello Ann, Here's just a little note for you. There's not much to say about things over here. By the way, Sis, when Oct 5[th,] your 12th birthday, comes by and I'm not there with something for you, don't feel bad. Just give me a rain check and when I'm home I'll make it all up to you. OK. Bye. Lot's of love, Rex

Fath didn't usually write to Bettie's mother, whom he called "Mother," but he did so when he learned about the death of Moth's beloved grandfather who had inspired her love of poetry.

Thursday night, October 26, 1944

Dear Mother,

Tonight, Mother, I'm writing a letter the like of which I've never written before. Maybe I'll say something that doesn't fit; I hope not. In Bettie's letter last night she told me of Grandpap's passing on.

Words are cheap, Mother, so I'll not try to tell you how I feel about it. Just imagine how Jimmy [Bettie's older brother, fighting the war in the Pacific] feels when he reads of it. I feel the way Jimmy will feel. The only difference is Grandpap and Grandmother filled an empty place in my life. Before I had them I never knew but one grandparent.

It's hard for me to realize that one so close and so loved by everyone he knew can be gone. I'm enclosing a poem and a small article from the Army Chapel Magazine Link. They say better than I what I'd like to say.

Take good care of yourself, of Grandmother Cecilia and Bettie. God bless you all. Goodnight, Mother. All my love, Rex

All of the men of Crew 74 survived and went on to fly a total of 35 combat missions by late November, 1944. All but my father received orders to return to the States. Fath was assigned to a newly formed detachment that flew unarmed B-24's equipped with radios and weather gathering devices. He flew weather reconnaissance over the North Atlantic for another three months.

V-MAIL

Sunday Night, November 12, 1944

Dear Mom,

All my hopes of making the U.S. by Xmas have gone sky high. Looks like I'll be here still by then. My new address you can see at the top on the right.

Just what I'm to do can't be told but don't worry, it isn't combat. I think it would be a good deal for someone who wanted it but I don't want it and can't do anything about it.

If you care to send me anything, Mom, please make it something to eat. No other things. Please spread the word around to anyone who's interested. Bettie is going to be very unhappy at this. Goodnight, Mom. God bless you always. Love and kisses, Rex

Both Rex and Bettie were disappointed he wouldn't be able to come home after completing his required 35 missions. They had expected he would be back in time for their baby's birth.

Fath wanted to bring something special home for Moth. He had his heart set on diamond earrings and on his next weekend pass, visited a London jeweler. The jeweler, upon learning how little money his potential customer had, delivered the bad news: Fath couldn't afford diamonds. The merchant suggested he check antique stores because used jewelry didn't carry the 100% tax that new items did. Fath followed the man's advice and purchased antique aquamarine drops for his bride.

V-MAIL

18 Jan, 1945

Dear Mom, Guess I've been a bad boy for not writing anymore than I have the last few weeks but if you'll notice the return address you'll see the surprise I've been waiting to spring on you. Things are moving now, Mom, and I'm really on my way at last. I just wrote Bettie about it tonite. Couldn't keep it to myself any longer. Don't write any more, Mom. Haven't had a letter in over a week now. Still don't know anything about the baby. I'm sure I'm a proud papa by now. With luck you'll get a wire by Bettie's birthday [Feb. 10]. God bless you, Mom. Tell Dad the news. Love & kisses, Rex

Shortly after writing this V-mail, my father received a telegram announcing the birth of "Andy." Knowing "Andy" was not one of the names he and Mother had considered for a son, Fath assumed – correctly – that he had a new daughter, Candace Sue.

"I was in England, at a cold damp and foggy place near Blackpool," Fath recalled in a birthday letter he wrote to me forty years later. "I was anxiously waiting for word of the arrival of a baby in Covington, Kentucky. I also was chafing at not being able to get home in time."

"The day I brought you home," Moth wrote in January 1981 on the occasion of my 36th birthday, "the streets were icy. In those 'olden days' you and I came home in an ambulance and were bundled up on a four-wheeled cart and delivered to Grandma's door, on a hill at Latonia Terrace."

The baby announcement - a "certificate of citizenship" - that Mother sent by mail never caught up with Fath and was returned stamped "address unknown." On the line for "parents" Moth had written "Bettie and the handsomest, sweetest navigator in the ETO."

V-MAIL

Wednesday Nite, Jan 31, 1945

Dear Mom & Dad,

Guess what!! I got stacks of mail today. Lots of back mail from Bettie and one from you, Mom. It was written New Years Day. Sure is swell to get some word again. You said you and Dad were going to celebrate your Silver Wedding anniversary in Cinci. I'm so happy for you, Mom. Bet your rings are pretty. Bettie told me about your visit. It's a shame Candace didn't arrive while you were there. I'm writing this V-mail tonite, Mom, but tomorrow there'll be a long letter. It's midnight already so I'd better be getting to bed. Still haven't heard from Max. Can't figure out why. Goodnight. Mom. God keep you always. All my love and kisses, Rex

Chapter 7

Reunited, Rex Meets New Daughter

Rex's family after his return from war. Mom, Annetta,
Dad, Bettie showing off slacks, Jeffersonville, February '45

Rex with Candy, Miami, March '45

By the end of February 1945, Rex was back in the U.S. at a reception station at Camp Atterbury, Indiana. A month later he, Mother and I travelled to another redistribution station in Miami Beach. There they bought a 1935 Pontiac 4-door sedan for $510.00 cash, money Moth had saved from the allotment the Army Air Force send to her while Fath was away.

Fath was transferred to Ellington Field at Houston, Texas in April 1945 where he spent a little less than a year as an instructor supervisor in an advanced navigation school.

While we were in Houston, Howard (Moth's father) and his second wife Margaret visited us. Howard's attempts at finding a job in New Orleans had been unsuccessful, so he and Margaret were heading to southern California, hoping to improve their fortune. They presented my parents with a footed, black enamel and brass box they had purchased in New Orleans. The box had delicate inlays of white flowers and colorful birds on the lid and sides.

Despite Howard's fall from grace over the years, my parents always kept the box on display. As far as I know, it was the only memento of her father that my mother kept.

Tuesday, Nov. 13, 1945

Houston

Dear Mom, Ann, & Dad,

I know it's been a long, long time since I've taken time to write. But at last here I am. Your letter written the 8th was swell, Mom. So full of news and everything.

Reason number 1,650,562 why I haven't written: The furniture finally arrived last Tuesday. [My parents had to wait six months for their furniture to be shipped from Jeffersonville to Houston.]

We were happy and disappointed. Happy to have our own things once more, but disappointed in that everything was so filthy with coal dust and soot and three pieces were damaged. The chair to the desk was broken beyond repair, the old chest of drawers of Bettie's had the front legs broken, and Bettie's beautiful range [stove] was pretty beat up. The porcelain was all chipped. I'm attempting to file claim for damages on all the things.

Bettie and I worked like demons Thurs, Friday, Sat and Sunday nites. Scrubbing and arranging things. Of course, Bettie worked most of those days, too. Sat. afternoon we went down town and bought a mahogany magazine rack, 5 pictures, and a white shag rug for the living room.

Monday the Army celebrated Armistice Day by giving us a day off. So while Bettie worked on other things, I cleaned the living room furniture. I used an upholstery shampoo on it. It really looks nice. Then I mopped and waxed the floor good.

Now we're all caught up with things except the bedroom needs a little waxing. We're real proud of our things. Everyone who sees the place now just raves about the furnishings, especially the dinette. There still isn't a scratch on that table. Enough about the work.

Now about our Candy. The little musical rocker came last Monday. It plays Rock-a-bye-Baby and Candy's crazy about it. At first she tried standing in it but she can sit in it and do just as well. So now she takes her little raggedy doll, Diane, and rocks the chair. If Bettie or I sing along with the chair she'll try to sing too. It's real cute. Thanks a million for it, Mom.

Oh, yes!! Candy (the little devil) has 2 more teeth. She chewed some more paint off her bed cutting them. She is walking pretty good now. Takes 6-8 steps at a time, stands up from the middle of the floor and off she goes. She still crawls when she wants to move fast, though. In the morning about seven we'll hear her talking and jabbering at her doll. Sometimes she'll play for ½ hour before she gets noisy enough for us to hear her from the kitchen.

Back to the furniture. Sometime while the things were in storage someone helped themselves to 6 teaspoons and a tablespoon, 3 strings of Xmas tree lights and the metal ash tray we got from Raleigh cigarette coupons. I think it was a pretty low trick but we have no claim on things inside drawers because they weren't listed on the contract.

You asked about California. So long as I'm in the Army and I can have Bettie & Candy with me, I don't much care where they send me. (Inside the U.S. of course.)

Bettie and I have been going to a Baptist church for the last two weeks. We like it fine. Last Sunday nite we both had parts in the program. It's more a Bible study and discussion. [Bettie, raised Lutheran, was baptized by immersion in this Baptist church in 1945.]

Oh, Mom, I hate to do this. But if you have any sugar sitting around getting hard or any to spare, have mercy on your big boy with the sweet tooth. We're on the bottom of the jar again. Oh when will sugar rationing end?[1]

That's about all for tonite, Mom. It's bedtime in Texas. Goodnite, God bless you always. Write soon again. Lots of love and kisses, Rex, Bettie & Candy.

P.S. It's hot as H....!! Send some winter, please.

It was decision time for the Pares - Fath had completed his military obligation. Would they return to the Ohio River Valley or would he pursue a career in the service? They made a list of pros and cons and cast their votes for the military life. Fath elected to "continue on extended active duty for an unlimited length of time" according to the official document dated 31 December 1945.

In early 1946 he was sent to special training for two months at Mather Field in Sacramento, where he, now-pregnant Bettie and I lived at the Los Robles Motel.

In the meantime, Moth's brother Mickey's English war bride Mary and 1½ year old daughter Rosemary arrived in the United States. Mary was eager to reunite with the dashing GI from Kentucky who hadn't yet met his daughter. Once in Covington, twenty-one year-old Mary learned her husband had moved to California; she and Rosemary got back on the train and headed west. She found Mickey in Vallejo, not far from Sacramento, married to another woman with whom he had a son.

After this blow, Mary tracked down my parents in Sacramento. They gave her emotional support at a difficult time. Mary agreed to wait for Mickey to get his second marriage annulled before she filed for divorce so that he wouldn't be exposed as a bigamist. And then, short of cash, Mary spent nine months working as a domestic in several cities on her way back across the country.

When she and Rosemary eventually arrived on the east coast, Mary discovered she had overlooked the federal tax on her third-class passage when she was saving for her voyage home. With only $125 to her name, she was about $50 short. Not only had her dreams been dashed, but she was stranded in New Jersey for another month until she earned enough for the ticket back to England.

Candy & Bettie, pregnant with Jennifer, 1946

Chapter 8

Bettie: Private Institution for Army Wives

Toward the end of April 1946 Rex was sent to Las Vegas to set up a navigator school. In August, when Mother was about to give birth to their second child, he was deployed to Okinawa, Japan, the site of the bloody final land battle of World War Two.

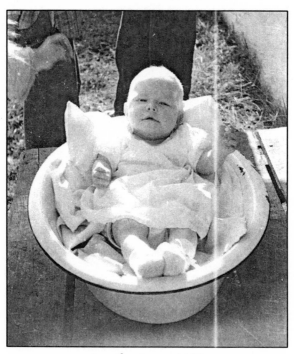

Jennifer, August 1946

Back in the States, daughter Jennifer Dee was born in an Army hospital in Henderson, Nevada. In Okinawa, Rex received another misspelled birth announcement. The telegram printed his daughter's name as Jennifer Die.

Mother, with two babies in tow, returned to Indiana to live near Fath's parents until Jennifer was old enough for the shots required for Okinawa.[1]

Rex, headstand, "See! I told you I didn't know which end was up."
Okinawa, November 1946

By the time Moth received notice to apply for her passport, an event that made the local newspaper, she was more than ready to rejoin her husband. She mailed Fath a mock ID from "U.S.A.'s Private Institution for Army Wives."

"This certifies that Bettie George has gone completely off the beam. Reason: 1) two daughters, 2) no husband. Cure: none in sight. Condition: dangerous. Eyes: open and shut. Hair: oh yes! Teeth: paid for. Ears: unfortunately. Hands: full. Heart: broken. Attitude: !*#XX!**^^!! (censured)"

Bettie's passport.

Her travel orders arrived in late January, 1947. Accompanied by Rex's mother "Mom," Mother, Jennifer and I took the train to San Francisco. We hugged Mom good-bye and boarded a troop transport ship for the voyage to Okinawa.

Bettie wrote to her mother and three youngest brothers, about her adventures crossing the stormy Pacific and her long-awaited reunion with Rex. She wrote of food and fuel shortages, intermittent water and unreliable electricity. She heralded Fath's skills and ingenuity in turning a Quonset hut into a livable home on war-scarred Okinawa. She filled pages with her growing toddlers' antics. She despaired over gaining weight, all the while reporting baking daily and eating desserts after every lunch and dinner.

Thirty-two years later Grandma Lona returned the letters to Moth. I didn't become aware of them until the mid-1990s when Moth occasionally spoke of writing a book about her Okinawa experience. I was intrigued by the letters and in 1998, I talked Fath into allowing me to take them home to Chicago. He seemed hesitant to let go of them, but I promised I wouldn't let them out of my sight on the flight home.

Bettie reading Okinawa letters to Candace, Santa Rosa, CA, 1997.

When I first read Moth's letters, I was struck by her positive, upbeat outlook on life. Until then I had always suspected her of faking it. From my perspective, she resembled a too-perfect Betty Crocker – never angry, never sad, never raised her voice, always found the bright side. I recall talking with her about it when I was a college student, complaining she and Fath hadn't prepared me for the real world.

The Okinawa letters dispelled my disbelief. The woman I saw in them was the same optimistic, enthusiastic person I had known all my life. As a young woman she had experienced family strife and hardship and was determined to take a different path. She chose to make her own future - to enjoy life actively and enthusiastically.

I photocopied and bound the borrowed letters and presented a copy to Mother in 1998. Enthused and appreciative, she added a dedication on the first page.

"To my mother, Lona Gibson, to whom I wrote these letters, who saved them and gave them back when I was old enough to appreciate them. Without her forethought this book would not have been possible. Thank you, Mother."

Part Two:
Bettie Writes Home -
Letters from Okinawa, 1947 – 1948

Chapter 9

Crossing the Pacific,
February 8 to March 4, 1947

Moth and her two infants, Jenny and I, boarded the USS General A. W. Greely[1] at Fort Mason in San Francisco for what would be a longer-than-expected 33-day voyage across the Pacific.

Moth wrote the first letter in four installments during the trip. A fifth installment announced our safe arrival in Okinawa.

I've done minimal editing and correcting for clarity, and have deleted many references to friends and family unless they contributed to Mother's story. I have not changed misspellings. Moth spelled "Manila" with a double "l" throughout, and always misspelled the abbreviation for "etcetera" as "ect".

February 8, 1947

Aboard S.S. Gen. A.W. Greely

3 days out of S.F.

Dear Mother & boys;

I'll start my first letter now & perhaps mail it in Manilla. Hope that you all are very well & happy. We are.

Had a fairly nice journey to Frisco. Didn't think so much of the Challenger, our train from Louisville. We had lots of service men on. One sailor took on the job of entertaining Candy. That was lots of help & fun for her.

Saw snow all the way. Didn't go to Salt Lake City. Turned off at Ogden and crossed the Great Salt Lake - 30 miles of it. That's quite a lake. The train went slow over it.

The land from Reno on we slept through. Arrived in foggy Oakland right on time 8:15 A.M. Monday. Crossed on the Ferry to San Francisco. Got a cab to Fort Mason. San Francisco is quite an unusual sight with all its hills. Makes Cincinnati look flat. I'd love to see more of it.

Fort Mason is a beautiful place right in Frisco. The Hostess House was much nicer than I had dreamed of. Everyone was so nice. The room was lovely. You could wash & iron in the laundry, fix formulas or use the refrigerator. They called for all your baggage & tended to every detail.

Candy had a terrible cold from the train. Took her to the dispensary. They gave her an exam & sulpha pills.

Tuesday we roamed around. Candy was improving. The ship was right there to see. Alcatraz was beyond us & a beautiful sight. S.F. really looks pretty at night. I'd love for you to see it.

Tuesday night I took a walk & saw lots and climbed hill after hill.

Mom seemed unimpressed. I was very disappointed as I thought she would enjoy the trip.

Mom left early Wed. A.M. and at 12:45 P.M. we boarded the ship. Since we didn't sail till 4 P.M. had lots of time to get settled. Our ship commissioned in March '45 is a transport. We are to stop first at Manilla then Okinawa.

The stateroom is roomy & comfortable. I share it with Mary Bates, a bride of 18 who is grand & helps with the children. Four bunks & a crib for Jennifer, one desk, dresser combination, 4 lockers, four chairs, sink, connecting shower & toilet ect. Plenty of lights & bed lamps, a fan, & one porthole. We're on the main deck, port side, just aft of midship.

The dining room is near by. We eat at 7:30, 11:30, & 4:30. The food & service is wonderful. We with children have a separate dining room, high chairs & all & stewardesses to aid us.

There are 19 children on board. The oldest is five. Four are babies like Jennifer. Two other girls have two children also.

Civil service employees, officers, 200 white troops, 100 colored, dependents, construction workers, & Philippinos are aboard. The ship is manned by the Merchant Marines.

A portion of the boat deck has been fenced in for the children. Movies are on the sun deck, church services also, song fests, dances, bingos, ect.

Feb. 22nd – Pacific

Still going. Here it is the 22nd. We will arrive in Manilla on the 26th, Okinawa probably March 1st or 2nd.

You see, we had quite a storm & it lasted six days. Changed our course twice. One day we even lost 100 miles. It was really rough. The eating was next to impossible. Dishes slid off the table & someone else's food would slide to you. Chairs & high-chairs with children went skating this way & that frightening all the children till they would cry all together & loudly.

Jennifer's crib went banging around & got a hole knocked in the end. The boat rocked day & night & at times we weren't allowed to be on deck or to have our portholes open. The sea was angry & foamy, the waves high.

Every little thing had to be anchored down. At night we'd stack our chairs, pack the glasses in towels, tuck the kids in tightly & try to sleep.

But after those six days & since, the sea has been calm & we are averaging 400 miles a day. It's warm & sunny & we spend most of our time on deck. All the wives are acquainted.

I've seen several good pictures, "Leave Her to Heaven" and "Home Sweet Homicide" included. Our stateroom is number 32. Number 38 is vacant so we girls from this section congregate in there evenings after the babies are asleep & gab & eat.

The mothers with babies have access to the diet kitchen & raid it for midnight snacks. (unauthorized)

One girl shared her Bon Voyage booty with us last Sunday night & we snacked on Vienna Sausages, shoe-string potatoes, crackers, cheeses, relishes, & date & nut bread.

We're really enjoying the trip. Or I am anyway. A few are complaining.

Now for us.

I had one day of sea-sickness (the first day of the storm). Found fresh air was the best thing for it. Felt fine since.

Candy had her spell of sickness & loose bowels as did all the children. She gradually got used to things & now is fine & eats very well.

Jennifer only last week had her trouble. She got so sick and for four days didn't keep food down. We changed her to canned milk. This frozen milk isn't too good & isn't homogenized. Since then she's fine. Eats at the table with us. Her smiling has won her a large circle of friends & loads of attention. She has grown so. Crawls very well, but backwards. Enjoys her Taylor Tot on deck or crawling on a blanket up there.

Candy is the pet of the diet kitchen. The enlisted men down there give her all sorts of things from sugar to ice-cream & cake while I fix the formula.

We passed the Hawaiian Islands the other week & could barely see them. Early today we passed the Marianas but it was not yet light enough to see.

Sure wish I had more summer dresses in my suit-case. Four pair of nylons were stolen from the B-4^2 bag when it arrived at S.F.

The stem fell off my watch; I got my hand caught between the table & a sliding chair during the storm. It got cut up a little & my birthstone came out. But I have it.

I'm going to close now. Haven't written a soul yet besides you. Always have company or am out on deck.

Rec'd a letter the day we sailed. It was from Rex addressed to the U.S.S. General A.W. Greely. He had just learned of our sailing. We were due in Okinawa around the 22nd but surely didn't make it.

Goodnight now. It's still warm so guess we'll turn the fan on again. Will be glad when we leave Manilla & head north.

Oh yes, we have a daily paper too. And those chairs on deck to sit in just like those people in the movies! The P.X. has fig Newtons. Candy calls them "pig bars" & eats a box a day.

Just came a knock at my door & two M.P's [military police] & four G.I's came in & said there was a fire around. I smelled the smoke but insisted it wasn't in here. It was a can across the hall. Some one had put a lighted cigarette in it. Good thing they found it.

Love - Bettie.

P.S. Valentine's day, two huge heart shaped cakes, decorated with red & white frosting were put on the children's table.

Crossing the Pacific, Susan McGough and Candy, January 1947

Sunday - Jan. 23rd

Flash - So you teased me about eating at the Captain's table! Tsk. I did.

I was one of the three wives aboard who received an invitation to dine with the ship's Captain & Major Johnston the Transport Commander. Don't know why I was chosen but was sure glad.

We were ushered to the Captain's quarters about 4:15 P.M. Quite spacious & comfortable ones. There we met him. He's very nice & nice looking. The five of us chatted around a round table.

He offered us cold cokes (it's rare to have a cold one). At five he suggested we go to dinner. A few mates, the ship's doctor, & a couple others were at the table.

Ate the usual food (might mention that the other wives took the children off our hands). After dinner he suggested different things we might do. We all chose to look the boat over. He took us up to the top deck & showed us everything & explained in length.

We went still higher & watched the sun set.

At 6:45 we thanked him & left. All in all it was wonderful & we were very honored.

The other girls are teasing us about it.

Am eager to get my mail there & learn how you all are.

Nite - Bettie

Feb. 28, 1947 - Friday

Aboard S.S. Gen. A.W. Greely

10 hours out of Manilla

Dear Mother & Boys;

Here 'tis. Feb. almost gone. Two years ago today Rex came back from England.

As you can see this is a tour of the Pacific. Seems our next stop will be Okinawa & we hope for that Monday morning - March 3rd.

We awoke Wed. A.M. & saw we were going through the straits. Islands on both sides, some close enough to see the trees on them. About 8 A.M. we spied Manilla.

The harbor & bay is still full of sunk ships. You see them sticking out of the water everywhere. We docked beside the USS Admiral Benson (which left S.F. the day after the General Greely & has been to Yokohama, Shanghai & is now en route back to San Francisco) On the other side of us was a British cargo ship.

The native boys swam to meet the ship & to catch money thrown them. Most of them are naked. Sure are good swimmers.

Meant to mention that the water looked so different going through the straits. It was calmer & blue. Into Manilla it was green.

We let off lots of troops & three wives, including my cabin-mate, Mary. Learned we weren't to sail till Friday A.M. (Turned out to be noon.) This really discouraged us.

It was so beastly hot too. Thank goodness we're going on & not staying in Manilla.

Most of the civilians, all the ship's crew & the officers (not to mention a few of our more flirtatious wives) got off Wed. night & saw Manilla. Girls had to be escorted by two or more fellows (armed).

Thursday A.M. a motor tour was arranged for the wives. The stewardesses kept Jennifer. I took Candy along. Went in Army trucks. The truck the children & mothers were in had a top to protect us from the sun.

We rode for two & a half hours. Visited the Chinese Cemetery, The American Cemetery, San Tomas, & saw the whole town. You just can't imagine it till you've seen it. The walled city is a wreck as are the many beautiful buildings. But Jimmy can tell you about that.[3] Was glad I got to see it but also glad to get back.

Candy was impressed by the horses & carts. And gosh lots of new cars!

One of the girls' husbands who flies regularly from Oki to Manilla came aboard. He said the fellows are all waiting & worrying about the USS Greeley. They expected us ages ago.

Right before sailing I acquired a new roommate. Gosh she's not like Mary. I miss Mary. This one is a Red Cross worker. Quite a gal (or so she thinks) & quite busy trying to impress me with her travels, spending, & all. Don't think I'll see much of her though. She'll be on deck till the last listener turns in. She's O.K., just not my type.

I'll close for now - Nite - Bettie

Okinawa - March 4, 1947

Arrived yesterday. Like it fine. Rex is wonderful. Home is nice, all clean for me.

Here's the $200 said we'd send you in Feb.

Will write more later. Temperature in the 50's. Kids both well.

Love - Bettie

P.S. from Rex

Wrong again!!! Post Office too far & too crowded now to get Money Order. Pay yourself from the Gov't checks to Bettie. We'll be able to get M.O.'s later to send our cash home. I'm writing this in a jeep with the motor running. I'm not really this nervous.

Love,

Rex

Chapter 10

Arrival in Okinawa,
Rex Meets Daughter Jennifer
March 16 to May 11, 1947

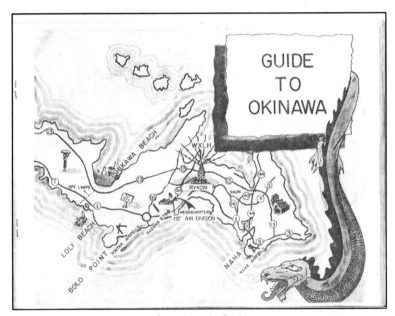

Map of south end of Okinawa.

Okinawa was the site of the final land battle of World War Two, the last stop of the Pacific stepping-stone campaign north toward Japan. The island is a prefecture of Japan and the largest of the 160 island Ryukyu archipelago. It is strategically located on the

China Sea, within 600 – 800 miles of Japan, the Philippines, Hong Kong, Taiwan, Korea and the coastline of what is now Communist China.

Throughout the Orient, Okinawa was known as the "Island of Tombs," for the thousands of turtle-shaped mausoleums - family tombs called "hakas" - where Okinawans prayed for the souls of their ancestors. To many visitors, Okinawa is the "Isle of Smiles" because of its genuinely warm, resilient and hospitable people.

One of many nicknames service-men gave to Okinawa – which means "rope in the sea" - was "The Rock." This may have been because the island was solid coral and volcanic rock, or perhaps it reminded some GI's of Alcatraz. Another name, "Operation Iceberg", was code for the U.S invasion of the island. Later, in the mid-1950s during the Korean War, the island was called "The Keystone of the Pacific" due to its strategic location.

The island is roughly half the size of Rhode Island, 62 miles long and 2 – 20 miles wide. Its climate is similar to that of Southern Florida, with high humidity and average annual rainfall of 80+ inches. The period from June to October brings destructive typhoons with winds up to 200 MPH, often accompanied by as much as 17 inches of rain in a 24 hour period. The climate encourages rust, mildew and mold as well as a great variety of crawling and flying pests including four different kinds of disease-carrying mosquitoes.

On Easter Sunday morning, April 1, 1945, 30,000 American troops landed on the beaches of Okinawa. Their goal was to take the harbors and the four operational air fields on the flatter, more populated southern end of the island. U.S. Marine troops had been briefed to expect 80% – 85% casualties during the landing, but the beaches were not defended and the Americans met almost no resistance.

Most of the 110,000 Japanese soldiers defending Okinawa were holed up in a vast network of underground tunnels dug into the limestone hillsides, waiting for the Americans to come to them. From the air, the Japanese sent more than 3,500 Kamikaze planes plummeting into the Allied fleet off Okinawa.

During the fierce 82-day battle, President Franklin D. Roosevelt died and was replaced by Harry S. Truman. Nazi Germany surrendered on May 8, 1945, but the bloody battle for Okinawa raged on until June 22. In all, over 500,000 American troops took part in the Okinawa campaign. Over 100,000 Japanese soldiers died as did 42,000 Okinawan civilians, more than a third of the island's population. The U.S. lost 12,520 troops and counted 37,000 wounded. On August 15, 1945, after the U.S. dropped two atomic bombs on mainland Japan, the Japanese surrendered.

Less than a year later the first U.S. dependents, twenty-seven families, arrived at Naha port on July 27, 1946. My father's bomb group landed at Kadena Air Field in early August.

The battle for Okinawa had left the formerly lush southern end of the island treeless and barren. The 1400-year-old imperial city of Shuri was destroyed, and the capital city Naha, pre-war population 60,000, was leveled and resembled a pulverized graveyard.

When the USS General Greely arrived at Naha port seven months later, Mother looked out over the bombed-out former capital city where 95% of the buildings had been destroyed and spotted Rex on the dock, waiting to meet his newest daughter, Jennifer.

The arrival of our ship was noted in "The Daily Okinawan" on Wednesday, March 5, 1947. "We're front page here!" Mother penned above the photo of herself and me. The caption below our picture read, "'Daddy!' little Candy George shrieks with happiness as, from the USAT General Greely, she spies her father, Lt. R.H. George, on the dock while her mother, who had previously located her husband, smiles above her. Mrs. George and Candy arrived Monday to join Lt. George, a navigator with the 22nd Bomb Group of the 316th Bomb Wing VH." Before sending a copy home to her mother, Bettie added, "Jennifer was asleep in stateroom."

Sunday - March 16th

Okinawa – Kadena Air Force Base

Dear Mother & Boys,

Yep, it's about time I wrote. Really it's easier said than done. I like it here fine, it's a pretty island & people are nice. Rex is as handsome & sweet as ever so I'm happy too.

Been here about two weeks now. Rex has to fly to Manilla tomorrow. He'll get the Money Orders there & mail these letters. Hope he gets back Tuesday. I'll sure miss him & so will the kids. He just stuck a spoon full of the best ice-cream in my mouth. We make it all the time. Same kind as at home, just packed for the Army. Add water & freeze. We stir every half hour till frozen. We have a 9 ft. Servel [kerosene-powered refrigerator]. We are the only ones on the street with a refrigerator. Good thing it is big. Everything is scarce & we all share. I borrow a roaster to bake & roast in and neighbors use our refrigerator. Thank goodness it's not an electric one. The electricity goes out from midnight till 6 or 8 A.M. & several times during the day.

Now, the water is off more than it's on. Usually we carry water. But today Rex put up a storage tank & we'll always have water. He also piped the fuel oil into the space heater so we wouldn't have to carry it in.

Hot water - tsk what's that? If we ever had water long enough & enough pressure we'd have it. So far there's been none.

We're eating fine. Nothing fresh. Every morning I open the refrigerator & the butter is so strong that it comes carrying the eggs out. They are too old to come out on their own.

Lotsa nice neighbors, all with the same problems so it's fun.

Yokasho, our inexperienced 18 yr old maid, is very pretty & sweet & willing but I can't make her understand a thing. She had never washed dishes before & she thought you washed them like clothes. She was on the third rinse when I stopped her.[1]

Friends took us riding in their jeep a couple times. (We will have one when we can find a clutch to put in one that isn't being used.) Saw lots. Really enjoyed myself. Still can see caves & pill-boxes [roofed, concrete emplacements for machine guns], native villages, pretty hills, coral, the China Sea, ruined buildings at Naha. Boy those back seats of a jeep have Cinci's Coney Island rides beat by a mile. Next Sunday we're taking some cigarettes & joining the neighbors on a trip north to trade with the natives for mats, baskets, brooms, ect.

Jennifer is very contented. Was really a stinker after the boat ride but is her old self again now. Lives in the teeter-babe. Jumped out of it today! She also likes to be in Candy's doll buggy.

The native girls love babies. Two who work in the neighborhood came in one day, looked the place over, and commented, "nico, nico" (nice, nice). They played with Jennifer till I put her to bed with a bottle, then played with the kids' toys awhile. Soon they put their shoes on & left. Such is life.

Candy is doing fine. She & Rex had a long hard week but she's good now. Plays out all day. Several nice children near by. She comes in & tells me she's been to a "tea party" or that she played "horses". She is going to be broken hearted if anyone ever tells her she's only two years old. She thinks she's as big as the other kids around.

Rex gets home for lunch most of the time & for supper around 4:00 or 4:30. He's lots of help & awfully nice to have around.

When I arrived he had our house so clean & nice, a chocolate cake for me, & birthday gifts. The prettiest shoes, bag, & belt set from Manilla. The shoes are blonde mahogany. The heels are carved like a Japanese house & gardens. The top part of the shoe & the bag & belt are of a fiber similar to white straw but softer & silkier.

I gotta close now 'cause Rex has finished writing Mom & we're sleepy.

I'll tell you about our house & furnishings next time.

Love

Bettie

Our family of four lived in a Quonset hut, a pre-fabricated, semi-cylindrical building made of corrugated metal.[2] Ours was 20 feet wide and 100 feet long. We occupied 60 feet of it; the neighbors at the other end had 40 feet. Many of the Quonsets in the area where we lived had not been finished on the inside. Fath's ingenuity, resourcefulness, and his carpentry and plumbing skills came in handy.

George family Quonset Hut

April 10, 1947

Kadena, Okinawa

Dear Mother & Boys,

I'll not let this happen again I promise you. You just can't imagine how busy and tired we are.

Last time I wrote Rex was going to Manilla. He left that Monday and returned Thursday P.M. Prices in Manilla are outrageous but he got a few things, paint, miracle whip at 40¢ per ½ pint (my home made mayonnaise is better), raisins, crackers, lettuce, ect. Bought a coffee table & two end tables. You see, the furniture issued to us is rattan & mahogany so we bought the tables to match. Couldn't find anything suitable for your & Mom's birthdays.

Sure was glad when he came back.

Our Quonset & a couple of others close by were never finished up. No Masonite, just board partitions you could see through, & like all others, leaks rain. The cabinets had no doors.

Now, scrounging is a legal profession here. So Rex found a construction company dump, borrowed a weapons carrier & hauled away two loads of Masonite. It is now neatly piled in our living room. The kitchen & living room are covered but that's just a start.

Every Saturday or Sunday friends take us jeep riding. Neighbors & friends buzz around every pretty day. We visited one point where we could see both sides of the island from a hill - sure wasn't very wide there.

One evening we all dressed up in our best, Candy in pink coat & white gloves, Jennifer in her blue dress, & borrowed the neighbors' jeep. Jennifer sat in a box & Candy on the back seat & we bounced over to Rycom (Ryukyu Command Headquarters) to visit friends we'd come over with on the ship.

Took blankets & wrapped up coming home. Jeeps aren't built for comfort, but we do fine.

Last week we attended our first dance. It was the pre-Easter formal. We felt quite proud - Rex in his red lined battle jacket & I in my red & white silk taffeta & my long gloves.

We gave a child to each neighbor & started out. (That was O.K. cause we've done our share of baby sitting.)

Rex had his 45 revolver strapped on, & off we went (always a gun). It was a beautiful night, big moon with a ring around it. The music was perfect, the club cozy, & the dance very dignified and enjoyable. All in all it was a grand evening.

You asked about Easter. There was an Easter egg hunt & Candy attended. We made her basket from a coffee can, colored paper, cut-outs from "The Lively Little Rabbit," & a paint-can handle. The grass was gauze from disposable didies dyed green. You sure must be original over here.

Now this week it has rained & rained. This mud is like glue, the lake at our back door will either have to be drained or we'll have to build a pier.

Servants! Yokasho proved too vain, but, in time, the truck she came to work on was discontinued. After awhile we acquired Haruko. Now she's doing very well, likes the children & works well. She brought me some clog-like Okinawa sandals, called "getas," brought Candy three pair of tiny shoes for toys. She is grateful for the soap, cigarettes, dresses, and baby clothes I give her. Gave her an old dress one day & the next day she had made a beautiful blouse from it. She brings her clothes & washes & irons them here. She wants to live with us but we don't want that so tell her "sorry no bed."

Our house is one you must "see to appreciate." We foresee a very comfortable home after several months, though.

Candy has "tea-parties" and plays outdoors with two girls (ages 5&7). Today she told me to help her look for her baggage because she had to make a train. She said "darnit" & I persisted she say "sugar" instead. She looked irritable & said "Well, I say 'oh darnit' outside."

She has been a problem about crying - loud & long over nothing. She'll get over it. She's very determined & won't give in.

Jennifer is no angel either. She has quite a temper & holds her breathe till she's blue & I'm frantic. She won't stay off her feet. Won't stay in her teeterbabe much. Just jumps out head first. She's small & can scoot out of the walker. The play-pen holds her, though.

We sure keep Rex busy. I can think of a million things a day for him to do. But he's so sweet & loving.

Hot water is pretty regular now - we have it sometime most every day. Power isn't so good. The big generator is out & power is low. Can't even cook on our hot plate around meal time when everyone in the area is using electricity. So I black my pans and burn my food using a gasoline affair that is as bad as a blow torch.

Lights go out around midnight. During the night we use candles and late guests sit around our Coleman lantern.

We've had oranges, lemons, apples, & lettuce & celery this week. Sometimes we really hit the jackpot.

Thanks for the Easter cards & the letters. Really I'll write once a week from now on. We borrowed (Everyone lives by borrowing.) a Sears & a Wards catalog last week & ordered a few things, also presents for you & Mom. We ordered you the album "Annie Get Your Gun."

So today when your letter came mentioning you already had the album & disliked it, my heart sank. Rex read it & confessed the letters & orders were still in his desk. So for once a husband was praised for forgetting to mail the letters. Now for your birthday, how about buying yourself a nice house-dress? Let the sky (and $6) be your limit.

My financial affairs seem in good order so I guess I'll have the detective to stop following you.[3]

How about fixing up a box sometime in your leisure? Include 3 Bakers Baking Chocolate, some white syrup, shredded coconut, Gerber's baby cereal, a bolt of white pigtail ribbon and 5 yards of white ribbon for hair bows. I sure would like for Candy & Jennifer to have some balloons (Kindly do not inflate before sending.) and I'd like 3 pair of pretty nylons.

Put all of the next check in the bank & we'll send some more for the Safe Deposit box.

The roaster sounds fine. Thanks for being so prompt. I knew Westinghouse would be hard to get; the other will be fine. I bake a lot when the power is up & the neighbor's oven is empty.

Rex says I must retire now & I still have a million things to say.

As of today we have our own jeep!

Loads of love, Bettie

Jeep with Rex, Jennifer, Candy and maid.

April 15, 1947

Dear Mother,

Here is your daughter to report on your grandchildren.

How's everyone? Hope you are all well & happy. We are well & were happy till we had a letter from Mom today. She says our household goods are still at the J.Q.M.D. [Jeffersonville QuarterMaster's Depot].

All the others who came on the Greely with me already have theirs or have been notified it's on the sea. I'm so mad I could <u>spit</u>.

Rex is writing to them now. So if you're called upon as my power of attorney to sign, that's what it's about.

Mother, Candy is really getting fat. Besides that, tall. I can hardly pick her up. Oh but she's devilish though. We spank & switch & punish her but it seems to do no good. Take yesterday. She was all dressed & went out to pick me some flowers. She comes back without her clothes & very casually informs me she had to tinkle so took them off. After due punishment, I put her on the front porch with Jennifer. Five minutes later she had pulled a potted plant out by the roots & was pouring the dirt down Jenny's back & rubbing it into her hair.

For this I really took her apart & put her to bed. She retaliated by taking her hair down & tearing the bed up. She was very sorry finally & was going to be a good girl. But today she rubbed more dirt in Jennifer's hair.

Jennifer is getting impish too. Rex says he guesses neither will be a sweet little lady. Jennifer isn't happy awake till she has Candy awake. She'll stand in her bed & fuss & call to Candy. As soon as Candy moves Jennifer howls with joy.

Rex starts a two day leave tomorrow. We hope to finish covering the walls, get cabinets in & floors painted.

Now that we have a jeep we spend our evenings in it. Sunday we packed our little family in & explored the island all afternoon. It was a gorgeous day, our jeep is all open & no top, time we got home we all had red noses, arms, & cheeks from the sun. Jennifer rides in the laundry basket & Candy bounces on the back seat. She has a blanket & nestles down when she's tired or sleepy.

Goodnight now. Say hello to Mary for us. When you send Rosemary's birthday gifts send a nice dress & socks or sweater & mittens from us.

Love, Bettie

Wed. April 24, 1947

Dear Mother & Brothers,

"Life in a Carpenter Shop" or "Who Fired that Shot?" is our theme for tonight. Hang on - don't go away!

Rex's leave started Wednesday. Immediately our living room became a carpenter's shoppe. Sawing & hammering - all in hopes of a livable house.

By Thursday Candy managed to get completely in the way and I thought of millions of "little things" for Rex to do.

He put up with it till Friday. Friday we took the babies to the hospital for their Pediatrician's check-ups. They each had a slight cold (their first here). The prissy doc seemed to think we shouldn't take them jeep riding in the night air.

Friday P.M. we pushed Jennifer off on an obliging neighbor, took Candy & rode over to the Griffith Theatre (outdoor) to see "California". The gum & pretzels in my pockets kept Candy satisfied till she fell asleep. Enjoyed the picture. Went to get in our "el jeepo" & there was the figure of an M.P. [Military Police] He said we had a stolen vehicle. Showed him our trip ticket, ect., but ended up with him in the back seat, with another M.P. car following, heading for headquarters. Tsk - my social standing went XXXX! Turned out the jeep had been lost & recovered long before we ever had it but the number was never removed from the list. So we got to come home.

Saturday was wet, very wet. Haruko was dismissed at noon to go home early. We (the carpenter, kids, & I) would have a lovely day alone. As I sliced some baked ham for lunch (we buy ham only by halves here) I decided I'd trim off some fat. Turned out it was my fat I trimmed & we promptly left our kids & work & rode in the rain to the dispensary where the doctor put two neat stitches on my right index finger at the joint. Didn't hurt none. So Saturday turned out to be a busy day for Rex, as I was pretty helpless.

What a life! Thank goodness I had borrowed the neighbor's roaster Thursday & baked for the week end. An apple pie, a temptation spice cake, & a batch of honey-nut cookies.

Sunday, too, it rained, rained, & rained. Candy couldn't understand why she couldn't get out & pick flowers. Rex was near crazy. Jennifer was in the way, & the lights (electricity) didn't come on till nearly 5 P.M., but we survived.

Monday was a pretty day. Candy could pick flowers, Haruko could wash, Jennifer could be outdoors, Rex could work, & I was using my hand pretty well. So at the supper table Rex said "Let's take a ride before the sun goes down." Quickly we dumped the clothes out of the basket, put Jennifer in it, loaded the jeep & took off.

Rode around Bolo Point & viewed the China Sea and the hills of Okinawa. They are really pretty. Pines & palms grow together. Everything is so green. The gardens & rice fields are doing fine. We wave at the kids & women as we ride by native villages. Kids all holler "nico" (native word for nice & the main word in their vocabulary).

After coming home & putting our two sleepy girls to bed we were putting away our coats & the gun when Rex said he'd show me a thing or two about loading the gun. Trustingly I looked on. Well, thank goodness it was pointed away cause those durnd contraptions really work (when you least suspect). The bullet went through the kitchen, back porch and then where?? We lit the Coleman Lantern & went out to see. Say, they really travel - clear across our yard & to the next Quonset (now a plumbing supply house).

So Rex missed his chance. And I'd always thought him the most wonderful, handsomest, husband in the world!

Tuesday was yesterday. Rex labored on. He'll be so glad when his leave is up & he can rest at the Bomb Group again.

The house really is looking grand now. The kitchen, hall, living room & 2 bedrooms are done. Tonight Rex is working on the little bedroom & has the bath yet to do. He's covering all the walls with Masonite. Formerly they were bare, rough planks. He can do anything!

Candy is getting so fat & tall. She's strictly an outdoor girl & lives to pick flowers for me. She's so cute. By the way there are millions of varieties of flowers around. Haruko, Rex & Candy bring me flowers. Had I known, I'd have brought a dozen vases. I always have four full of fresh pretty flowers. Candy brings mostly wild violets which she picks carefully so they'll have long stems. Today Haruko brought some that are like Gladiolas.

Candy still calls you Gan-Gan. She never forgets you all. Talked about playing Hi Ho Silver with David today. [Bettie's youngest brother, 10 years old at the time.] She pretends all the time. I must "watch her youngest baby" while she goes to the P.X. or Commissary for food. She gives them medicine, irons, cooks, & uses Jennifer as a toy.

Jennifer is still loving; still holds her breath, too. She is happy, still no teeth but her hair is thicker. She is in her playpen mostly. The doctor will run a blood test on her next week as he doesn't like her color. She's little but not skinny. Stands alone occasionally in her playpen. Crawls too fast, and right now has a black eye from falling out of bed.

Rex is quitting now. It's 10 P.M., so let's say Goodnight.

Next week I'll send a Money Order.

Love – kisses, Bettie

In the following letter, Mother identifies the place as "Yontan," which is where a Japanese airstrip had been located. We lived in Area C of the Yontan area, a few miles north of Kadena Air Force Base.

May 3, 1947

Yontan, Okinawa

Dear Mother & Boys,

Hear that rain? We just got home in time. The twerps are in bed & Rex is reading. Raining so hard that all of our leaks are in action. Just moved my foot further under the desk and ran into a puddle. The water seeped in between the floor & wall.

Responding to your letter we received today: The records from "Lady in the Dark" sounds nice.[4] Rex'll like them. Thanks so much. Pack them good.

Rex wears his gun in a shoulder holster. Says I should learn to use it but I'm not eager.

Gee, contests, hope you win. You know, it seems if you'd enter enough of them you'd surely win something sometime.

The other week it rained so badly I couldn't go to the doctor so Rex took the stitches out of my hand. He was scared the rain would stop & he wouldn't get to do it.

By the way - next month is typhoon season. Will we be blown your way?? (That puddle under my feet is now a lake.)

We were to go to a dance last night but Rex flew Wed. & last night. Next Wed. he flies to Guam & won't return till Saturday. Then he's O.D. [Officer of the Day] from Sunday noon till Monday noon. What a week!

Heard dependant travel was authorized, so this fall we may go to Tokyo.

Jennifer was out all morning & the sun was bright so her nose & arms are burned. They are bright pink. She's getting so cute. Stands alone, looks like one of these kewpie dolls. Very friendly; her hair is growing. No teeth!

Candy is terrible when I take her anywhere. I dress her so pretty and she wants to roll in the dust on the bus or wade in mud or crawl through barbed wire. Touch her & she cries like you murdered her.

She & Jennifer play nicely together. They had their baths together in the kitchen sink today.

Two neighbors now use my refrigerator. Well Sunday A.M. I was in the kitchen sink bathing & humming a tune when people started coming for their meat. Bessie chatted for 2 hours while I sat with a towel over me. But then it could have been the husbands! Can't complain.

Prices have gone up so at the commissary. They must be making us pay for getting the food here "air-mail special".

We in Area C live quite a way from the Kadena commissary and P.X., so every morning at 9 A.M. & afternoons at 12:45 a bus (Don't imagine it resembles any you've ever seen. It's yellow, crude, dusty, crusty, dangerous, and we sit on a wooden board along the side.) Picks up those who wish to shop and takes us to the commissary & P.X. The driver carries our packages, helps watch our kids, & brings us home inquiring when we'd like for him to wait for us again.

Now for requests. With May's check we should have $494.86. We are sending a money order for $30. Put $5.14 in the bank to give us $500.

Send - by airmail - 1 lb. Lykins Opera Creams.[5] Rex's request.

For Mother's day (course we're late as usual but we're a long ways off) send Mom a 2 lb. box of opera creams & get yourself 2 lbs.

In the next box send us two boxes of tea bags and one box of tea. Think I'd like a new spread for Candy's bed, too, but now that the mosquito nets are up I'll wait till fall.

Goodnite now.

Love

Bettie, Rex, & girls.

Always take your car-fare, lunch, & show (if desired) out of our money when you shop for us.

Flash - Jennifer has 2 teeth! Stands on (not in) her Taylor tot.

Sunday, May 11th

Dear Mother,

Rex was to return this A.M. but hasn't.

A mouse moved in yesterday so I'm very anxious for Rex's return.

Candy "killed two wolves & cut up a man" yesterday. Guess she shouldn't play so much with these older kids.

Love

Bettie

P.S. Monday Noon - Yippee.

Rex came home last P.M. with lots of good food.

Roaster came today, it's perfect & in perfect condition. Keep look out for the broiler & grill attachment.

Furniture en-route. Good day - treat the family to ice-cream on us tonight!

May 26, 1947

Area C - Okinawa

South Pacific

Dear Mother & Boys,

While Rex saws & hammers away I'll start a letter. He's making, or building kitchen cabinets & doing a good job on them. I should be washing the dishes (the ones from the States) but the water is off. Have had water for quite awhile now so this is a surprise. Perhaps the fellow who tends the water pumps wanted to see a movie tonite.

Rex got me coconut in Guam but I'll welcome the Baker's chocolate as I've found such a good recipe for coconut crisps, with confectioner's sugar. Nice of you to think of the food coloring.

The last visit to the Pediatrician, Jennifer's color had improved so he decided against a blood test. Little did he know that her little arms were sunburned & started to peel the next day. But she is just tiny. She's round & cute though & as peppy as can be. She can stand alone for ages so should start walking real soon. Still only two teeth.

Tried cream puffs - half of them weren't done, so didn't stay puffed. Going to try again soon.

Sears & Wards orders are coming through pretty good. This will save you lots of shopping. The furniture arrived & in perfect condition - well almost - on May 16th. Rex unpacked the radio-phonograph first thing & we've played & played our records. New ones will sure be welcomed.

By the way if you ever see a few boxes of tapioca get some for us & put it in the next box.

Father's day is coming in June. Please send Daddy & Rex's Dad each a card & a box of stationary. Also Daddy a birthday card.

For all your trouble & time this month we'd like to contribute $5.00 towards your Mixer.

Guess you wonder why we aren't buying Bonds. We will start in August. Want to have $1000 in the bank first for emergency. Sold our furniture from Manilla, the baby bed Rex made for Jennifer, & my lounging pajamas that were too small. This may sound silly but with no stores over here we trade, borrow, buy, & sell to & from each other. Traded a rubber sheet for two boxes of baby cereal Sat.

We've spent most of our time these last two weeks at home. Since the furniture came we've surely been busy. The washer was really welcome. We teased Haruko & said the scrub board she has been using was better and that we'd not use the washer.

She calls Jennifer "Jenny-Penny"! Rex comes home for lunch at noon. So Haruko & Jennifer take a walk visiting & chatting with other maids while Candy, Rex & I eat.

Candy's room is a dream now. Her tea set & set of aluminum cooking utensils really thrilled her. The couple next door made her a little round table & she has plenty of chairs.

There's always a "tea-party" on. She showed her pans to everyone so when our neighbors bake they come for one of her little pans. She had a devils food cake in her little tube- pan, & a coconut cream pie in her pie tin. Sunday I made her a miniature meat loaf in her loaf pan & put little pieces of potato around it, put jello in her little mold & fudge in one of her pans. So she had dinner in her room. She ate every bite. She plays with the older ones so much & knows how to pretend & imagine. Feeds & bathes her dolls, irons clothes (hankies & wash clothes) by the hours on her little ironing board.

Jennifer is sweet but won't put up with any foolishness from Candy - screams right out.

Rex has quit for the night so I must too. I've still lots to say & millions of questions to ask so I'll write again soon.

Rex sure works hard here. Just hope we can stay two years.

Love to all now, Bettie

Chapter 11

Joys of Living in the Tropics,
June 3 to August 27, 1947

June 3, 1947

The Gem of the Pacific

Dear Mother & Boys, & Mom, Dad, & Ann,

Bugs - yes, all kinds - they fly. Ordinarily we'd spray every evening with aerosol & the skeeters, flies, gnats & fleas would be gone. But some dope forgot to list Okinawa as a tropical isle & we have no more bombs (aerosol). They tried spraying by plane; that harms the rice crop so didn't work. So till things improve we'll stumble in & out of mosquito nettings. Right now the island has a siege of a termite-type bug. Look quickly - you'll see two on my cabinets! This is evidently their mating season; I pray it will be short & futile. They come in pairs, shed their wings all over the house & then crawl under things & die. Tut - so much of my good writing paper for bugs.

Baths - The shower leaks so badly we can no longer use it. So we all bathe in the kitchen sink - it's a blue metal affair about 2 ft. by 3 ft. & 1 ft. deep. Rex isn't happy there & won't sing even. To make matters worse, we took down our kitchen door, replacing it with a screen door to allow more light and air in. When you collect soap, clothes & towel you must also bring the shower curtain & put it up on the screen door to insure privacy. Cleanliness is a troublesome habit.

Food. The island is out of potatoes, the bakery has been broke down nearly a week now and there has been no meat besides liver, chicken, & bologna in the commissary. The food prices are sky high. A half ham is $5 a pound, jar of honey 61¢. Fruits & jams have soared. Hamburger is 60¢ a lb. Bacon also 60¢, and it's canned. Four boats are due in this month & we hope there will be some food for us.

Cooking – oh, today was good for baking. I turned out two beautiful crusty loafs of bread. I'm so proud of my bread. Also today, a sea-foam cake with delicious butterscotch filling. I've baked every kind of muffin, roll & biscuit you can think of.

The last time I made cookies I had to sift weevils (neat brown animals) out of my flower, sugar, & then pick them out of the coconut. I was making a delicious honey nut cookie till honey jumped to 60¢ a jar.

So much for eating. We enjoy it & are gaining. No salads, always starches & sweets. Everyone gains here.

Adventures in El-Jeepo. Saturday we snatched 2 kids, the thermos jug, a few goodies & some fruit & headed for Yanaburo - a naval base south of Buckner Bay. We enjoyed the ride - such as you do in jeeps & just as we were in the eating & returning mood it started to pour - the rain of course. Now, El-Jeepo has no top. We drove frantically hunting shelter while the kids fought over an apple & refused to stay under the blanket I was using for a tent. Ah, we spy a motor pool. There was a work shed with a top on it. We drove under & ate amid greasy automobile parts, native mechanics & flies. We had to move twice as the canvas roof on the shed got saturated & leaked. The rain slacked up & we decided it wouldn't hurt us. We looked like tramps time we got home - only to find it hadn't rained on this side of the island. We must be a pair of idiots, cause we think it's fun.

Entertainment - neighbors come in, we ate out Monday, we saw "Sea of Grass" and we're going to a formal dance Thursday.

Kids - They are cuter every day. Jennifer is beginning to walk. Today she really got going & is doing fine. She's little, happy, & cute. Loves to reach through her playpen & pull the "tea party" dishes off Candy's table. She's a little spoiled & doesn't like it when Candy leaves her.

Candy is so proud of Jennifer's walking - won't let her crawl but drags her up on her feet & says "No, you walk to me, you little rascal. Come on now". Every time a neighbor comes in she drags Jennifer in & says "Now you take a few steps for Bessie & show her what a big girl you are".

We have tea-parties daily. She loves her dishes & cooking utensils. She is always thinking of something to send for - "a little frigerator, a tiny stove, a bell for her bike, a washing machine - just a little one." Always it's "just a little one."

Really we're very proud of our girls & they are good (at times).

Jennifer and Candy, 1947

Eavesdropping last Friday I heard Candy coaching Jennifer. "Say 'dammit,' Jennifer, go ahead, say 'dammit.' You'll be bad then, dammit, dammit, dammit." I ignored it & she hasn't said it again. Jennifer just laughs.

Rex works so hard around here. There is yet linoleum to lay and the complete Quonset, floor & all to paint. But our place looks homey & nice now.We often sit listening to records & reading. We're very happy & contented with ourselves.

Hope we can stay in the army & if not, talk about going to South America or Alaska.

Max & Marie's [Rex's younger brother and his wife] little girl came April 13th. Deborah Marie called Debbie. Think it's a darling name & from Max's description a darling baby, plump, white, & red-headed. Rex was so thrilled about it. Poor Mom - all these girls! Marie got along very well for which I'm thankful.

The light will go out soon & I can't write by flashlight, so must wind up.

Rex is flying tonight & will be home between 1 & 2 A.M. Tired, hungry, and dirty.

Well the light went out as I started page 9 so I'll have to finish tomorrow. I'll take my little flashlight & go to bed. It's 12 P.M. now. Goodnight & God bless you all. You're swell folks.

Love - Bettie, Rex, &

the two widgets.

June - 5th.

Back again. Rex got home at 1 A.M. - had flown to Iwo Jima & Tokyo but not landed.

Give Jimmy & Jeanie our love. [Bettie's oldest brother and his girl friend.]

David [Bettie's youngest brother] will be in the 5th grade. Hooray! My last hope. Hope you get him Boy's Life magazine & that he likes it.

Mother, sometime when you send a box send a couple lipsticks for Haruko & a little box of powder.

Monday 10:30 P.M.

June 23, 1947

Okinawa

Dear Mother & Boys,

There's an orange loaf cake in the oven, two kids in bed, one husband asleep & me writing.

June is the last month in the Army's Fiscal year & they are flying nights, days, & weekends to get time in. Rex has twice the time he needs but still must fly. He briefs at midnight, takes off at 2 A.M. for a ten hour flight somewhere below Manilla, turns around & comes back.

Summer is here & man is it hot! There is a breeze every night but our Quonset seems determined not to let any of it get in.

It rained for ten days. Everything from clothes, to books & luggage got moldy. Now it's been dry for four days (a record) so we sun the moldy things & put them away to mold again next week.

The few pieces of furniture we have that are veneer are coming all apart.

Spent Sat. & Sun. at Ishykawa Beach [on the Pacific side of the island, just a little north of where they live]. Saturday we went late, were in the water about an hour & took the long way home.

It was real pleasant & a lovely sandy beach. We buried each other, got sand in our ears, nose, & eyes, & swallowed salt water.

Sunday before lunch our neighbors suggested a picnic & a dip in the ocean. They have a weapons carrier for a vehicle so we rode in that. It was hot & windy. Quite a bumpy ride in an open truck but we made it.

Enjoyed a fine picnic dinner. Jennifer & I didn't go in the water on Sunday. Candy had a time with some little girl friend she found & wasn't afraid of the water. The beach was crowded & you saw everyone you knew. Jennifer & Rex got sun-burned. Little Jenny really gets red. Her hair was bleached white. So she looks red & white.

Tuesday - June 24th.

Rex is carving handles for the kitchen cabinets. I'm going to answer your last two letters.

Congratulations to Jimmy & Jeanie. Any date set? Bet that ring is pretty & looks pretty on Jeanie's hand. Next time Rex lands in Manilla we'll send something for Jeanie's hope chest.

You asked what was the matter with Candy. She had scabies - a little mite that burrows under the skin. Had spread quite a bit before anyone thought they were other than mosquito or flea bites. Doctor gave us some emulsion that dried them right up. They were really bothersome to her though.

Now when you spank Candy she says "Now you've made me sick, just sick!"

She seems to cry a lot anymore. She'll cry & I'll ask her, "What's the matter?" She'll stop completely & tell me, "I'm not happy." The other day when asked she said "Well I want to go to a dance, that's why I'm crying. When can I go to dances?"

Jennifer just walks around getting into things and grinning that grin that shows how short she is on teeth. She used to sleep in the jeep but now she won't even sit down.

Mother there's lots of things I want. If this shopping is too much for you please let me know. Mom would probably do some of it. Don't mind telling me cause I know it takes time and trouble.

We're enclosing a $50 money order. Twenty-five for the bank account and twenty-five for the safety deposit box.

Little things that don't weigh much send first class or airmail.

1 pkg. emery boards

2 pair white shoe strings

8 white buttons - size of one included

1 gold identification bracelet for Jennifer - it's for her birthday. Just "Jennifer" engraved on it.

2 spools white thread

12 pair training pants for Jennifer. She weighs 18 lbs., so the very smallest size, preferably elastic all around.

10 pair of same for Candy; she weighs 30 lbs. Her waist measures 19 inches. Think she'd take size two but not sure. If you see any fancy ones a couple pair of those would be O.K. She's wearing those you sent for her first birthday now.

1 dozen Pro-phy-lac-tic pocket combs. (brown & black)

1 year subscription "Ladies Home Journal". Have it in my name % 1st Lt. R.H. George, ect.

1 rubber scraper for an electric mixer. They're to scrape the bowl while the mixer is in action.

1 Book - Robert Lewis Stevenson's "Child's Garden of Verse". Preferably illustrated - plain O.K.

The darned P.X. had better get some paper in. I'm now writing on pages from my recipe book. Send some paper, a couple tablets. No envelopes. We got them all over the place.

Candy & I attended a delightful cocktail party last week. She wore her white organdy pinafore over a pink linen dress, white gloves & her black patent slippers. She was so dressed up that she wouldn't even be sociable.

Our hostess had twenty girls in. She had delightful refreshments including finger sandwiches and tarts. The tarts were so pretty. Some filled with pineapple cubes topped with a cherry, others with vanilla or chocolate pudding with a drop of meringue in the center.

The marvelous part was the way she bakes. She has no roaster or oven, only a hot plate. She turns the hot plate on, inverts a deep sauce pan on it, sets or balances her pie plate or muffin tins on that & covers all with a large dish pan. Has meat loafs, baked potatoes, ect., all the time that way!

I've gained 8 lbs. Everyone gains here. No salads, only starches & heavy foods. You'd think the jeep riding would take it off but it only causes your seat to get calloused & your tail bone to ache.

Goodnite & God bless you.

Bettie

P.S. Rex has the handles on the kitchen cabinets now. They sure look nice, he does everything right. Now he's reading a mystery.

July 8, 1947

Dear Mother,

Rec'd 2 letters & a pkg. from you. One jar of syrup was broken; everything else was sticky, but O.K. Thanks so much; everything was fine.

Your black walnut cake sounds good. Sometime send me the recipe. Then if you send it you'll have to send the walnuts too.

Sorry David did not pass. Hope that it doesn't discourage him. Next year I'll send for Boy's Life for him & maybe he'll read that in place of those d—— comic books. That's the trouble with most kids, they don't read the right literature.

We spent the week end of the fourth at the Beach. Candy & I have nice tans. Rex just gets red & Jennifer blisters. We don't take Jennifer anymore unless it's late afternoon. Sometimes we swim in the Pacific (Ishikawa Beach) sometimes the China Sea (Lolly Beach).[1] Often we take our lunch. We always meet others there.

There is no use trying to have good kids. The couple next door have Candy spoiled rotten & Haruko spoils Jennifer. She won't let her cry at all.

Candy can color & stay in the lines now. They still have tea parties but there isn't much left of the tea set.

The P.X. got some magazines in - the first in 6 mos. They charged 30¢ for a Saturday Evening Post, 50¢ for Lady's Home Journal. This is the only place in the world where it's cheaper to go to a movie than to stay home & read a book.

Made raisin bread the other week. Had creamed chicken on hot biscuts today. Baked a marble cake. Keeps me hopping fixing breakfast then two big meals every day and only serving potatoes once. In the next package send some packaged cheese - Old English & Velvetta - 2 each.

Got a new G.E. refrigerator Monday. It's a seven ft. box but seems small after my 9 ft. Servel. The Servel stopped running & we couldn't fix it. At the same time a boat load of refrigerators came in so we got one. It's electric; with the poor power we have it won't last long. The electricity is worse than ever. I'll be glad when we are put on the new power plant.

Candy is awake. It's about time for Rex to come home & I'm still in shorts. If I knew what was on at the movie I'd ask Haruko to stay & we'd go out.

Love - Bettie.

When you do the shopping have lunch & a movie on us.

August 11, 1947

Dear Mother & Boys,

Now here I am with umpteen letters to answer and loads to say so I'll get started.

The shoes & socks came, perfect. You did fine. The crystal for the record player & bracelet came; they too were just right. ('cept we found out it wasn't the crystal but the amplifier tube that needed replacing.)

The silver spoon and fork for Jennifer's first birthday are precious. The pattern is so neat & pretty. We're using the spoon & Jennifer knows it's hers. Candy's having a fit cause hers doesn't have her name on it, so Rex will have to put her name on hers.

Rex left early Sunday (yesterday) for Yakota Air Force Base, Japan. He will be gone four days. They put our jeep in the bomb bay of the B-29 so they would have transportation to Tokyo to shop.

He was in Japan last week end. That was cause of B-29 engine trouble & he didn't get into Tokyo. He is scheduled to go to Manilla next week. Candy says she's "not happy" when her Daddy is away. She wants him to bring her a present - a parasol and a teeter-totter - hope she forgets the latter.

A young Baptist couple (civil service workers from California) has started a Sunday school for children. I teach the Primaries. In five weeks we have jumped our attendance from four to 35 & gotten bus service. Rex & I still contribute to the church in Houston & they are sending us some of the literature we use. We've ordered crayons but need little blunt-nosed scissors. If ever you see any send 15 or 20 pair. Don't pay over 20¢ a pair for them. When the word gets around I'm sure we'll have 70 or more children.

We have attended a couple very nice parties, (well one was nice, the other left the neighborhood in an uproar for weeks), several movies, & a picnic at the beach every Sunday. Last two Sundays I've taken the kids & gone with friends to swim & picnic.

Now, if there is a lone wife in the area, & there always are 2 or 3 husbands gone, someone always offers help, and entertains you. Makes time go faster. A neighbor girl whose husband is on the Yakota mission is sleeping over here with me cause she's scared.

You almost lost your only daughter last week. I'll start from the beginning.

We Kem-toned [a brand of paint used in the tropics] our living room. It's soft, pale blue & beautiful - for a Quonset. Then we had to do something about the floor! So last Monday we tried to put blue lacquer on it. We were using pure acetone to thin it. Took turns painting & sitting. It was 10 P.M. & I mentioned how much like ether the acetone smelled. I sat down &

immediately went to sleep. Rex talked to me & tried to wake me but couldn't.

He dragged me outside & tried to get me to breathe deeply. Neighbors came to help & a former nurse kept shoving the ammonia bottle under my nose. I couldn't stay awake. So down to the dispensary in style (in another neighbor's state-side car) I went. Rex stayed to get the kids out of the house. They slapped me all the way down. Every woman in the neighborhood beat me around that night.

The doctor gave me a double dose of caffeine in my blood stream & said I must drink coffee & be kept awake no matter what, for four hours.

By that time I was so silly it was funny. I cut-up, flirted, got loud, & giggled constantly.

I even sat in cold water to stay awake till 2 A.M. & wow! What a hangover the next day!

The doctor said if I'd just gone to sleep with all that acetone in my lungs I would have smothered & never awakened. So Rex was fooled again! He came on down to the hospital. Was he embarrassed! I was the life of the party in my little sun-suit, my hair in pin curls, & paint & dirt all over me. (And to top it off, I had laryngitis & squeaked & strained to talk.)

Jennifer had a cake with pink frosting & coconut for her birthday. She also dropped her one penny in the birthday box at Sunday-school & stood proudly while we sang Happy Birthday. She's still tiny but not thin. Her temper fits are getting worse. I just ignore them. She doesn't eat much. Has started to climb all around. Fusses with Candy & screeches if she isn't first for a drink or cookie. Looks for the world like a little banty rooster strutting around. She's sway-backed & her chest & rear stick out. Has a little barrel chest.

Miss Candy, using her imagination, can spin a yarn that would put other fairy stories to shame. Of all things, she chases imaginary rats all day. She has lots of expression & uses phrases like "Well now, what do you know about that?", "Can you imagine it?" & to Jennifer, "You're too little to understand, Honey". I'd give anything if you could hear her. She came in one day & said, "Mommy, Janie has two maids at her house, we'd better get another one too".

Oh yes - we have a gardener - Matsuda - He speaks no English & I can still only count to ten in their language & say "jato" - which means "nice." He persists in making a fence when I want the yard cleaned up first. I've given up. Haruko now does all the talking between us. I feed him, too, of course. The first day I let him eat in the kitchen. He ate everything, but I found 2 cigarette butts, matches, ashes, & a dozen cherry seeds on the floor. Now he eats on the back porch.

Truthfully, living conditions over here are very sorry & utilities inexcusable. We have a put-put [small generator] we scrounged so can have power when the main generator is out. It was out of order for five days last week. The low power burned the motor of my washer out already. We women in this area (because it's far away, & no high ranking officers live out here) have it worse than the other areas. So we got together & went to see the Base inspector about conditions out here. We didn't accomplish too much but something happened last week that did.

A wife on the next street got Jap-B-encephalitis (sleeping sickness) & died this A.M. Since she took ill things have been changing cause the Command is scared. She's the 3rd death from it in two weeks. We now have power; Colonels actually came out & inspected this area and had a meeting with us families. Airplanes sprayed the area, garbage cans & lids were distributed, and our screens were painted with D.D.T. A mosquito carries the disease. It's almost always fatal & if not, leaves you insane. We have had the shots for it, thank goodness, but still are taking every precaution cause Jennifer was too young for the shots & they aren't positive protection anyway. Many girls are going to return to the States because of it.

I figure that there are diseases everywhere. At home there's polio this time of the year. Time you were booked for passage home the season would be over. Nothing like that worries me.

Wednesday, the bus that takes us weekly to the dry cleaners, laundry & Post Office, will take us to the Chapel for the funeral service first.

I'll stop chattering & answer your letters now. By the way, try adding chopped onion & bits of Old English cheese to cold mashed potatoes & heating in the oven - really delicious.

Say, I've got to go to bed. It's after 11 now & Candy & I are going to the commissary tomorrow. We're getting some pretty good food in now & more variety. Even mayonnaise, fresh boxed cookies, Whitmans & Johnstons candies, graham crackers, frozen cauliflower & broccoli.

Goodnite now. God bless you

Bettie

August 27, 1947

Kadena, Okinawa

Dear Mother & Boys,

Me again! Was supposed to go to a Sunday School Teachers meeting but because of storms I'm staying home. Seems a typhoon is several hundred miles away and we are getting wet from it.

Read about your heat wave. We have had hot weather but there is always rain, wind or sun the next minute. Weather changes every minute. Can always sleep at nights comfortably though. The kids don't have heat rash anymore but Rex & I do. It isn't very pleasant either.

Was going to ask for certain foodstuffs but Rex & I just discussed my weight & decided I'd bake less. I'm loosing my waist line. Foods are so different over here and with fixing two big meals a day I naturally eat them. Oh me. The scales said 121½ lbs. last week. Most of the time there are no salad fixings or fresh things at the PX.

Right now Candy is eating ice cream with chocolate sauce & Rex is drinking a can of cold beer & eating cheese & crackers. (Crackers were in the commissary for the first time this week.) They won't give me a bite. I told them my Mother wouldn't starve me like that.

Please don't spend much money for Christmas. We're going to try to do our shopping by catalogue & have them send the gifts. Gee! Can't want for the fall & winter edition of Sears & Ward's catalogues to be sent. Do send Haruko a gift at Christmas - a scarf, pretty combs, mittens or the like. Whenever a pkg. comes she is as excited as we are.

Rex brought us lots of nice things from Tokyo. Two darling dresses apiece for the kids, a silk parasol for Candy, a child's fan, some odd souvenirs, also some cologne (Chanel #5) for me.

Jennifer plays right along with Candy now. She's still got only 6 teeth, those are large, her front ones are far apart. She's a cute looking little one.

Candy & Janie, our neighbor girl, found a red pepper tree & sampled the fruit thereof. What a time I had. They screamed, jumped, howled and cried. I gave them ice, water, cookies, apples, & still they were miserable. Their mouths got all red & swollen. I called the dispensary & they had me give them bread & jam & make them chew & chew it before swallowing. What a time. Candy was so exhausted afterwards that she asked to go to bed.

Got rid of my gardener yesterday & am not very happy. It was troublesome & expensive to feed him and he didn't garden; he was just a fence-builder & after so many fences our place is beginning to look pretty silly.

I'm going to bed now. I can't think & am writing worse.

Love

Bettie

Tired Bettie, fall 1947

September 5, 1947

Dearest Mother & Boys,

Friday P.M. Just finished dishes, Rex just tucked our babies away for the night. Now we're writing our Mothers. Then we'll have a piece of chocolate pie and settle down to our new mystery novels.

Rec'd your letter a couple of days ago. Please never worry about us; we're very happy here & wouldn't think of leaving. Just remember: It's bad news that travels fast. Also rec'd the first issue of "Lady's Home Journal" (August). Get it, look at the fashion section. I'll never come back to the U.S. if I have to wear or see clothes like that - icky-poo - such a shame.

First I'll answer your letter.

I repeat - we're happy. It's civilized here. We want to be here. When we come back to the U.S. we'll try to go to Germany or somewhere. As long as we're able & Uncle Sam buys the tickets we're going to see what we can.[2]

It's plenty sticky here all day but we can always sleep at nights. I have heat rash pretty bad. Rex & I went to a dance last night & I embarrassed him cause I couldn't stop from scratching all the time.

Rex decided I should take exercises. So Monday - Labor Day - we started. After 40 minutes I could barely limp down the hall to bathe. Then I heard the mixer & soon Rex brings me in a vanilla malt - thick & creamy - to cool me off. What hope is there?

[Bettie and friend Marian McGough played volley ball to keep in shape. In a 1991 letter, Marian recalled, "After the game, we would go back to the George's Quonset and eat cherry pie. Great diet!"]

Mother, do get an electric mixer, they are so handy. I use mine every day.

By the way our typhoon last week broke up into several storms. Had lots of wind & rain for a week but no typhoon.

Any time you see black walnuts get a half pound or lb. & send them. I'm all out & had been making a honey-nut muffin that was so good & easy.

Mother, my girls are getting so they cry when I walk out of their sight. Such kids. Candy isn't so bad but Jennifer can blink her eyes & pucker up in a moment. Candy told me that when she goes back to the States she was going to get a black silk car with red wheels. Oh me.

We have been taking care of Candy's friend Janie while her mother has a new baby. So Sunday Janie goes with us to Sunday school. Afterwards we go to the club for a second breakfast. You should've seen us with the three girls. Jennifer wouldn't sit down, Candy wouldn't eat - Janie wanted to argue. From all appearances we were happy & smiling. Next day a Major asked Rex how he could have so many kids & stay so young looking.

I'm going to close. Love to all. Will write soon.

Bettie.

Chapter 12

Typhoons, Security for Life, Theft
September 15 to November 17, 1947

Typhoons could do serious damage to a fleet of airplanes sitting on the runway. Therefore, it was critical to get the planes off the ground and into the air where they would be safe during the storm. One of the duties of B-29 flight crews on Okinawa was weather reconnaissance. They flew into approaching typhoons[1] to determine their direction and severity.

Flying into a typhoon was dangerous business and most crews did it as infrequently as possible. Rex's crew, however, flew typhoon recons repeatedly. Under present-day rules, a flying mission into a hurricane qualifies for the Distinguished Flying Cross commendation.

We were lucky when it came to typhoons. In July, 1949, a year after we left, 175-mile winds from Typhoon Gloria destroyed 92 Quonsets housing American families and damaged many others. Within a couple years, typhoon-resistant construction made life in Okinawa much safer.

September 15, 1947

Kadena, Okinawa

Dear Mother & Boys,

We are all very well & happy, especially these last few days cause a cool breeze is blowing & it's so pleasant & comfortable.

We've been gadding, gabbing, & going so much of late that we go to bed early when we are at home. Last week attended Bingo, movies, a formal dance, entertained the Sunday school teachers, spent 2 evenings visiting friends & the other p.m. had company. A YWCA is being organized in the area & I'm in on that also.

Rex has been quite busy flying typhoon recons but we never have any typhoons. They always go somewhere else.

The bread making deal gets simpler each time. I can now start when I get up & have fresh bread in time for lunch. It stays fresh longer than bought bread so only have to bake twice a week.

We have a top on our jeep now. Don't think that means it's a closed jeep. It's just a top.

One of the girls going home next week just brought over a darling black & pink taffeta formal. I needed another one so will buy it. Sold that summer pique one last week. Everyone going home has a sale. People - as soon as they know someone is leaving - call up to speak for their dishes, toys, furnishings, even for their maid. Some really ask outrageous prices & get them. A kerosene stove ($75 in a catalogue) was sold for $150 in our neighborhood last week.

Mother, just stop eating before you go to bed so you won't have bad dreams about us. Leave us in peace here on Okinawa. Gosh, we've never had it so good! This would be a poor time to return to the States anyway. Couldn't buy a new car even. But here we have a house & a jeep, cheap help, loads of entertainment, the best friends in Army people, good food, & a chance that, before returning, we will get to see Tokyo or Shanghai. Right now we could fly to China but it is so high & would be full fare for each child.

About Christmas presents for these angels - neither needs any dresses at all; nor pants or socks or shoes or coats. I'll list a few things they could use but really it's just what you see or like or pick from the list. Please don't spend much. I mean it.

Candy - handbag (red or green), rubber boots (big enough for over size 7½ or 8 shoes), any kind of tea set or washer, or mixer, or any miniature kitchen item. Maybe a little sewing set. A sweater perhaps or a robe.

Jennifer - a kiddy-car, winter pjs, or gowns, a pull toy, tin tea set.

Well they are awake now so I'll close. Candy is reading your letters. Jennifer is into the dish cabinet. Jennifer weighs 19 lbs. Candy 30 now. Jennifer can act so hurt & blink her eyes & draw in her lips when corrected. Candy sings "Away in a Manger" now. Took her to the club to Bingo Sat. P.M. She knows where the Ladies' Room is, so went alone. She comes running back, pants down around her knees, hollering, "Oh Mommy, their toilet is broke!" Naturally we got a laugh but it was embarrassing.

Love

Bettie

October 1, 1947

Kadena, Okinawa

Dear Mother & Boys,

Hello! I haven't had a letter from you for awhile but will probably get one tomorrow.

Candy's patent slippers came today. They are perfect; & came at just the right time. Candy & Jennifer attended a birthday party today and Candy would bend over every few seconds to wipe her "new patent slippers" with her lace hankie.

Haruko isn't with us anymore, so I was ironing this P.M. Want to bake cookies tomorrow as the Women's Club of Area C meets here Friday. There will be about 20 or 30 attending. Just business & social gatherings every week or so.

We are all fine. The Sunday school is coming along nicely. Had 57 in attendance Sunday. I had the devotional at the Teachers' meeting.

We sat down a few days ago & made out our Christmas lists. Getting most everything out of the Sears & Montgomery Ward's catalogue. I'm getting Rex & he's getting me, & we're getting the kids & they are getting us a Kodak Movie Camera so when we come home we can show pictures of our life here.

There are a few gifts for you to get & I think there will be enough money in the S.D. Box. Of course Mary's & Rosemary's which you have probably already purchased. And send Connie, Mary's Mother, a subscription to the "Ladies Home Journal" - 1 year - I think it's $6 for England but send it anyway. And that should do it.

Now send us (at your leisure) some black walnuts, some pecans to use in baking & some Bakers Choc. Also 20 balloons, candles (pink) & holders, & 20 napkins. (These things are to be for Candy's birthday party in January.)

Candy is such a help, she takes Jennifer's shoes & socks off for me & talks to Jennifer like a Grandma. Tells her to eat & she might grow up next week & be able to talk.

When I cook or bake they are both right there. Candy kneads her little loaf of bread as I do mine.

Jennifer is getting to act so cute. She flirts & blinks her eyes if you try to correct her. She eats no vegetables but lives on fruits. She loves her doll & teddy bear.

How are Jimmy & Jean doing? Has she got her ring paid for yet? Tell Jimmy we've never seen any pearls yet. Perhaps when we go to Tokyo in the spring we shall.

It's still warm here but not so downright hot. We're enjoying an unusually dry spell to.

We must now share the Jeep with another couple, Willie and Doris Williams. They live a block away & are close friends so there is no conflict or inconvenience. We always went to most of the dances, Sunday-school, ect. together anyway.

Rex isn't flying much because they have so few good airplanes.

Take good care of yourself Mother & don't work too hard. Never worry about us because we do fine & are very happy. Rex still beats me (of course) & I can drink either a weak Tom Collins or a half a can of beer now without getting dizzy. Ah, soon I'll learn to smoke (an opium pipe) "Cigarettes, Whiskey, & Wild, Wild Women" - perhaps you've heard the tune - Yippee!

Love & God bless you.

Bettie

P.S. Try Carnation Milk's "Pink Velvet Pie." It's quick, easy, delicious & economical. Featured in August magazines.

Ah, bananas are back![2] Try a delicious banana cake with caramel fudge frosting - moist & flavorful.

Wed. P.M. - Oct. 8, 1947

Kadena, Okinawa

Dearest Mother,

Just returned from Sunday School Teacher's meeting, Rex is reading, he has tucked the kids in & they're asleep, so I'll answer your last letter.

We are all fine. Well, Rex is getting a cold, Jennifer has a little runny nose & I have laryngitis, but Candy is fine.

I'm still without a maid & thoroughly enjoying it too. Seven girls have been to my door, but I want my house to myself for a little bit, so have refused them all. Why, my ironing is always caught up & it never was before. I can't gad as much but we can borrow a girl when we want to go out.

Want to bake bread early tomorrow so Rex can take a loaf back to some fellow in his office at noon. Now all of our flour has weevils in it, also tiny tan worms who are soon to be weevils. You sift & pick for hours before you bake.

We had 62 children in Sunday school Sunday. That's good for this base. Just four months ago it started with 4 children. We're planning a Christmas party for all the children on the Kadena Base - even a Santa Claus.

Thanks for the balloons. They lasted 2 hours & the kids sure enjoyed them.

This is just a note. Best I go to bed now.

Love to all

Bettie, Rex & girls

In her next letter, Bettie announces that Rex has been awarded a "permanent commission." This means their decision to make the military a career has been blessed by the Army Air Corps and seals their future.

Rex, Bolo Point, fall 1947

Okinawa

October 23, 1947

Dear Mother & Boys,

It's a beautiful sunny fall day & the kids are taking their afternoon naps, so I'll start chatting with you all.

Best news first! Rex is now a 1st Lieutenant in the U.S. Army. His permanent commission came last week. Dated as of Feb. 5, 1947. That's what we've always hoped for & now we have it. That means security for life. Of course you can't settle down to your vine covered cottage for years to come but we like & enjoy traveling & seeing new places & knowing new people. We no longer have to wonder & plan on what we'd do or where we'd go if he were discharged.

And just call me "Widder George," cause Rex left Oct. 21st for - guess where - the U.S.A. It's on a mission (can't tell you much more cause it's a secret). They are to go to Texas (it's rumored). Don't know how long it will take. They guess & hope to be back in a month. I'm not the only wife left. Almost all the fellows in the Group go sometime before Oct. is over.

A friend called last night & said Rex's plane feathered an engine [lost an engine] in Guam so was held up & won't leave there till Friday. Hope they don't have any more trouble to hold them up.

He'll probably call you by phone - maybe before you receive this letter. He was kind of excited about going but hated to leave us.

The girls have been very good so far. The weather is fine, & the work is caught up.

Candy had a shampoo before her nap & I put her hair up on the curlers & am awaiting the results. I now tie her pigtails back cause they were long & thin. If the curlers work I'll trim her hair slightly.

Jennifer still hasn't enough hair to mention & its white as ever. I'll tell her to talk & she'll shake her head & say "no no."

Saturday before Rex left we attended a formal reception for the new Colonel. Had a grand time & got to wear my new formal.

Say, the mixer really makes good Sponge Cakes. Made some good cream puffs too. Also we're all frying doughnuts. They are easy and so good & crisp.

The old commissary has cranberry sauce, grape juice, Bakers Choc., & Bisquick this week. It's getting to be like a regular grocery.

Haruko was a good worker but we (quite by accident) discovered she was stealing from us so sent her back to Ishikawa.[3]

My washer is fixed now & I'm doing fine alone. People think I'm crazy but it's kinda nice to have your house to yourself for awhile. When I'm ready, I'll get another maid. But I won't be so darned good & generous with her.

As for how long we'll stay, to be truthful we haven't made up our minds yet. We planned on extending our tour here but now that we have regular army we probably won't. Anyhow, we don't intend to tell you now cause it isn't entirely our decision. Families come & go on every boat.

Tsk, tsk those typhoons never seem to get here. They don't even worry us. Just means wind & rain & another mission to fly.

Gosh here is another letter from you that I haven't answered!

I'd still like small scissors. Send 15 or 20 pair & a bill for them & I can pay for them out of the Chaplain's Fund. Or pay for them out of the S.D. box, but do get a receipt.

Since its cool I've given up my ½ can of beer a day. Stopped drinking Tom Collin's cause one would give me a hang-over. Oh me, my drinking days sure didn't last.

I'm reading "David the King" now. It's about David in the Bible.

Rex may buy a car while he's in the states (a used one & put it on a boat). Kinda hope not. We don't have a jeep to ourselves anymore & you can't lose on a car over here but I hate to invest when we can't afford it yet.

I'm going to close now. Love to all. Thanks, Mother, for doing my shopping so well. Bettie

Wed. Oct. 29, 1947

Kadena

Dear Mother & Boys,

Thought I'd jot down a few lines before I retire & answer your letter which came yesterday.

Rex is still flying towards the States & should have called you time this arrives.

After I wrote you last Thursday I heard from him. Our neighbor has a Ham Radio and Rex called from Guam by short wave. We talked for quite awhile. They had to stay there a week.

So we made a date to make contact Sunday at 7 P.M. to talk again. Some of the other wives came & for an hour & a half we chatted with our husbands.

Tuesday at 6 P.M. they contacted us from Kwajalein in the Marshall Islands. They were to leave there today at sundown. So we'll try tomorrow at 2 P.M. to contact them in Oahu, Hawaii.

Talking to Rex is grand. It makes the time go faster to know where he is & what he's doing.

Any time you even have a chance to use a radio you can call for J9AAI. Don't lose that call number as some time you may need it. It's on the 10 meter band.

Capt. Corzine (our neighbor) has contacted every state but Vermont so far.

So much for that. My girls & I are really busy this week. Today at 3 P.M. they attended a birthday party. Cake, ice cream, hats, poppers, candy in fancy cups & all the candles on the cake were little girls. So cute.

We got home at 5:30 & left at 6:30 P.M. for another party. It was given by a fellow & his wife in Rex's office for 5 children & parents.

Jennifer was the life of the party. She flirts & teases & makes faces & isn't shy at all.

They brought us home at 10 P.M. I just got the kids in bed. I was so proud of them; they were so good. Candy's hair was curled & was she vain!

Now tomorrow I must set my bread to rise & catch the commissary bus at 9 A.M. That trip takes two hours on Thursdays. Then talk to Rex at 2 P.M. & take the kids to a Halloween Party at 4 P.M. At 6 P.M. they are to go with the mothers & little children of the area to trick or treat.

Friday is the Sunday-School Halloween Party at 7 P.M. Don't think I'll take Jennifer there.

Sure enjoyed your letter. No, you can't send a fruit cake. We have them at the Commissary already. Those weevils I spoke of come in the flour when you by it. We don't raise them around here. But what you keep here you keep in tin or don't keep.

Jenny is tiny but very well filled out. She isn't serious like Candy was but very gay. Says no, don't, down, & apple; & a variety of strange noises. Sings every time she picks up a book.

Candy is still my girl. Such a help & more fun to talk to. Before we left for the party she gazed in the mirror & said. "When I go in Bob's house everyone will say, "Here comes Candy; don't she look pretty with her fluffy curls?" She's very prissy about her clothes. She wants something changed soon as it's dirty and is forever wiping her shoes off.

Going to close now. Glad to know everyone at home is happy and doing so well. Send us some snapshots soon of everyone.

Goodnite now. Love & God bless you all,

Bettie

November 17, 1947

Rain, rain, & more rain.

Dear Mother & Boys,

Oh where is my wandering husband to-nite? It's almost a month now! Got the last cable the 14th from El Paso & think he'll be home the last of this week or first of next. Sure is getting lonesome around here.

Guess Rex has called you by now. Had a long letter from him from Honolulu.

We have been fine till this week. It's rained now for 9 days straight, the motor (the second one) on the washing machine burned out, Jennifer got a cold, five gallons of diesel oil leaked out around the space heater in the living room and Candy has decided to sleep with me. Flour has jumped from 45¢ to 73¢ for 5lbs. &

the flour is all moldy so I'm buying my bread. Ah me, also the shower leaks again and the hot water pipe in the bathroom, too.

A rotten floorboard on the back porch gave in & went through. We were put on the main water line and immediately all the toilets went out of commission from the pressure. We have the kind that have the flush box away up on the wall & you pull a string, or rather a chain, to flush.

I've got a new maid as of today. Her name is Tomako. She works faster than Haruko but hasn't managed to do a thing right yet. Guess I'll tell you why Haruko isn't with us. One day I discovered - quite by accident - that she was slowly carrying away everything in the place. Not till after we'd fired her did I discover that, in addition to linens, silver, & china, she had taken every hat I own. We should have just turned her over to the M.P.'s. (Candy calls them P.K.'s) She was a good worker & good to the children; it broke my heart when I found she wasn't honest, after all we'd done for her & given her.

Jennifer has finally gotten an appetite. She's over 20 lbs now & looks cuter every day. She feeds herself & makes a terrible mess but will have it no other way. She does every thing Candy & her friends do and loves her dolls & having tea parties. She sings & dances & tries to act cute when she's corrected. Doesn't talk much or show any interest in looking at books. Ah me, no future!

Candy can say her ABC's - no foolin' - without any help she can go right through. Now I'm trying to teach her to recognize them. You know, she's counted for quite awhile but just now can realize what or how many of something there are. For instance, she can now count the oranges & tell you there are 12 there.

After a spanking or if she's put to bed against her will you'll hear her fussing like this. "I'm just a little girl, a pretty little girl, & you've spanked me. I danced for you today and we sang songs &

now you spank me. I don't have anyone to play with; my Daddy is to the States. You said you loved me, that's what you told me — —."

And on & on it goes. I'm in the other room, trying not to giggle. She often comes to me & says - "Now are you sorry you spanked me?" Her excuse for being bad is always that she's tired & needs rest.

The nice part about being alone over here is that everyone looks after you. I've never eaten out so much. Someone is always asking us to the club to eat with them. I've taken in several movies, rides, ect. Friends even drove us over to Rykom (ground forces headquarters) where the P.X. has a real pop corn machine & we all had a bag of popped corn. Yesterday Candy, Jennifer, & I were asked to tea (by another "widow") & served hot chocolate & some fancy dish which was a meringue shell filled with crushed pineapple pudding & topped with r.s.p. [red, sour, pitted] cherries. Quite tasty.

Now I'd best answer your letter. Hum, nothing to answer. You remember the movie "The Rains Came"? Well, 'samo-samo Okinawa.' They'll last till March. Ah well, only three of our six rooms don't leak. Some Sgt's wife flew back from here & told reporters (from the Tulsa, Oklahoma "World") all the secrets of the island & even how many planes were here. We're waiting to see what happens!

Goodnight now. It's been a good three months since we sent that film in, so can't understand why the prints aren't back.

Love & kisses, Bettie

Chapter 13

Nursery School, Rats, Weight, Christmas, November 30 – December 28, 1947

In the following letter to Rex's family, Bettie mentions the religion of the "natives." Traditional Okinawan religion includes aspects of animism, ancestor worship and Buddhism. By 1952, seven years after U.S. occupation, there were estimated to be fewer than 5,000 Okinawan Christians in the civilian population of about 700,000.

November 30, 1947

Kadena, Okinawa

Dear Mom, Dad, & Ann,

Rex is typing some papers about his commission and the kids are taking their naps. It's a nice Saturday afternoon and I'm going to write till the kids wake up & then finish tonight.

Rex got home Nov. 20th. We were sure glad to see him and hear about the States. Wish he could have seen you all. He had a quick trip home.

We had a typhoon here on Tuesday before he came home on Thursday. It didn't scare me, it wasn't a real bad one & very little damage was done. The kids and I just ran around emptying pans of water that blew or leaked in & mopping other places. The old

Quonset won't blow away! The bad part is we have no power or water at such times. We had only two candles & our storage tank of water, but in two days everything was normal again.

The Sunday school I've mentioned is non-denominational & is for children up to 15 years of age. Our superintendent is Baptist, the chaplain is Presbyterian and our teachers are a variety. Most of our material is Baptist. We're planning a Christmas program to hold in the Chapel now. Rex attends Chapel while I'm in Sunday school.

No natives are included. They have a Sunday-school & church at Ishikawa. Rev. Haggi (native) is pastor. Only a small percentage of the natives are Christians. Friends of ours - who organized the S.S. & visit us often - have visited the native church & are friends of Rev. Haggi. The Reverend's wife is now ill & was sent to the leper colony in the northern part of the island. He says it isn't leprosy, though.[1]

The weather here is still pretty decent. We need a little heat early in the morning & towards evening. You need a sweater outdoors.

Gracious, Mom, I'm stouter all the time & the cleaners here ruin everything. They shrink everything - even Rex's clothes are getting too small.

We just plan on coming home & going on a shopping spree. Rex got a new civilian outfit in Honolulu. Guess he'll wear mostly civvies, instead of his military uniform when we return. Looks fine in his sport outfit but of course can't wear it over here.

Candy starts in Nursery School Monday. She'll go from 8-noon. I'll miss her so much but there aren't many children around here since the one outfit moved to Naha. She'll learn lots as they read stories to them, color, draw, play, & sing. Her teacher is a friend of ours. They usually take kids at 3 yrs. old, but will start

Candy about a month before her birthday. She goes on a school bus and Jennifer and I will be out there to wave bye-bye. Jennifer will get more attention, but will miss Candy.

Jennifer is sure an imp. She's saying more words now, & is she sassy! She'll holler - "no!" & run as fast as she can. Wants to be outside all the time & wanders off the minute Candy or I look away. She plays with the dolls & wraps them in blankets & brings them visiting for me to hold & kiss just like Candy does.

We had Thanksgiving dinner at home. No turkey cause we don't care for it that much; the commissary didn't get any chickens either.

Then that evening we attended a dance. Had a grand time, fair music, & a nice buffet.

I have another girl – Tomako.[2] She's 18 & kinda cute. She is doing pretty well now but was sure exasperating for several days. She eats any & everything & isn't demanding. She lives at Sabe which is just a 15 minute walk so there are no transportation difficulties. She has worked around here before & the couple (who had to move to Naha) said she was honest & had never stolen that they knew of.

Can you do some shopping for me, Mom? The enclosed $10 is for 1 pair of shoes - Stride-rite, brown, size 8½ C for Candy and 1 cardigan sweater for her - prefer navy-blue, second choice red. Please send the sweater air-mail as soon as possible. She will need a sweater all the time in school as their Quonsets aren't well heated.

Guess the shoes will be around $6 & don't pay more than $4.00 for the sweater. Here's another American dollar Rex still had. Have lunch with it.

Sunday - P.M. just about midnight.

Had guests all day so didn't get back to writing. Have some snapshots I got back & will send tomorrow as I will have to sort & divide them. And I want this in the A.M. mail. Love to all, Bettie

Kadena, Okinawa

December 1, 1947

Dear Mother,

At last here are the pictures we promised you. Received a letter from you and also one of my Christmas packages.

Gosh I haven't written since Rex got back. He got to see Max, Marie, and Debbie when he went through Los Angeles. He said Debbie was sure cute. He just was with them a few hours.

Rex has never let me mention when we were coming home. It will be sooner than it would have been if he had not made regular army. We would have extended six months otherwise. We will be ready to come home, though.

As you can see, I'm using a typewriter this time and Rex is criticizing my typing and spelling. Little does he know it is just this machine that isn't smart.

THESE KIDS TYPE EVERY TIME I TURN MY HEAD

TUESDAY

Candy just got home from school and is teaching the games she learned to two other little girls in the neighborhood - ring-around-the-rosy and London Bridges. She brought home a picture she colored and is using new expressions already.

2:00 PM

Tomako is doing fine now and getting more done than Haruko ever did. I at last have more leisure. We went to a bingo game last night and Rex won a Parker 51 pen and pencil set in pearl grey with gold heads, also a pair of book ends. The book ends are teakwood busts of some Philippine Presidents. That's the first time Rex has ever won any thing and he was sure surprised. We have gone to 4 bingos since we got here and won at two so that is not so bad - we should go oftener I guess.

Jennifer still has only 6 teeth. She is saying more words now. The doctor claims she is not slow about her teeth, so I am not worried. I am glad they are such strong ones.

10:30 PM

There is no use, Mother, I try to write a few lines and someone always comes in. Company just left and I will just sign off for now and write you again soon.

These snapshots were all taken way back in the summer and since then Candy has a new hair style and Jennifer has new hair. But the snaps are better than nothing.

All my love now, and don't work too hard for the holidays.

Bettie, Rex, Candy, and Jennifer

Monday - Dec. 15th

Merry Christmas

Dear Mother & Boys,

Rex just put the kids to bed and I finished the dishes & we're writing you & Mom; and it's about time.

Have had several letters from you, a check and a box.

The kids' toys came fine. Jennifer will sure be thrilled with her little tricycle. It's so cute. Everything is fine. That washer is cute. Gave Candy the songbook but they haven't seen any of their Christmas things.

'Course we've already started to read "Treasures of the Kingdom" - a very good book that we're proud to own. My hose are exquisite. Ah me, how styles have changed. Every time a boat comes in we stand & gape at the long skirts & queer styles. But the hose part is O.K. because they are so sheer.

Tomako is doing fine so we'll give her a nice Christmas present. She claims she is a Christian, too. Jennifer calls her Ko-Ko.

We have been busy lately with Christmas coming. Our Sunday school has planned a program & there is one by the Base Women's Club & also one by the area club. So I've got a finger in too many pies. We've gone out quite a bit, too. Bingo & movies, & to a nice wedding & reception. Had 3 guests for dinner yesterday, & we eat at the club occasionally. Saw "Dear Ruth" at the movie - gosh I hope you saw it, it was a scream. We sat 2 hours in a downpour to see it. We really got soaked. We don't take the kids out at all in the evenings since Candy started school & it's gotten cooler.

Jennifer is growing by leaps & bounds. Her dresses are getting too short & she says more words. Plays very nice by herself while Candy is in school. She says "coat" & gets excited every time the closet doors open.

Candy seems to be able to remember & memorize anything. She likes school & does well. As soon as she comes home she tells me who has been bad or good & who sat in the corner. She is always teaching Jennifer games & dances. Jennifer is a mimic & does or tries to do everything Candy does.

Just took a few minutes out to chase a rat. He wasn't a baby one either. Wouldn't you know: He got away. Rex has his '45 loaded with birdshot & we're just waiting for friend rat to reappear.

Answering your letters.

Talk about reducing - I weigh 123 now. Consulted the Dr. & am going back Sat. I am hoping he'll give me some medicine to help reduce but he doesn't seem very helpful. Says everyone gains here.

Bettie , Bolo Point, late 1947

Do give me Bruce's address. [Mother's next to youngest brother, age 18, who has had a hard time keeping a job, had enlisted in the Army.] Let's hope he's contented & will come out in three years more settled. For him, I really believe the Army will be a good thing. I think he'll get along alright & his health even will improve. Rex says so, too. I know you'll miss him & that it will be hard for him at first. But there are lots of nice young fellows I see over here & none are overworked or mistreated. They get lonesome but so does everyone.

We want a new car when we get back but guess we won't stand a chance in the world. We'll have to get a used one if nothing else. Would like a station wagon.

Jennifer has blue eyes. Looks just like Candy did only so very fair. Her eyes aren't as blue as Rex's though.

Rex is still a pretty good husband & father. We enjoy ourselves in everything we do. We have lots of nice neighbors & friends. More & more families are returning home. We're now the established, old residents. These new ones arriving are having it lots easier than it was a year ago; they don't know how well off they are.

Goodnight now, Mother, & God bless you all. We hope you have a wonderful Christmas; we'll be thinking of you. Still hope to go to Tokyo this spring. So many are going to Shanghai but that's so expensive because you have to fly there via Pan-American, but you can go Army Transport to Yokohama.

Love

Bettie, Rex, Candy & Jennifer.

Sunday - Dec. 28th

Dearest Mother & Boys,

Christmas has come & gone & we're still stumbling over toys. The whole week has been wonderful & we had a lovely Christmas & hope yours was as happy.

All the packages arrived, too. But first I'll tell you about the week.

Saturday, a week ago, there was a party & program in our little club here in the Area. All the children participated & the maids were invited also. Santa came in & had gifts for the kiddies.

There was a tree, a log fire & all. Neither Candy or Jennifer were afraid of Santa; they liked him. Rex enjoyed the taffy apples one lady made & decorated.

Sat. P.M. we attended a formal dance. Had a wonderful time. Had a party of 14, mostly from this neighborhood.

Sunday the woman's club gave a party for the kids at the Bomb Wing club & Santa was there too. He had lovely gifts for them. A pull toy for Jennifer & a wagon of blocks for Candy, besides balls, candies, ect. All the kiddies sang there.

Monday was a busy day with shopping. Also started baking cookies, as the women's club was taking home-made cookies to the hospital for a Christmas treat. My neighbor & I baked & tasted cookies till we were sick of them.

Tuesday night we were busy putting up the tree, preparing the turkey, ect. Giving shampoos & all. What a mad house. T'was 1:30 A.M. before we got to bed & had to get up at 5 A.M. to pop the turkey in.

Now, this turkey wasn't my idea at all. Rex's pilot & wife decided to have a big turkey dinner the 24th for the crew & we were invited. There was a catch - Would I bake one of the two turkeys & make either biscuits or rolls for 18 people? Phoo!

I put the turkey & dressing in the roaster & left for practice on the Sunday School program. When I returned, friend turkey was very well done & falling off the bones. For a neglected turkey he was delicious.

Her dinner was really very nice but we couldn't stay long as the kids had to have their naps.

Then at 7PM Christmas Eve was the Sunday School program with Santa - again. Candy stuck her fist in her mouth to say her piece but lots worse occurred. It was a beautiful program & very successful, but one little boy tried to start a riot & beat up every kid in sight.

All these tiny kids got up with pieces to speak & you've never seen anything so cute. One girl ran off crying, a little boy preferred to tell his life history, another did acrobatics. The older class had the manger scene & sang beautifully. Before Santa came I was supposed to sit on stage in a rocker, reading. Candy - in pj's, slippers, & her pretty new robe – was to run in with a book saying "read me a story." So she does, then climbs up on my lap & I start reading "The Night Before Christmas." A little girl in the audience hollered she wanted to see the book, too, & trots on up beside us. That wasn't supposed to happen but made it cute.

Afterwards we visited a few friends & came home. We put the toys around the tree & were glad to get to bed. Christmas A.M. we took movies of the kids & their toys. They just walked around amazed for awhile before they touched anything. Neighbors came in & we ran over to their house. The usual robe & slippers Christmas morning. We finally dressed about noon.

Had people drop in for eggnog later. Spent the evening alone in the dark cause the power went off.

The tree is beautiful. We have 64 lights, icicles & 3 dozen ping-pong balls for decoration, also cotton & radar tape.

Friday our neighbors came over for eggnog. Boy, Rex can really make it. We have to make up our own recipe over here & it consisted of ice-cream mix, lots of eggs, nog, sugar, & heaven knows what else.

Saturday I baked an Angel Food cake & a Gold Cake & two couples came over that evening. Ah-ha, another excuse to make eggnog. But I thought I'd help & grabbed the paprika instead of the nutmeg & shook away! Ah me.

Today it has rained & blown all day. No one from this area even went out to Sunday school, as you would have drowned in a jeep. So it's been a lazy nice day all in all.

That's just about enough of our doings.

Thanks so much for all the wonderful gifts. Everything was perfect. The kids are pleased with their toys, needless to say. We have never appreciated presents so much as we have this year, so thanks to you all again for your grand selections.

Rex's parents' 28th anniversary is Jan. 7th. I'd like for you to go to Pogue's or Shillitos' china department & buy 8 glasses - nice ones. Let them run about $5. Have them packed & sent with a card.

Then buy yourself an Elizabeth Arden lipstick & get a nice fattening lunch! Take David home some blessed comic books too!

I sent Dad & Margaret [Bettie's father Howard and his second wife] a gift & wrote on their card. Sent them to the Rexford address in Los Angeles.

Jennifer is talking more now. She's no baby anymore by any means. Always wants "coat, coat, go, go" & as soon as I get her coat out she giggles & jumps up & down like she'd never been out of doors before. Candy imitates her teacher & uses Jennifer as her pupil. And the words Candy uses - never wants to disturb anyone, Jennifer looks just adorable today, or Daddy is aggravated.

I'll close now & go to bed. Jennifer has two more teeth at last. Rex has a terrible cold. The water tastes & smells terrible. There is, at last, good bread on the island. P.X. prices have soared, & the put-put is broke down. We want to put our application in to go to Japan in a month or so.

Love – Bettie

Chapter 14

Anticipating Return to the States, Bad News From Home January 4 – May 1, 1948

January 4, 1948

Dear Mother & Boys,

Rec'd your letter this week. This will just be a note as it's late & Rex flies early in the morning.

Your Christmas sounded swell - but I'll answer the letter later.

Please send me - by first class mail

1 pair shoes - size 6 A; color - red leather; style - pump - no platform sole; heel not less than 2 inches or more than 3 inches

I'd like I.Miller's or similar good brand. Price - not over $20. Also 3 pair of hose to match. Included is a money order for $20.

Love - Bettie

P.S. I need them.

January 14, 1948

Cold & Windy

Dear Mother & Boys,

It's 8 P.M. on a Wed. and the kids are sound asleep, Rex & I have pen in hand.

Notice my hair? Finally it's shorter & curled. My neighbor & I gave each other permanents yesterday. Looks pretty nice; could be shorter but we were afraid to risk it.

Candy thanks you all for the cute cards; she took the one with the ice-cream cone on it to school today. Sunday was her birthday. She dropped her three pennies in the birthday box at Sunday school & was sung to.

Sunday afternoon I baked the cakes for her birthday party. The living room floor was freshly painted & just got dry in time for the little angels to track it up.

Monday at 3 P.M. was the party. Fifteen children & 10 mothers were here. I had a lot of fun with the cakes.

There was a pink & white angel food with butter frosting & decorated in delicate pink & green for Candy's cake. There was a devils food with a boiled frosting, and an 8 egg gold cake with fudge frosting. Also ice-cream, pink & green too.

Also 2 pots of coffee. All the ice-cream was eaten & all but ¼ of a cake eaten. The house was a wreck & Candy's toys were scattered in every room. Candy was trying on slips & socks & hair bows when the last guest departed at 5:45 P.M.

The party was a success & the furniture survived. Wow - that was 13 too many kids! In spite of all the mothers present, there was fighting, kicking & howling.

We have had lovely weather for awhile & it has just turned cold again today.

Jennifer can say anything now but doesn't make sentences. She's finally cutting 2 more teeth; that will make 8. She's no angel.

Now for some business. We will have to have a car when we return to the States. They are high & hard to get, especially on the west coast.[1] From all reports, the situation grows worse instead of better. But we'll have a car regardless.

Now, the P.X. has automobile raffles – they started last week. They got in 7 Buicks (super 4 doors). They were $2650. You pay $1000 cash for a raffle ticket & if your number is drawn you have 1 month to pay the balance & collect your car. (If your number isn't picked, of course you get your $1000 back.) They are to get more cars & other kinds in. So it would be to our advantage to try to get one. It would go home on the same boat as we would.

Rex is writing the bank now for most of our money to be sent immediately and I want you to send all of our Bonds - registered air-mail. Do this as soon as you can as we'll have to endorse them & send them to San Francisco to be cashed.

I know it seems terrible to cash our Bonds & I hate to do it, but when we return to the States we'll have to have a car. Just hope that we do get one here instead of having to get one at San Francisco or Seattle.

The kids really are enjoying their Christmas gifts and want to thank you & the boys again. Do I feel snooty in my black sheer hose!

Well, Rex has his letter for the bank all worded & ready to type. We'll mail yours & his at the same time. So when you go for the bonds you will take this letter & ask them if they have received Rex's letter, & if they are going to do as we ask. We don't want any ickle-bickle or red tape from them. (It says here!) We want our dough to pay my husband's gambling debts & get the kids out of hock!

Goodnight Mother, you let us know as soon as possible.

P.S. Rex says to send any old jewelry, insurance policies, coupons, beer checks, or loose change, too.

Seriously now - take care of yourself.

Love, Bettie (formerly of great wealth) George.

Rex H. George. X his Mark

January 20, 1948

Dear Mother,

Received two letters from you yesterday. There hadn't been any mail come in for over a week so it all poured in yesterday & everyone got a stack.

Guess you thought the last letter was queer but we were serious & hope the money & bonds are en-route. We (like many others) borrowed $1000 here & there to get our name in the car raffle. Every time you turn around some one is asking if you have an extra hundred or two they could have till they can get money from the States.

We didn't intend to tell anyone when we were coming home but guess I'd better do so now. We're to leave Okinawa around July 28th. We'll be back in the States before the 1st of September, at any rate, & it should be earlier. Our plans are - I should say "dreams" - cause you can't depend on the army and you can't plan cause the best laid plans of Bettie & Rex oft go astray. (unquote). We'd land in San Francisco or Seattle. (About half of the fellows won't know where their next post will be till they get to Ft. Mason in San Francisco.)

We'd drive down the coast highway to L.A. & visit Max & Marie if they are still there. Gee, I forgot, we'd like to go to Yosemite first, then to L.A. Then to the Grand Canyon and from there north to Denver, then zoom across to Kentucky.

We really hope & pray our next post is in the East so the army will be paying our way home to visit family. If it would be on the west coast we'd get no travel pay.

Did Daddy say if he'd received my card, pictures or Christmas gifts? What is his address?

Do send us a picture of you. Candy still points to the stout woman with the upsweep in her "Tooth" book & says Gan-Gan.

Rex is devilish - oh me, what I put up with! Tsk, his three females get him down at times too & he learns more about daughters everyday. Candy told him yesterday that her patent slippers were getting scratched up & he should get her some new ones right away.

Candy now sings the alphabet, so I'm teaching her to recognize the letters & she's doing better this time. Candy's robe was just exactly the right size all around.

Thanks for doing the shopping, everything sounds fine. Next time I feel generous & tell you to get Elizabeth Arden lipstick you do as I say! So there.

So Goodnight, Love, Bettie

January 30, 1948

Dear Mother;

This is a pretty day & started out fine, but now it's 10 A.M. and we have neither lights nor water. Tomako was going to iron too! Oh well.

Sold the washer last week (boy, are we hard up). We couldn't run it on the low power out here in the area & our put-put has been out of commission for ages so the washer was of no use to us. The other areas do have good power now. The first person who showed up bought it.

Our Buick deal fell through. You must be here for 6 months after purchase and the next drawing is Feb. 2nd, which is too late for us. Still glad we sent for the money & bonds, though. We'll have the money with us when we reach the coast & the bonds too so won't have to fool around waiting for it.

Attended a tea yesterday welcoming all the new arrivals. Boy every time a boat comes in, the people here look shabbier. These new styles aren't so bad either.

Jennifer is here pestering me. She's cutting several teeth & has a slight cold. Her hair is getting shaggy now & won't stay combed.

Candy is in school. She washed in her toy washing machine for the first time this week. (I just give it to her now & then cause they have so many toys.) She undressed all the dolls, we used Lux flakes & started in. It was so cute to watch. When she was done - she rinsed too - she told Tomako to starch & iron them as soon as she was able.

Candy knows about half of the letters now. She picks them out from books, groceries, ect.

We got some of our movie film back. The Christmas pictures are grand. When we return you can see the kids unwrapping their gifts Christmas A.M. We use a neighbor's projector and will buy our own when we return.

Rex & I have been reading lots lately - murder mysteries now. Fried 4 dozen donuts yesterday. (Forgot I shouldn't mention these things to you because of your diet.)

How are you doing? Would you be able to eat Sponge Cakes or Graham Cracker Chiffon pies?

What does Bruce have to say these days? Tell Bruce we'd like a snapshot of him in uniform. Hope he's where we can see him next fall when we get back.

My, my, David has his eleventh birthday coming up. Let's see, isn't he old enough for the Tom Sawyer books? Go to a book store & get him a couple books for a boy his age - let him pick them out if you like. We'll allot $4 for that.

And now since I won't mail till Monday I'll sign off for awhile & get some lunch.

4 P.M. Sunday

Listen to the rain?! Hasn't stopped since Friday night.

Saturday A.M. Candy, Jennifer, & I dressed all the dolls in their clean clothes & repaired toys. Last night we played "Easy Money" – it's like "Monopoly" - at our neighbors. Course I won (for a change.)

Candy & I went to Sunday school on the bus today. Few were there cause of the heavy rain. Rex & Jennifer stayed home & straightened the house.

Whenever a group of us get together any more, all we talk about is when we get back to the States. Even the kids. No matter what they ask for we never say "no," it's always, "O.K., as soon as we get back to the States." Don't know what we'll say when we get back.

Bye now. Let us know how you're feeling, Mother.

Love

Bettie

In early February, Bettie learned that her father had killed his estranged second wife Margaret in a jealous rage. Based on Bettie's holiday letters, it's clear she hadn't been aware the two were no longer together. Howard was eventually convicted of manslaughter for a "crime of passion" and was imprisoned at San Quentin.

February 3, 1948

Dear Mother,

Rex got your letter yesterday A.M. He had to fly till 8 P.M. so didn't give it to me till evening because he wanted to be here when I read it.

I'm very sorry about what happened. I'll write Daddy in care of L.A. County Jail & meanwhile send me the proper address. Will it be a murder charge or manslaughter? Can't find out so far if California has capital punishment or not.

To write and pray is all that can be done. I hope, too, that he gets off as light as possible. There are two state prisons. One's at Folsom I don't know where the other is. We could see him when we return.

If Jimmie [Bettie's older brother] should decide to go out there I will contribute $100 toward his fare. Meantime, we will send you $30 each month starting now. [Note: this was to replace the child support Lona had been receiving from Howard].

You will hear from the lawyer & Daddy before I do, so if there is anything that can be sent to make him more comfortable let us know.

We can't condemn others because we never know what we'd do in the same circumstance, and if God is willing to forgive us our sins surely we can forgive others. This should be a lesson to all of us children to watch our tempers and beware of jealousy.

If you're going to tell Bruce, do it through the Army Chaplain or a Lutheran minister in that town. Don't tell David and be careful it don't get out in the neighborhood as children can be so cruel and David would feel it.

Candy is lots better today but had a cold that came suddenly & settled in her eyes. Used Penicillin drops in her eyes. At first the Doctor said it might be measles cause the S.S. General Pope brought dependents in a week ago with measles & mumps, but don't think so as she hasn't broke out & has no fever. I've kept her home from school Monday & today. She & Jennifer are having quite a time.

Made vegetable soup today, had some for lunch (it's now 2 P.M.) with orange loaf cake & ice-cream. I weigh 127 lbs. now. The doctor won't give me anything yet and I'm cross & unhappy if I don't eat. You can't diet decently over here on this kind of food.

Am anxious to see my shoes; they should come this week. The kids will need dress shoes again soon but think I'll wait till later & perhaps get white Mary Janes.

I'll close for now and start a letter to Daddy.

Love, Bettie

Two weeks after learning about her father's crime, and a week after her 25th birthday, Bettie confesses she spent her birthday in bed.

I can't recall my mother ever "taking to bed." She tended to bounce back from adversity quickly, but the news about her father may have been more than even she could handle.

February 18, 1948

Dear Mother,

Now I'm sure the kids will wake up any second so I'll make this brief. The red shoes & hose came Feb. 9th. They are really perfect; I'm so pleased with them. Thank you.

Things haven't gone too well this month. I spent my birthday in bed - just nerves mostly. My neighbor baked me a delicious cocoa whipped cream cake. Sure was good. Then Thursday we went to a Valentine Formal & had a nice time.

The kids had colds, Candy had that eye infection. So Monday Jennifer woke up with 102 fever. The doctor said it was her tonsils - her fever had gone to 103½ when we got her there. He put her on sulfa. She perked right up but today when I had to take both kids to the doctor he said Jennifer still needed something & the sulfa was showing in her urine so he switched her to penicillin. So she got a shot in her little bottom and will get another tomorrow.

Candy hasn't been to school cause of a cold & bad cough that hangs on. The doctor still expects her to come down with the measles but I bet she doesn't. Her eyes water but that's from the cold.

I've got an infection along my hair line on the back of my neck and in front of my ears. I put gooey salve on it 2 times a day.

Rex is just tired of hearing us fuss & complain, I guess. He got some Lincoln Logs and entertains the kids by building for them. They really need some new books though.

To answer your letters:

Haven't heard much about the pay raise. No one here thinks it will go through.

Candy & I made valentines & also valentine cookies for her class at school - heart shaped cookies with red frosting. Also baked some for the hospital.

Please send Tomako 3½ yards of some pretty cotton material - she likes green gingham.

The bonds came also, thanks; you & the bank did pretty good.

I'll close now. Perhaps my next letter will be longer and more pleasant.

Love, Bettie.

By the time she writes the next letter, Moth seems to be back to her typical – almost Pollyanna-ish – self. She was a champion of positive psychology before it even had a name.

Kadena, Okinawa

Feb. 25, 1948

Dear Mother & Boys,

Rec'd a letter from you yesterday also Candy's birthday book. It's a grand book and she really needs books. She rec'd a book & a sweet white purse from Mary last week, I wish Mary wouldn't send things; I know she can't afford it. She always sends such cute things.

Candy & Jennifer are better now. Candy is in school again. She attended another party this afternoon & came home like a busybody & told me what they had & did & who was bad or good.

I attended a party given by my neighbor for the 3 women in this area who leave in March. We played "Tripoly" & I won - the booby prize.

Monday was Washington's Birthday. We attended a "Come as you are - no rank" dance. Had a swell time.

Jennifer is at last a little girl. Rex combed her hair differently & cut bangs. No, she still hasn't enough hair for pigtails or anything.

Had a letter from Daddy yesterday. T'was very nice. I wrote him awhile ago.

Have you ever made potato salad (hot) with Hellman's mayonnaise? It's really something - super & tasty. T'was in Nov. magazines - cut down on the amount of vinegar. Go look this up or ask me for it; you'll like it. Also, Carnation's fudge recipe in February magazines – no, January - is easy, creamy, & cheap.

The 30 dollars was for you. We'll send 30 each month. Glad you have decided to go ahead with the gall bladder operation as I truly think it best. You'll be fully recovered by late summer & feel fine. And don't be afraid! So there.

By the way, send me some red shoe polish, please - maybe 1st class.

Jennifer has tea parties by herself now & talks to the dolls. Never sits on the toilet without hollering for a book. Fact is we always have the latest reading material in there anyway.

I'll close now as it's late & Rex & I haven't had a good night's sleep in ages - just can never get in there till midnight or later.

Love,

Bettie

There are no letters between February 25 and May 1. It seems unlikely Mother would have gone two months without writing. Maybe some of the letters Grandma Lona passed on to other family members weren't returned once we got back to the States. Another possible explanation could be that they contained sensitive information about Moth's jailed father and were purposely destroyed.

Saturday - May 1st

Dear Mother,

The girls are fine. They are still hollering goodnight! Candy is getting so brown & Jennifer's cheeks just keep burning & peeling. Can't wait till you see them, Mother.

We dined with another family at the club this evening & Jennifer stood in her high chair & hollered "Hello there" to every officer who came in.

[We've been taking care of Tommie Williams while his parents are in Shanghai.] He was sure a good little boy & no trouble at all & we enjoyed the use of the William's car. The last evening we had the car we bathed the kids after dinner, pajama'd them & took them for a ride. Came home with Tommie asleep on the back floor, Candy asleep on the back seat, & Jennifer sound asleep, sitting straight up next to Candy.

Tommie's parents, Doris and Willie, had a nice time in Shanghai & brought us lovely gifts for caring for their son & car. They gave the girls each a pair of oriental brocade & silk lounging pj's & me some slippers and a 4 piece set of matched leather luggage. The luggage is gorgeous to look at but none too sturdy. Such things are amazingly inexpensive there. We were so surprised & happy with the gifts & felt we didn't deserve so much, Tommie being so good & all.

Time marches on - 24 hours elapse - It's May 2, Sunday.

I left you last night at the end of page two & played poker with the neighbors. Neither couple of us know beans about it & no money was involved. I did drink a beer - my first this year. Made me miserably warm cause it was a sticky night. She served coffee, ice cream, & a delicious fresh orange loaf cake about 11:30, so we came home full, happy, & just worn out.

Rex cooked breakfast this morning while I dressed the girls for Sunday school. We had 74 children there today.

Entertained Lieutenant Roy Smith from Rex's squadron this evening. He said he enjoyed his dinner.[2] 'Twas his first home meal since he's been on The Rock. We had baked ham, sweet potato-marshmallow casserole, frozen green beans, slaw with tiny green onions diced in (compliments our neighbors' garden) and celery, pickles, iced tea, mince pie with whipped cream, coffee, & oh yes, hot biscuits.

The latest on our Japan trip is still that we will sail May 20th. But that's nearly three weeks away and most anything can happen.

~~Realize~~ Really. Oh heck - can't even write when I do think of something to say. Just 80 more days & we'll be heading your way.

We attended a dinner & dance Friday P.M. Tomako stayed with the kids. Quite a few couples attended in costume. About 200 were present. We ate at long tables that were 8 inches high & sat on grass mats, & ate from special China brought from Shanghai. The soup we ate with a china scoop, like spoon (more like a little shovel). All the rest of the meal we ate with chopsticks. It was surprisingly easy and the courses were tasty & exciting.

We did get very tired of sitting on the floor & everyone took their shoes off. The club was elaborately decorated for the occasion. During dinner we were entertained by natives doing their dances, Japanese & Okinawan. They alone were something to behold. After dinner, about 9:45, we all retired to the bar & lounge while the dining room was cleared & converted. The orchestra was nice & we danced till midnight.

The whole affair was by invitation from the Headquarters Squadron of the Bomb Group & it really cost them. They presented all the ladies with souvenir scarves & had prizes for the best costumes. The meal was served in courses by Okinawa girls in their full costumes. You ate everything of out of one little bowl & if you didn't like one course the next was just dumped in on top. The club officer is a clown & advertised black-market silverware for those hungry ones who couldn't manage chopsticks.

Now I'll answer your letter.

Yes, Mother, you know that if something happened to you, we would raise David & love him. When David is grown & we have a tour overseas we would take you also. Once the boys are married & gone & you either have no desire to keep a place or have no place, we'll always have room for you in our house trailer, tent or what have you. (Guess you'll keep this as a binding document.)

I think its fine that David has some art ability. We're real proud of him.

Really hope Jeanie finishes high school but I know Jimmy wants to marry & don't blame him either. But she's so near done now.

Going to close now & say Goodnight to all.

Love & God bless you,

Bettie, her wonderful, handsome husband & her two widgits.

Part Three:
Career Air Force Means
Always on the Move

Chapter 15

Salina, Sunnymeade and a Son,
1948 - 1952

Ready to go home to the States, May 1948

As Mother said in her final Okinawa letter, "Most anything can happen." Less than two weeks after writing that letter, Mother, Jenny and I, along with other wives and children of the 22nd Bomb Group were on the USS A.W. Brewster, heading for San Francisco.

Rex, his crew, and approximately 1,000 men in his bomb group, had been ordered back to the States to join the Strategic Air Command (SAC) at Smokey Hill Air Force Base in Salina, Kansas.[1] There they would be attached to the remnants of the 20th Air Force that had been based on Okinawa and Guam during the war.

After the women and children were on their way, the men flew their B-29s to Fairfield Air Force Base (now called Travis) east of San Francisco. When he landed at Fairfield on May 26, 1948, Fath learned our ship was about to arrive in San Francisco. He requested permission to leave his crew, met us at Fort Mason and accompanied us on the train to Salina.

Crossing the Great Salt Lake in Utah, Fath was wide awake, fascinated as the train sped past miles of murky salt water. He had never seen anything like it. He filmed more than two minutes of uncountable telegraph poles as the train whisked by them.

Upon arriving in Salina, the Pares discovered housing was tight. Eager to continue east to see their families, they rented rooms in a farmhouse out of town. They bought a used 1947 Nash Ambassador and we took off for Jeffersonville. On the Sunday of the Pares' 7th anniversary (and Fath's 27th birthday) we surprised his parents and sister as they exited their small, red-brick Baptist church. Annetta spotted her brother first, gasped and ran toward him, her hand covering a big grin. Mom, in a smart, fitted navy dress and a wide-brimmed navy and white hat hurried toward us in her high heels, arms out-stretched. Dad, dignified in his double-breasted brown Sunday suit was right behind her.

Back at the house, Mom baked Rex's favorite coconut cake and we drove up-river from Jeff to Clifty Falls State Park for a birthday picnic. As he had done since he was a teenager, Rex teased Mom about her poor baking skills by pretending to pound the knife into the cake. It was a short but happy reunion, then on to visit Mother's family in Covington before heading back to Salina.

We were still living at the farmhouse two months later on Jenny's second birthday. Shortly afterwards we found a day-light-basement apartment in town, closer to friends from Okinawa, the Williams and the Howzes. Mother was grateful to be in town near friends when, in mid-November, the men flew their B-29s to Lakenheath Royal Air Force Base in England for a 90-day TDY (temporary duty).

"The Berlin Blockade situation became difficult," Fath told me years later, "and we started sending B-29s as a show of force to threaten the Soviets with being bombed off the map if they didn't straighten up and fly right."

In Salina, both Moth and Doris Williams were pregnant and spent Christmas without their men. In England, Rex visited sister-in-law Mary and her daughter Rosemary whenever he could, often bringing them food items that were still in short supply. He didn't return to Salina until mid-February, 1949.

Typical of most SAC families, we became accustomed to packing up and moving frequently. We lived in Salina for less than a year before Fath was transferred to March Air Force Base near Riverside, California in the spring of 1949.

Grand Canyon on way west. Bettie pregnant with Christopher.

The Pares found a house in a walnut grove on Indian Road in Sunnymeade and awaited the birth of their third child. In those days parents didn't know the sex of a child until it was born; with two daughters already, they were hoping for a boy.

In mid-August Moth announced she was ready. Fath piled us two girls into the Nash, dropped us with a friend from Okinawa days, Anita Howze, and sped some seventy miles to the Long Beach Naval Hospital. He paced the maternity ward until he received the news. They had a son, Christopher, born at 2:17 AM.

After being assured that Mother and baby were fine, Fath drove (probably exceeding the speed limit) back to Riverside. Arriving at the Howze house, he rummaged through the Nash's glove box, found a pad of paper from a hotel in Salina and scribbled a note to Anita. "Christopher Alan George arrived at 0217 PST and weighed 9 pounds 6 ounces. No hair hardly. Bettie is fine. I'm gonna get some sleep and then I'll be over this

afternoon. Tell my girls they have that little brother. Thanks a million, Rex." He slipped the birth announcement under Anita's front door at 5:00 AM.

Now Jenny and I had a real live baby-doll to play with. Chris had intense blue eyes and never stopped moving and grinning. He shook the daylights out of his playpen. He bounced in his Teeter-Babe. He stood and swayed in his high chair waving one hand while eating a cracker with the other. No safety belts in those days!

Candy and Jenny in walnut tree, Rex and Chris

Christmas time arrived and Fath was away again, this time to Bermuda where his 22nd Bomb Wing practiced rapid deployment techniques in their B-29s. Moth soldiered on, managing the finances, making all the local decisions and raising three children on her own.

That December, while Fath was in Bermuda, Grandma Lona went to New York City as one of 100 finalists in the first Pillsbury Grand National Recipe and Baking Contest. In celebration of Pillsbury's 80th anniversary, company President Philip Pillsbury wanted to recognize the achievements of "the unsung heroes on the home-front" and "give them public recognition in the most glamorous place in the country."

The announcement of the contest attracted over 200,000 entries. Grandma's "Aunt Lou's Dixie Spice Cake"[2] – her walnut spice cake mentioned in the Okinawa letters - was one of the 100 recipes chosen to compete at New York's Waldorf-Astoria Hotel. The Waldorf, known as the "Unofficial Palace of New York," was then the world's largest and tallest hotel, rising 47 stories. The contestants were treated like royalty with a tour of the city and breakfast in bed the morning after the competition.

The only ingredient required in the contest, soon referred to as "The Bake-Off," was a minimum of ½ cup Pillsbury flour. In 100 individual kitchens set up in the hotel's grand ballroom, the contestants cooked from 8:30 AM to 5:00 PM. Each kitchen was equipped with a worktable, electric mixer, recipe ingredients and a General Electric stove, "probably the largest collection [of stoves] ever in operation in one place at one time," marveled the New York Times. The cooks, only three of whom were men, ranged in age from 22 to 74 and represented 37 states, Alaska and the District of Columbia. They used 580 pounds of flour, 127 dozen eggs, nuts, spices and one onion.

Former First Lady Eleanor Roosevelt presented the awards at a luncheon in the Waldorf's eighteenth floor Starlight Roof, a room that faced Park Avenue along the entire length of the hotel. The First Prize of $50,000 went to a Detroit housewife for sweet rolls called "water-rising nut twists."[3]

Each contestant received a souvenir program with their name on the front in beautiful hand-written calligraphy. Lona's table mates included the food editor of the New York Sun, the president of Foley Manufacturing Company of Minneapolis, Phillip W. Pillsbury himself and Art Linkletter, all of whom autographed Lona's program.

Lona was featured in one of the New York newspapers, under the headline announcing, "Kentucky Woman Spills Custard, Keeps Cool." "Mrs. Lona Gibson of Latonia, KY brought from her oven two beautiful layers of black walnut spice cake and then turned around and knocked her pan of custard filling to the floor."

When asked if she was upset, she replied, "Have to make another batch of filling. Upset? Anyone who has raised six children isn't supposed to lose her temper, is she?"

In addition to the all-expense paid trip and her picture featured in a local newspaper, Grandma won $200 cash, a GE Stratoliner Range, a Hamilton Beach Food Mixer and a variety of other baking equipment, spices and extracts.

Grandma Lona Gibson receiving Bake-Off check, December 1949

Back at March Air Force base the following summer, the 22nd Bomb Wing was about to put their Bermuda practice to use. On June 25, 1950 North Korea fired the shots that started the Korean War. On July 4, Rex's crew received deployment orders to fly to Okinawa where they moved into a hastily constructed tent city. On July 13 they began bombing runs over North Korea. The crew flew 29 missions before returning home four months later, just one day before the first Soviet-built MIG-15s entered the combat.

One member of the 22nd Bomb Wing was a man named Manuel Argimiro Torres, a fun-loving bachelor from Puerto Rico known to all as Argie. He and Fath developed a friendship that would last throughout their lives.

Chris turned one year old while Fath was in Korea. Chris loved the mint patch and the drippy faucet under the walnut tree in the front yard. Clad in a blue romper, or sometimes just a diaper, he would sip from the drip coming from a pipe that was just a few inches taller than he was.

Rex with bombs,
September 1950,
Okinawa

When our cat Smokey had her first kittens, Chris was at first squeamish about touching their fur. But by the time the second litter arrived, he handled them as a mother cat would, grabbing them by the scruff of the neck to transport them. He delighted in moving the kittens in and out of a large cardboard box set on the grass. Home movies of Chris transferring the kittens entertained us for years. We would beg Fath to run the movie backwards, so we could see the kittens magically elevate to Chris's hand.

By the time Fath returned from Korea, he had been away a total of seven of Chris's first fourteen months.

Despite our father's frequent absences, the area was beginning to feel like home. Many of our family's lifetime friendships started or continued during his time at March Air Force Base. Several friends from the Okinawa days were stationed there, including Doris and Willie Williams and Mary Bates, Mother's roommate on the ship to Okinawa.

Argie was there, too. He was famous for his mouth-watering preparation of arroz con pollo, frequent extravagant parties and legendary generosity. His signature dish converted Rex, a lifelong rice-hater, into someone who salivated over the mere thought of Argie's dish. Argie spoiled Jenny and me with expensive gifts. Once he gave Jenny a walking doll that was as tall as she was.

A couple months after Fath and Argie returned from Korea, our family moved into our first purchased house. The Pares had fun decorating the small, three-bedroom, one-bath house on David's Road in a new three-street development in Perris, CA. The red and white color scheme they chose for the living and dining rooms – red carpet and red and white checkerboard wallpaper – made quite an impression on friends who would remember and comment on it 41 years later on the Pares' 50th anniversary.

From our front stoop, we could see the San Jacinto Mountains in the distance. One of my memories from this period is of watching an Air Force plane spiraling down from the sky, streaming smoke, and disappearing into the mountains. Even though I was only 6, I could sense the anxiety along our street, realizing the father of one of my friends, or even my own father, might not be coming home for dinner.

Fath finally got rid of our old tan Nash Ambassador when it hit 64,220.0 miles. It had a bad habit of conking out in the middle of nowhere. He flew to Flint, Michigan where he picked up our first new car, a '51 Buick Special for $2,405.

Fath took leave in June and the five of us piled into our shiny two-toned blue Buick and headed to Columbia, South Carolina where Uncle Bruce was stationed at Fort Jackson. Grandma and Uncle David, now 14 years old, were living there also.

From South Carolina we drove to Washington, D.C., where Fath's brother, our Uncle Max, his wife Aunt Marie and cousins Debbie and Christine were stationed. We continued our grand tour of relatives by going to Covington, Louisville and Jeffersonville.

That same year, 1951, Rex again had to spend three months in England, but this time he made it home for Christmas. He returned sporting a mustache. It was so pale he had to darken it with Mother's mascara so it would show up in the photo she took before he shaved it off.

He also brought back two English bicycles for us girls. Unlike American two-wheelers with fat tires and pedal-operated brakes, our bikes had skinny tires and hand- brakes. Jenny and I were the envy of the kids on our street; no one had ever seen bikes like ours. They were too big for us, but Fath solved the problem by connecting blocks of wood to the pedals so our feet could reach them.

A year or so later, on another visit to D.C., I got my come-uppance for being so smug about my "English" bicycle. I hopped on cousin Debbie's bike and headed down a hill, only to realize I didn't know how to stop an "American" bike. I crash-landed into a garbage can and ended up in the emergency room with a split lip and a scar to remind me that "...pride cometh before a fall."

Rex with mustache

Chapter 16

Houston, Sacramento, Allowances, Fire, 1952 - 1953

Barely a year and a half after purchasing the house in Perris, Fath was transferred to Houston to attend an aircraft observer training course. We moved into a house on Lazywood Lane just in time for the hot, humid Texas summer. Every time the ice cream truck came down our street, we ran inside to ask for a nickel to buy popsicles. After a couple weeks of this, our parents decided it was time for Jenny and me, now six and seven, to have an allowance – 25 cents a week. We could spend our new wealth on anything we wanted, including popsicles, but we could no longer ask for money. I promptly gave up popsicles and saved my quarters.

Aside from the allowance, I remember very little about our time in Houston; I can't recall anything about school. I do have a fuzzy mental picture of the entire family dressed in Sunday best to attend our first live theatre performance at The Alley Theatre.[1] It was the beginning of a family interest in theatre, sparked in no small part by Mother's performance in high school plays. Later, when we lived in New England, it would lead us to Broadway shows in New York City.

My most vivid recollection of Houston is a discussion my parents' had one Sunday after church. They had been eager to reacquaint themselves with the Southern Baptist church they'd joined during their brief 1945 posting in Houston. This was the church where Mother had been baptized by immersion and the church to which they had been tithing (sending 10% of their income) for seven years.

As we rode home after the service, the parental conversation in the front seat was getting heated. I heard them say they were shocked and disgusted that the minister had preached from the pulpit against other religions and races.

My parents resigned their membership and never went back to that church. Although we attended church everywhere we lived, it would be several years before they found another that they wanted to join.

Looking back, I now realize how well this incident illustrates my parent's respect for other opinions, religions and beliefs. They valued – in fact, sought out – diversity, long before it became the popular concept it is today. As much as they believed in their chosen religion, they didn't believe theirs was the one and only way. They had Catholic friends and Jewish friends. They lived among Buddhists on Okinawa. They didn't feel threatened by other religions or races. Quite the contrary – they were attracted to them and interested in learning about other views, beliefs, perspectives and traditions.

After Fath retired they would travel the world, learning about other cultures and making lifelong friends wherever they went. It was this same spirit of adventure and curiosity that influenced their decision to choose the military life which, in turn, fed their passion for exploring the unknown.

When Fath completed his Houston training in October, 1952, we moved to Sacramento. We rented a house on Verna

Way. Jenny and I joined classes already a month and a half in progress at Del Paso Manor grade school. Mother's youngest brother David, now 15 - on the notion that he needed discipline and a paternal influence – was sent from Covington to live with us. He chafed under Fath's strict rules and high academic expectations and only lasted a few months with us before returning to Kentucky.

Jenny and I spent afternoons after school catching tadpoles in a nearby creek with Susie McGough, a friend from Okinawa. One afternoon we lugged our buckets of tadpoles home, filled the bathtub and released the little squirmers. Fifty-five years later, at the Pares' memorial service, Susie recalled, "Captain George returned home after flying late and, eager to shower, stepped into a tub filled with pollywogs. We were afraid we would be in big trouble, but he thought it was very funny, so we were saved."

Ironically, after having lived in Okinawa without contracting any of the mosquito-born diseases that Moth mentioned in her letters, Susie came down with encephalitis - sleeping sickness – in Sacramento and was hospitalized in serious condition. Mother took care of Susie's younger brother Greg while their mother Marian, Bettie's Okinawa volley-ball weight-loss friend, stayed in the hospital with Susie.

In early December 1952 our rental house mysteriously caught fire. Although the fire was contained in the attached garage and adjacent kitchen, everything in the house sustained smoke damage and had to be cleaned, repaired or replaced. The fire even melted the copper off the bottoms of Moth's Revere Ware saucepans.

We spent 5-6 weeks living in a $45/week efficiency unit at a motel until the house was livable again. We – the five of us and David - were there for Christmas and my birthday in January. In the minimally equipped, oven-less kitchenette, Mother made one of our Okinawa favorites for my birthday - pink velvet pie, decorated with marshmallows cut into flower petals dyed with blue food coloring.

The fire caused us to miss the social event of the year - Argie Torres' mid-December wedding in Riverside where our bachelor benefactor married the lovely Betty Munoz. Fifteen months later, Argie and Betty named their firstborn "Rex George Torres," an honor and great point of pride for our father.

Years after the fire, the mystery of how it started was solved when Chris confessed to the crime! This is his 2011 recollection of doing so.

"A day or so earlier, the pilot light on the stove had gone out, and Mother didn't have any matches. I told her she could light a piece of ribbon from the hot-water heater pilot and use it to start the stove. Being only 3 ½ years old, I was close to the ground and could see the open flame at the bottom of the heater. I think I figured the method out by myself. We stuck the ribbon in the flame and used it to light the stove.

"I enjoyed helping so much that a couple days later I decided to burn the trash. Unfortunately, I didn't take it out of the garage. When Moth saw the fire, she called for me to make sure I was safe, but I assumed I was in trouble and hid. When she did find me, I was amazed she didn't realize I had started the fire, so I just kept my mouth shut.

"The Pares suspected it might be me, and for several months Fath questioned me when I was half asleep, but he couldn't break me. I didn't find out about the questioning until I was a teenager," Chris recalled.

"When I confessed - about thirty years later - I was too big to spank. I don't remember the details of the confession as much as I do the crime. The fire came up in conversation one time when I was visiting the Pares and I figured I was safe from a spanking, so I told them what really happened."

Chapter 17

Topeka, Forbes and SAC, 1953 - 1958

Jenny and I managed to finish the school year in Sacramento before the family moved to Topeka. We drove there via Eastern Washington, Yellowstone National Park and the Grand Tetons.

The Williams, our jeep-sharing Okinawa friends, had invited us to join them at their cabin on Loon Lake near Spokane. The guys - Rex, Chris, Willie and his sons, Tom and Dan - fished for trout which Doris later fried in bacon fat for breakfast. To this day, I've never had better trout. The large cabin didn't have indoor plumbing, but it did have a first class outdoor privy. We added the Williams' euphemism for outhouse – hoo-hah – to our family vocabulary.

The adventure continued as we drove east toward Topeka. Begging bears came right up to our car in Yellowstone and we marveled at the bubbling mud pots and at Old Faithful shooting smelly sulfurous water high into the air on a regular schedule.

Mother made each move a learning experience. Every factory, mine, mill, museum and historical marker attracted her. We toured the Anaconda copper mine, left the Wonder Bread factory with miniature loaves and scored bag-loads of samples at Proctor and Gamble in Cincinnati. Each time we moved to a new town we spent the first few weeks visiting the tourist attractions, museums and public buildings. By the time we had been there only a few months, we usually knew more about the area than many locals did.

Rex was now stationed at Forbes Air Force Base near Topeka where he was an Instructor Navigator, transitioning Strategic Air Command (SAC) crews from B-29s to RB-47s. During his five years at Forbes he was advanced first to Squadron Navigator and then to Wing Navigator. He was eventually moved into Intelligence and Planning where he created detailed war mission plans – material so sensitive that his office was in a vault and a walk to the copy machine required an armed escort.

In Topeka we three kids experienced many firsts - first snowfall, first "upstairs/downstairs" house, first basement, first front porch, first porch swing, first alley, first locusts and first tree house. Four-year-old Chris was given his first household chore – putting napkins on the table at mealtime. Jenny and I remember him moaning, "I always get the hard jobs!" as he circled the table, five paper napkins in hand.

For the first time, instead of living in a development we lived close to the center of town in an area with older homes on streets lined with tall trees that towered over our two-story Western Avenue house. Downtown stores were a walkable mile away, and the Kansas State Capitol building, where I worked as a page one summer, was even closer.

We walked to and from Central Park Elementary School, about six blocks away. Our route took us past the park with its swan lake, arbors and an old tree that was background for our family photograph every Easter. We walked past the mysterious and smelly "cat-lady" house, ever hopeful of catching a glimpse of the old woman reputed to be living with hundreds of cats.

Mother always sent us off to school with her mantra, "Good, better, best, never let it rest, 'til your good gets better and your better's best." Our parents never bribed or rewarded us for grades other than acknowledging a job well-done.

In Kansas, land of tornados that could carry away Dorothy and Toto, we practiced tornado drills - sit on the floor in inner hallways - and air raid drills - duck under your desk and cover your head. On the playground, I got good enough at double-dutch jump rope to get my picture in the Topeka newspaper. I also liked to play jacks and hopscotch and walk on the stilts that Fath made out of $1.80 worth of lumber. Jenny and I had platform roller skates that clipped to our shoes, but the buckled brick sidewalks made skating a rough ride.

I earned extra money by gathering and dumping leaves over the fence for our next-door neighbor Mrs. Collingwood. She used them as mulch for her rose bushes. Her husband owned banks in Topeka and western Kansas. We three George kids visited him in his imposing walnut-paneled office downtown where we each opened our first savings accounts. We returned home with our own bank books and cast-iron coin banks in the shape of the state capitol building.

Our parents joined Westside Baptist Church. We attended revival meetings and summer Bible school, Baptist Youth Fellowship meetings and Wednesday evening services in addition to services on Sunday morning and evening. Fath was a deacon; Moth taught Sunday school. They were tithing again and expected us to put 10% of our allowances in the offering plate on Sunday mornings.

Sunday evening service was my favorite. It was less formal and usually had livelier hymns than those we sang on Sunday morning. At this service you could request a favorite by calling out the corresponding number in the hymnal. I went prepared with a list of numbers to shout out – it could get pretty competitive.

It was in Topeka that Mother, already known as a gracious and generous hostess, outdid herself by entertaining two sets of out-of-town visitors on the weekend following the day she had all her teeth extracted. She had worn bridges since high school and, at age 31, was tired of the inconvenience. She had all her teeth pulled in one sitting. The new dentures were immediately inserted over her raw gums and she carried on, regardless of the pain.

For the first time since her involvement in the on-base Sunday school in Okinawa, Mother became active in the Officers Wives Club. Officers' wives were expected to participate and Bettie could no longer use the small-children-at-home excuse. By the mid-1950s, as Rex was waiting for promotion to permanent Major rank, his efficiency reports (performance evaluations) began mentioning his and Moth's participation in on-base and community activities.

As she did with every new venture, Moth brought energy, creativity and her unique sense of humor to the task. She orchestrated teas, planned meetings and menus, and wrote ditties sung to the tunes of popular songs. She organized assembly lines to produce elaborate themed name tags, and she sweet-talked the local department store into loaning window display props for club events.

Her most impressive effort, covered by the Topeka Capital Journal, was a tea honoring the wife of the new commanding general at Forbes. The wife of the Kansas Governor attended also.

Mother revived her high school interests in debate and performance when she became active in Forbes Femmes Forum, a Toastmasters-like group.

Another milestone for Moth was her first airplane ride. One weekend while Fath was on a 42-day TDY to McConnell Air Force Base in Wichita, she took a commercial flight 140 miles to visit him.

In those days airlines served hot meals even on short flights. When the tray of chicken, mashed potatoes and gravy was served, Moth, a little nervous and excited about her adventure, carefully spooned the small dish of gravy onto her potatoes and smiled at her seatmate. One taste and she understood the puzzled look on her neighbor's face. Moth had just stirred the prune whip dessert into her potatoes.

We were accustomed to hearing about Mother's escapades, but were usually unaware of what our father's job entailed beyond the navigator title. He never talked shop at home. The first thing he did when he arrived home at night was change out of his uniform. Unlike some service men, he never wore his uniform to church or to off-base social events.

Fath was in the 90th Strategic Reconnaissance Wing at Forbes Air Force Base from 1953 to 1958. One of his Bomb Group missions in the mid-50s was training units flying the Boeing RB-47 for potential photo reconnaissance flights to Siberia should a war break out with Russia.

Small children were allowed to go on the flight line with their fathers and Fath would occasionally take Chris to the base on Saturday mornings. At Forbes the flight line was a high-security area. Shortly before Chris turned seven – the age when he would have been too old to enter high security areas - Fath gave him a tour inside an RB-47.

Recalling some of the things Fath told him when he was a boy, Chris - some 50 years later - asked Fath for more detail about these missions. The following is Chris's recollection of that conversation about the missions the Wing would have flown in the event of war with the Soviet Union.

"The 90th Wing flew the RB-47E, a photo-reconnaissance version of the Stratojet B-47 medium bomber. The aircraft had a crew of three consisting of a pilot, co-pilot and navigator. (At the time, the Air Force called its navigators 'observers', but Fath always thought of himself as a navigator.) The only defensive armament was a tail gun (stinger) operated remotely by the co-pilot. Instead of nuclear bombs, the bomb bay held a camera and magnesium illumination flares.

"The wartime mission of the 90th was a combination of bomb damage assessment and photo intelligence. In the event of an attack, they were to fly over the Soviet Union hours after the B-52 heavy bombers had completed their mission. The RB-47E's photographs would provide the basis for an evaluation of the effectiveness of the B-52s and would develop intelligence in an era before the U-2, SR-71 and spy satellites.

"This was also before ICBMs and the "missile gap", so wars were expected to last long enough for the intelligence gathered to be useful in the ongoing prosecution of the war. The wartime missions were generally expected to last about 12 hours and involved flying about 6500 miles. The 90th Wing practiced for its wartime missions over northern Canada."

Fath's Bomb Group spent the entire summer of 1955 in Alaska – almost five years before it became a state - while the runways at Forbes were being rebuilt to accommodate more B-47s. He was stationed near Fairbanks from early May until August 31, missing both Jenny and Chris' birthdays. By the time the men were loading up to come home to Topeka the snow had started falling in Alaska and Fath was concerned they might get stranded there.

While I was verifying the dates of Fath's Alaska TDY, it occurred to me that, although he had been away from us so many times, I had no specific memories of family life without him. Some of this could be explained by my young age, but by 1955 I was ten and can clearly remember several other things from that period.

I checked with Chris and Jennifer; their recall was much the same. Jenny remembered sitting on the stairs of our first Topeka house, crying as she read a letter from Fath and telling Moth that she missed Daddy.

We received mail from Fath almost daily and wrote to him frequently. He sent me a postcard from Alaska addressed to "Miss Candace George."

"Dear Candy, your letter was wonderful. I've been trying to get to the North Pole to mail one back to you. You'll see by the postmark that I finally made it. ... Have lots of fun this summer. Kiss our Mommy for me. All my love and kisses, Daddy"

We three siblings have concluded that the reason we don't remember Fath's absences is because Moth was so capable and experienced at managing on her own. The changing of the guard was seamless, and her constant upbeat energy kept us so active we hardly noticed the change.

Fath's job as a Major and Senior Aircraft Observer was described in his February 1956 efficiency report as "Plans navigation, bombing and radar phases of missions, supervises target study, critiques observers [navigators] on their mission accomplishments, monitors training program."

His squadron commander wrote "Major George has an alert, imaginative mind and works methodically and carefully." The commanding officer from his summer 1955 TDY in Alaska added, "Quiet in manner but his resourcefulness, enthusiasm and ingenuity inspire confidence and respect in his associates. He is logical, precise and meticulously accurate. His reports and studies are models of clarity and thoroughness."

This is a spot-on accurate description of the father I knew. So is this one from 1957-58:

"Extremely idealistic and his integrity is above reproach. Principle strength and at times his principle weakness – tends to fight decisions if he believes they violate his code of ethics.

"Weakness: On occasion does not delegate and tries to do too much of the job by himself."

In Topeka our parents must have been feeling more confident about their financial status. Jenny and I took tap and ballet lessons. I went to Saturday morning French classes at nearby Washburn College. (All I can recall from that $4.50/month investment are a couple of songs.) Our parents purchased an old upright piano for $35.30 and installed it in the playroom, which was carpeted with the red carpet from the Perris house. They were spending about $15 a month on music books and lessons.

Fath traded the 1951 blue Buick for a canary yellow one in June of 1954. The new car cost $3,177.32. I was glad we owned Buicks because they were one of the few automobile brands I could recognize. The useless - except for identification purposes – portholes along the front fenders seemed special to me. In fact, our three-ventiport model was called the Special; the more expensive models had four portholes.

The downside of a new car was that Fath would be even more strict about enforcing the car rules. We already knew there was no eating in the car, not even when we went to a drive-in movie. "The car isn't a restaurant; we're here to see the movie, not to eat." And heaven forbid should one of us write with a finger on condensation on the inside of the windows.

It was before the days of seatbelts. We could move freely around the back seat, arguing over who got to sit where, fussing when one of our sibs edged over the invisible line into our space.

We leaned over the back of the front seat singing the same song until it drove the Pares crazy.

Every time we went on a long trip I worked at learning to whistle. Fath would give me verbal instructions from the driver's seat and I would blow - to no avail. No matter how many times we drove cross-country, I never succeeded in learning to whistle. (My husband, who is a good whistler, has long since stopped trying to teach me.)

Like many families, we had our own private vocabulary, much of which came from storybooks Moth read to us when we were young. Inspired by "Winnie the Pooh," an "aha!" always elicited "said Piglet." A "why?" triggered "All that George Adolphus said was 'why, why, why'."[1] Often quoted at the dinner table was "The Goops they lick their fingers; the Goops they lick their knives. They spill their broth on the tablecloth. Oh, they lead disgusting lives!"

When we asked Mother where she was going, she was sure to reply, "I'm going downtown to smoke my pipe. I won't be back 'til Saturday night and don't let the old witch in." If Jenny pouted, Moth sing-sang, "Jenny's mad and I am glad and I know how to please her - a bottle of ink to make her stink; a bottle of wine to make her shine; and ten little boys to tease her."

Fath taught us suggestive ditties such as "Dirty Lil" and "I love to go swimmin' with bow-legged women and dive between their knees." The arrival of a package would inspire a few bars of "The Wells Fargo Wagon" from "Music Man" or a recitation of lines from my first reader, still lodged in my brain, "A box, a box, a box for me. Open it, open it, open the box. A rabbit, a rabbit, a little white rabbit, a little white rabbit for me!"

Our all-time favorite private language was inspired by a mimeographed sheet I brought home from school when I was in sixth grade, titled "Center Alley." My teacher read this nonsense language version of Cinderella in class and I had been captivated by its cleverness. Soon the entire family had incorporated numerous "anguish languish"[2] words into our vocabulary such as "hansom horse barn" for "handsome husband," "ladle gull" for "little girl" and "warts garner hoppings garner hopping" (what's gonna happen's gonna happen).

Jennifer, Chris and I still use anguish languish among ourselves. Yes, we are all daffy, but we sure did have fun.

The Pares kept detailed records of their automobile mileage and household expenses beginning early in their marriage. Every night before they went to bed they noted their cash expenditures for the day and tallied their cash on hand. They didn't go to bed until their accounts balanced.

That may sound like an obsessive and onerous chore, but I believe it was an opportunity for them to talk privately about their plans, to stay on track and to be completely open with each other. And just like everything else they did, they had fun doing this.

Part of the entertainment was trying to remember where every penny had gone. Here are a few entries.

In June, 1955, one of us kids must have lost a tooth. Under "miscellaneous" is "10 cents - toothy fairy". In July, Mother spent 31 cents for a sewing machine needle. That same year the Pares started putting $1/month into the savings accounts each of us had opened at Mr. Collingwood's bank. They continued to contribute to our accounts – and occasionally borrowed from them - until we graduated from high school.

In March, 1957, they entered 3 cents as "missing". In August there's note of 35 cents for fishing worms; in October, 21 cents for Halloween masks. When they hadn't balanced and wanted to finish and go to bed: "$1.00 - I wonder" in Moth's handwriting, ".55 - Rex won't confess," ".08 - Bettie stole," written by Fath. Eventually, "Bettie stole" had a column of it's own in the ledger, sometimes titled "Bettie wasted" or "Bettie lost."

My parents felt a strong tie to and responsibility for Moth's English sister-in-law Mary Cooper Gibson and her daughter Rosemary, then age eleven. Bettie was ashamed at her brother Mickey's abandoning his British war bride and daughter. During Fath's many TDYs in England, he had created a strong bond with both of them. While we were in Topeka, the Pares began looking into sponsoring their immigration to the United States.

Fath completed the paperwork in December 1955 and sent it to the American Embassy in London along with a sworn affidavit certifying that he would be responsible for their financial support if necessary.

He was required to list his income and assets on the petition: gross monthly income $881.78, $300 in a savings account, $200 in a checking account at end of month before pay deposit, $250 in U.S. Government Bonds, a 1954 Buick Special and the house in Perris, California with a market value of $10,000 and a mortgage of $7,597.

Mary, Rosemary and Mary's mother Connie arrived in the States in the spring of 1956, settling near most of Moth's family in Covington. That summer Rosemary took the train to Topeka to visit us. We were fascinated by her accent and the broad smile we recognized from the home movies Fath had filmed during TDYs to the UK. She was only about six months older than I, but seemed so grown up and sophisticated. She wore red lipstick and swooned over Tony Curtis.

Also in 1956 (and unbeknownst to us kids until years later), Mother's father Howard, who had been convicted of stabbing his second wife to death on January 12, 1948 while Bettie and Rex were in Okinawa, was paroled from San Quentin at age 57. My parents made a contribution to the family collection for the lawyer who represented him in his parole request. Howard settled in San Francisco where he worked as a superintendent at an apartment building on Russian Hill.

We were in Topeka longer than we had lived any place else – five years - although we did go back to Sacramento for three months during that time. There was no risk of becoming too settled, though. We lived in three different houses and I attended three different schools - a grade school and two junior highs.

After four years in Topeka and living in two rental houses, the Pares purchased a ranch house on a large corner lot on Wayne Avenue. The house had a breezeway connecting it to the garage, a good-sized utility room with a concrete laundry sink just off the kitchen, a patio out back and what seemed like miles of hedges, especially when it was my turn to trim them. This was the tree-house house.

The tree-house was a deluxe model designed and built by Fath with Chris's assistance. It boasted a crystal radio set and an old-fashioned 1920s upright "candlestick" phone – the kind with a receiver that hung from the hook switch - connected to its twin in the kitchen. The lofty perch was mostly Chris's domain, but one time Mother invited the minister's wife to join her for afternoon tea up there – and she did.

Fath, self-appointed arbiter of women's hair styles, cut Jenny's bangs in Okinawa and chopped off my pigtails in Sunnymeade a couple weeks after Chris was born. My father claimed he had lopped my locks to simplify the morning routine in anticipation of my starting kindergarten. His hair involvement went beyond offering his opinion and giving us the occasional cut; he was also responsible for our weekly shampoos.

This ritual took place at the utility sink in the house on Wayne. We stood on a small stool so we could get our heads under the faucet. Our father's strong fingers worked our scalps, sometimes eliciting an "Ouch!" He followed the second sudsing with a vinegar rinse. After the washing ritual, Moth would take over and set our permed hair in pin curls or hard plastic rollers.

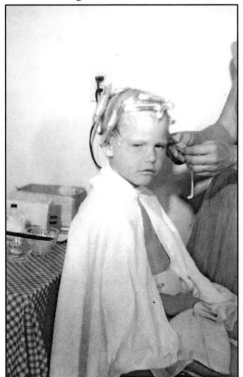

Ah, the home permanents - Toni or Lilt. Squirming on a high kitchen stool, draped in plastic so the toxic liquid wouldn't eat holes in our clothes, Jenny and I endured the nose-stinging fumes. Our eyes watered and our scalps were pulled tight as Moth wrapped our abused hair around small plastic instruments of torture.

Jenny gets a perm

189

The man of the house had very strong opinions about hair – his, ours and everybody else's. With regard to his own, he was meticulous to the point of being vain. He had a good head of hair, thick dark brown, which he kept regulation short and neat throughout his 30-year military career. He somehow managed to have a cut that didn't result in hat-hair when he removed his uniform hat. As he aged, his hair turned white but remained thick, just like his own father's had.

Fath preferred "his women" have short hair and was adamant that short styles on women were more flattering than long ones. He invoked the refrain, "A woman's hair is her crowning glory," to discourage Jenny and me from wearing hats to church. We didn't fight the hat edict except on Easter when we insisted on having bonnets like all the other girls. (Both of us rebelled when we went to college. We each let our hair grow long and wore it straight.)

Just when I had the numbers of my favorite hymns memorized, and a little over a year after The Pares bought the house on Wayne, Fath completed his tour of duty at Forbes. They sold the house at a loss and in June of 1958 we packed up and moved to Springfield, Massachusetts.

Chapter 18

Springfield, Bettie Coed, and Lt. Colonel Rex, 1958 - 1963

On the drive east we visited relatives and the Pares dropped me off at Uncle Jim and Aunt Jean's home in Covington. I spent the summer helping with their young daughters. Aunt Jean treated me like a girlfriend and taught me to play Canasta and Hearts. I felt so grown up that summer before ninth grade.

In August, Uncle Bruce, Grandma and Bruce's new wife Joanne, an attractive blond divorcee, drove me to Springfield. We went through the Pennsylvania Dutch country where Grandma's maternal ancestors had settled. Uncle Bruce and I bought giant pretzels and posed with them while Grandma took our pictures with my Brownie camera. I always enjoyed being with my favorite uncle; he had a quick, self-deprecating wit and liked to joke and make us laugh.

For the first time since Okinawa – where they didn't have a choice – the Pares wanted to live in less-expensive base housing to save for our college educations. Their plan was stymied by a waiting list for officers' housing at Westover Air Force Base. They found a "temporary" house in Springfield on Lloyd Avenue, off Boston Road across from Five-Mile Pond. We never did move to base housing and our temporary house turned out to be the first one we lived in for more than four years.

I started 9th grade at Duggan Junior High, my third junior high in as many years. Now that Jenny and I were older, our allowances were raised to $1.00/week; Chris got 65 cents. Allowances weren't tied to chores or behavior; we earned them by being members of the family and our chores were considered part of our family responsibility. Occasionally one of us would negotiate being paid extra for a special task or would successfully petition for an advance, which would be noted in the household expense register.

Springfield was a big change for us. Massachusetts seemed more complex and so much older than Kansas. We soon learned the area even had its own vocabulary. What we called milkshakes they called frappes; if we ordered a milkshake we got flavored, shaken milk. Our soft drinks were their sodas; our hamburgers were hamburgs there. The sandwich called a submarine or a hero in other places we had lived was a grinder in New England. Our jeans became dungarees.

In Springfield, "downtown" became "down-street." When school kids asked permission to go to the restroom, they said they needed to go to the basement. What we had always called the basement was referred to as "down-cellar."

We sounded like country hicks when we pronounced "aunt" like the insect and accented the first syllable of "cement" and "umbrella."

In Springfield, one of the biggest challenges for me was how to reply to the first question people asked when they met someone new. It wasn't "Where are you from?" - the question most military nomads dreaded. In Springfield the question upon meeting was "What are you?" The first few times I was asked this, I had no idea what the inquirer wanted to know. When I learned I was being asked about my ethnicity or ancestry, I went home and asked my parents, "What am I?" "You're American," they replied. The next time I got the question, I tried that response; it only seemed to produce suspicion and more questions.

The family frequently went on day trips to visit historical sites in New England - Boston, Mystic Seaport, Sturbridge Village. We explored new terrain, hills and mountains. We visited textile factories and paper mills and traveled to New Hampshire to watch harness races.

One year we all went to New York, financed with Moth's refund money. For every coupon she used at the grocery, she'd stash the "saved" amount in a jar. Eventually she had enough to pay for a hotel and five tickets to "My Fair Lady" on Broadway.

Soon after we had settled in, Mother began planning her next adventure. Now in her mid-30's, she announced she was going to college. She started as a full-time freshman at Westfield State College in 1959, the year I was in 10th grade at Classical High School.

I had always assumed Moth's motivation for going to college was to eventually be able to earn a good salary that would help pay for our college educations. Now I believe there was much more to it than that. She had an insatiable thirst for knowledge and loved to share what she had learned. Our constant moving had, to some extent, satisfied her thirst. She liked to read – mostly non-fiction, especially biographies – and enjoyed writing. She welcomed a challenge.

I think she also realized that within a few years, the main part of her "job" – as a mother and homemaker – would be phased out. She had never been one to sit still for more than a few minutes. "Sit down, Bettie," was Fath's familiar command to get her to slow down and relax. He was seldom successful.

Going to college provided a new focus for Moth's energy. It also required changes in our family dynamics. We all took on more responsibility for maintaining the house. Jenny and I were in charge of vacuuming and dusting on Saturday mornings. Ten-year-old Chris, already an acknowledged math genius able to do long division by second grade, helped Mother solve algebra word problems. Fath, a surprisingly fast two-finger typist, typed out most of Moth's handwritten assignments. Fath had enrolled in a work-related correspondence course, so the entire household had homework at night.

No surprise to anyone who knew her, Moth exemplified the off-to-school mantra she recited to us each school morning: "Good, better, best, etc." She graduated in four years with a B.S. in Secondary Education, a minor in Latin American Geography, and a 3.98 grade point average, ranking third in her class. Both her mother and mother-in-law came to Springfield for her graduation, although they never did seem to understand why she had wanted to go to college in the first place.

Bettie graduates from college, June 1963

Following Grandma's example, Moth began writing jingles and entering contests. During a visit to New York City, she and Fath attended the taping of "The Price is Right," hosted by Bill Cullen. Moth was chosen from the audience to be a contestant on an upcoming show. A few weeks later, she and Fath returned to New York for her scheduled appearance. She didn't make it past the first round of the game, but came home with a Polaroid camera as a consolation prize.

Moth was an ideal candidate for game shows – attractive, energetic, enthusiastic and smart. In 1962 she was chosen to be on "Concentration," the longest-running game show on NBC, hosted by Hugh Downs. It was filmed before a live audience in NBC's Studio A at 30 Rockefeller Plaza. Mother didn't win big on this one either; she returned to Springfield with a "Concentration" board game and a Bulova watch that ended up being my high school graduation gift.

We hadn't owned a television until we moved to Springfield. We must have been the last hold-outs in the entire United States. Up until then, our parents had refused to buy a TV because they had seen television supplant family activities in friends' homes. By the time we finally got one, I had already survived the embarrassment of not knowing who Zorro was and had managed to live without seeing Elvis on the Ed Sullivan show or the latest dances on American Bandstand.

The TV was set up in a cozy corner of the basement (down-cellar), delineated by wardrobe packing boxes from our last move and the stairs down from the back door. Our TV room was furnished with the old red carpet from the Perris house, a couple of plastic-wicker bucket chairs and two beat-up footlockers.

The well-travelled trunks were full of old photographs, a silk parasol the Williams had given Jenny and me in Okinawa, and some military medals and paraphernalia. How we loved to rummage through the black and white photos, laughing at Mother's short skirts and her pigeon-toed stance.

I've always been glad we didn't have a TV when I was growing up. Otherwise, when would we have managed to read a Bible chapter every night - even all those "begats" so we could honestly say we had read the *entire* Bible? When would we have shared what we had done during the day? What about getting sent away from the table for giggling too much or for gagging on some food we didn't like, but had to "at least taste?" Would we have ever played cards and board games or assembled puzzles? We might never have read poetry around the table after dinner, as we often did.

All of us eagerly anticipated poetry nights. Moth recited "The Highwayman" with great drama and she would give us the shivers when she read "Little Orphan Annie." We passed our hefty, well-worn volume of "A Treasury of the Familiar"[1] around the table, searching for our favorite poems. Fath often chose "The Cremation of Sam McGee" or tickled us with his animated reading of "Abdul A-Bul-Bul A-mir."

And every Thanksgiving at our house was accompanied by a reading of "When Father Carves the Duck" as *our* father – unlike the "duck" father – skillfully wielded his just-sharpened blade over the turkey.

The five of us always had breakfast and dinner together. Dinner time was sacred. Almost nothing was so important as to allow us to miss family dinner. Weekday breakfasts were routine, efficient and occasionally the cause of indigestion for our father. In uniform, he waited impatiently until we all were seated before saying grace. I guess we'd had one too many spills leading up to the morning when he intoned in his command voice, "From now on, everyone will drink their juice first."

We kids knew it was the wrong time to challenge this arbitrary new rule, but later we began plotting our revenge. One Saturday morning, when he wasn't under so much time pressure to get to the office, we made our move. After grace, we stood up, raised our juice glasses to our father and in unison proclaimed, "The Mighty Highty Tighty says, 'Drink your juice first.'" Bottoms up and we sat down.

Fath knew exactly who the Mighty Highty Tighty was – a little square-shaped dictator from Disney's "Surprise Package" storybook[2], who insisted everyone in his kingdom be made to look and act just like himself. Fortunately for us, Fath had a sense of humor and the capacity to laugh at himself, despite his dictatorial leanings. To our relief, we didn't get in trouble that morning and he soon retracted the juice edict.

Jenny and Chris both recall that dinners without Fath tended to be more relaxed. "We could eat frozen peas only when Fath wasn't home," Jenny reminded me. "Fath preferred canned peas, probably because that's what he grew up with. All of the rest of us, including Moth, liked frozen peas better.

"And there was the toast issue," Jenny continued. "When I was a teen, I liked my toast very light. 'That's not toast!' Fath would declare. He just couldn't stand it!"

Jenny's story reminded me of Fath and slaw. Standing at the deli counter, he would get all worked up about the "slaw" label on an item that didn't look like his idea of slaw. "That's not slaw!" he would insist indignantly, his lip curling in contempt. He took these heresies very seriously and in doing so, left himself open to our teasing.

Fath had rules for almost any occasion. Phone rules were especially important. We had been trained since early grade school to answer the phone with, "George residence, say-your-name-here speaking." (It was only recently that I learned most military brats were taught to answer the phone that way.)

As we got older, we were more successful at challenging - very carefully – some of Fath's rules, but we were never able to convince him to ease up on the "ma'am and sir" rule. Until we left home for college, we were reprimanded if we didn't follow every "yes" or "no" with "ma'am" or "sir" when addressing an adult - even if the adult *asked* that we not do so. Grandma hated being "ma'amed", but it didn't matter – that was the rule.

We did, however, pull off a major coup while on a camping vacation in New Hampshire one summer. That year Jenny, Chris and I had started calling each other by our first initial. I was "C", Jenny "J", and Chris was "Ch" – "C" having already been taken. I was about to start my senior year in high school and was learning to drive. I decided I was too grown up to continue calling my parents "Daddy and Mommy". J and Ch agreed so we set out to come up with monikers for our parents more fitting to our then advanced ages of 16, 15 and 13.

We tried several possibilities to replace "Mommy." "Moth Ear" didn't go over well, and "The Big M" resulted in a reprimand from Daddy for being disrespectful. By the time we came up with "Moth" (pronounced just like the first syllable of mother), it didn't sound half bad by comparison.

I knew we would never get away with using our parents' first names, so "Rex" was out of the question for our father. I'd gingerly tried out "Fath", which was not well-received. But by the end of our week in the woods, we were referring to our parents - Rex and Bettie, Daddy and Mommy – as "The Pares," and Fath had sternly warned us to stop all the nonsense.

Despite that command, the new monikers stuck and a year later, by the time I left for college, the Pares were referring to each other as Moth and Fath.

Sometime in the early '60s, Fath, a two-pack-a-day smoker who kept a carton of Lucky Strikes under the driver's seat of the car, quit cold turkey. He told us he quit so we three kids wouldn't start. It worked.

He said he had started down the slippery slope as a kid when he and his friends tried smoking Catalpa tree beans. "Perfectly vile," he reported when telling this story in 2004.

"Around age eleven, I picked lima beans from Mom's kitchen garden, sold them, and purchased a bag of Golden Grain tobacco. When I returned home I hid the bag in the cavities of the basement foundation, stuffing balled-up newspaper on top to cover it. The following Sunday after church, Dad took me to the cellar to 'show me something.' He put a chair on top of the work-table, pulled my bag of tobacco from its hiding place and rolled a foot-long cigar-sized cigarette. He made me sit on the table-top chair and puff the whole thing. I didn't mess around with smoking for a long time after that.

"I started smoking seriously about age 17 after I graduated from high school and was working full time. With my first pay check I purchased an Evans cigarette case with a built-in lighter, a carton of Phillip Morris, a box of flints and a can of lighter fluid," he recalled. "My entire start-up expenditure was about $6.00. I was only making $12 - $14 working a seven-day week.

"I went home, spread my purchases on the kitchen table where Mom was preparing lunch and announced I was smoking. Her reply was, 'Just be careful and don't smoke too much.'"

At Westover Air Force Base Fath was the Programs and Plans Officer for the Headquarters of the 8th Air Force, an element of the Strategic Air Command (SAC). Despite having a desk job, he maintained his flight status as a Master Navigator. By 1961 when he turned forty, he had logged over 4,200 hours in the air as a working crew member over the previous 17 ½ years.

He had been a Major for nine years and considered himself well paid. In 1961 his gross pay was $10,440. On that and $138 from interest and dividends, he paid $1,367.35 income tax to Uncle Sam.

His performance was rated "outstanding" in all categories of his 1960 efficiency report. The Director of Plans endorsed him, noting "one of the finest officers I have encountered during my entire service career." He recommended Fath for promotion from Major to Lt. Colonel.

The promotion came through in 1962. Lt. Colonel George had become known as a "polished and forceful speaker, excellent writer, with outstanding ability to communicate ideas to others. Considered an expert in his field [strategic planning] and sought out by higher headquarters because of his high qualifications ... has materially contributed to a currently-adopted weapons system realignment for the 8th Air Force and Strategic Air Command."

One day in June of 1961, Mother received a phone call from a woman in San Francisco who identified herself as "a lady friend" of Moth's father Howard. The woman, Rhoda Miller, told Moth that Howard was in the hospital. He was seriously ill and if Bettie wanted to see him alive she should come soon.

Despite Moth's conflicted feelings about her father, she and Fath decided she should fly out to San Francisco. The Pares sold saving bonds and borrowed cash from both Jenny's and Chris' savings accounts to pay for Moth's plane ticket and trip expenses.

Upon arriving she learned her father's "illness" was the result of excessive drinking. She was angry but didn't say anything to him about it. Nor did she confront him when he showed Rhoda a photograph of the grand house he claimed to have given his ex-wife Lona and their children. Moth immediately recognized the picture as the home of her father's well-off older brother Jim. When she returned to Springfield, Moth reported being "so mad I could spit." Very strong language for her.

To my knowledge, Mother never spilled the beans about her father's past to Rhoda. It was one of those things we didn't talk about. "If you can't say something nice, don't say anything," was a familiar saying at our house.

Fath recorded the loans from Jennifer and Chris for the trip to San Francisco in the household expense ledger and on June 29 wrote "all repaid." (I didn't learn about this "Howard" incident until years later.)

My parents told me about my grandfather's past in the fall of 1962 when they drove me to Antioch College in Yellow Springs, Ohio. They said they were telling me then because they didn't want me to learn about Howard from relatives who lived near Antioch. During this conversation, I mentioned recalling a visit to my grandfather at his workplace when we lived in Sacramento. "That was the gift shop at San Quentin," Fath explained, with more than a touch of irony in his tone. "Your grandfather was a model prisoner and was rewarded with a cushy job." I didn't ask any more questions.

After our parents died, Jenny, Chris and I were comparing notes and discovered that each of us had been told about our grandfather around the time we left home for college. We had never discussed this with each other nor probed for more information from our parents.

Neither the Pares nor I had ever seen the Antioch campus. Antioch was my first choice because of the required co-op program (work/study). I found the idea of studying only three months at a time, followed by a job for the next three months, very appealing. I was equally intrigued by Antioch's Education Abroad program.

I never cease to be amazed as I think back on the amount of responsibility and freedom our parents gave us. They seemed to know when each of us was ready; if it was difficult for them to let go, they hid it well. From giving us weekly allowances at an early age to dropping me off at a college with almost no rules, rumored to be overrun with communists and free-love advocates, their timing was almost perfect.

The Pares helped me cart my few belongings from the car to the cinderblock-walled third-floor double room I would be sharing with my assigned roommate, Kathie Sidner, from Oak Ridge, Tennessee. They chatted with Kathie a while, and left to visit relatives in Covington and Cincinnati before returning to Springfield. Their round trip expenses were $27.80 for motels and $15.40 for turnpike tolls. My parents would now be paying about $1,100.00 a year for my tuition at Antioch, not counting room and board. Moth's tuition at Westfield State College, where she was about to enter her senior year, was $100.00 a semester. Their gross income in 1962 was $11,445.67.

Perhaps the most dramatic example of the Pares' ability to find the balance between letting go and being supportive happened following my first quarter at college.

It was the end of December, 1962; I was 17, three weeks away from my 18th birthday. My first co-op job was as an assistant to the manager of the Morgan Memorial bookstore in downtown Boston. Definitely not a glamour spot, Morgan Memorial was the original Goodwill Industries, founded in 1895 to provide support to immigrants. In addition to the bookstore, this facility provided training and jobs for the mentally and physically handicapped.

Unlike Kathie and Karen, the two girls I would be rooming with in Boston, I had to start work the day after Christmas; their jobs began in January. The plan was for me to find a furnished apartment before they arrived; in the meantime, I was staying at the Boston YWCA.

The big news that year - reported in the Boston Herald and all over the nation - was the Boston Strangler. Seven women had been strangled to death since June. Women in the area were so afraid that police were offering escorts from MTA[3] train stops.

My roommate Kathie was nervous about being in Boston. The majority of the Strangler's victims had worked in the medical field. Kathie's co-op job was second-shift on the psych ward at Mass General. She would be returning to our apartment around midnight. Her father had given her a teargas pen-gun for Christmas.

I had been at home in Springfield for the Christmas holiday. Springfield was two hours west of Boston - an easy trip on the Turnpike. Early on the morning after Christmas, Fath drove me to Boston. I deposited my bag at the Y; he dropped me at the Morgan Memorial bookstore at 7:30 AM and drove back to work at Westover.

It was cold and dark by the time I got out of work, but after two nights of wandering around Boston with my trusty map and the newspaper for-rent ads, I felt fortunate to have found a furnished two-bedroom apartment in a large four-story brick building in the Back Bay area.

My plan was to take the Greyhound home on Friday night after work. The Pares had volunteered to drive me and my borrowed linens and kitchen utensils back to Boston on Sunday. I had a New Year's Eve date on Monday night with a former boyfriend who planned to stay with his aunt in Boston.

On Sunday morning, December 30, J, Ch and I piled into the back seat of the Yellow Buick, trunk loaded with blankets, sheets, dishes, pots and pans. A couple hours later we pulled up in front of 315 Huntington Ave. The building looked even bigger by daylight. Fath asked us to stay in the car while he and Moth went in to meet the manager.

After what seemed like a long time, the Pares reappeared and got back into the car. Fath turned around in the front seat and calmly said to me, "Now I want you to know it is entirely your decision whether you stay, but you have rented the very apartment that was the scene of the most recent strangling."

He suggested we go in and look at the apartment again while the rest of the family waited in the car. We entered the building, climbed a flight of stairs and walked down a very long hall. He opened the two new locks on the door. We entered the apartment and sat on the couch. Fath pointed to the carpet. "There's where the police found the girl's body earlier this month. The apartment has been vacant since then. If you decide you don't want to stay, the manager will return your deposit."

The Pares had learned the apartment's chilling history the night before from my boyfriend whose aunt had recognized the address. They then drove all the way to Boston so that I could make an informed decision. I believed then, as I do now, that they truly wanted the decision to be mine and they believed I was capable of managing, whatever choice I made.

When I look back, I realize what a gift their vote of confidence was. Although I thought it highly unlikely the Strangler would ever return to the same place, and I didn't relish starting the apartment search over again, I decided that finding another place would be best for all. We trudged back to the car and drove home.

My date and I celebrated New Year's Eve in Springfield instead of Boston. On New Year's Day the Springfield Republican reported that Strangler victim number eight had been found dead in her Back Bay apartment.

At 5:30 AM on Wednesday, January 2 the Pares and I again headed for Boston. They dropped me at work and started looking for apartments when they weren't going to the train station and airport to intercept Kathie and Karen, who otherwise would have gone to the Strangler apartment. By the end of the day when the four of them picked me up at my job, our belongings had been moved into the second floor of a single family house in Cambridge. The Pares treated us to dinner and drove back home to Springfield.

Chapter 19

Virginia, Korea, Germany, Retirement, 1963 - 1971

Six months after my Strangler adventure, the rest of the family moved to Arlington, Virginia. Moth, with a fresh Bachelor's degree in secondary education, worked almost full-time as a substitute teacher and in the summer as a bank teller. J and Ch attended high school at Washington Lee.

With two incomes, the Pares felt almost rich. They began havening dinner at nice restaurants now and then; Fath bought Moth a mink stole and a two-strand cultured pearl necklace. But soon they had to tighten the belts again; they had three kids in college.

Rex was stationed at the Pentagon in USAF Headquarters, Aerospace Programs for four years. In August of 1967 he was deployed to Korea for a year. The assignment didn't allow Mother to accompany him.

I had graduated from Antioch and was about to start training as a Peace Corps Volunteer for Venezuela. With Jenny now a student at Park College in Missouri and Chris in Oregon at Reed College, Moth moved from a large house to a new high-rise apartment building in Falls Church, VA.

For the first time since 1944 when Fath left her to join the war in Europe, Moth was entirely alone. She immersed herself in a full-time teaching job at Swanson Junior High, focused on doing the job well while having fun. At year end her principal gave her the highest possible performance rating and added, "Mrs. George is a loyal and dedicated teacher. She has excellent rapport with students and staff, and contagious enthusiasm that is felt throughout our community. It is a real joy to have Mrs. George as a member of our faculty."

When she wasn't busy teaching, Moth got to know her new neighbors. She mentored a young couple across the hall who were about to have their first child. She taught expectant mother Ann Polumbus how to make pie crust and Béarnaise sauce and got her hooked on saving grocery coupons and rebate money. "Bettie made my first year of motherhood work for me," Ann recalled. "She taught me not only the practical things like how to take a baby's temperature, but more important things about staying calm, loving each other and laughing and staying happy. She taught me the importance of the role of a mother and I thank her to this day for that."[1]

The Havlicks, neighbors who shared a wall with Moth, described her as "always so buoyant, bouncy, bright and ... vacuuming. We bet she had the cleanest rugs in Falls Church."

Mother experienced some dark days during her year alone. In November, 1967 her second youngest brother, Bruce, our favorite uncle, committed suicide. He had been unable to find peace as a closeted homosexual living in the conservative Ohio River Valley. This was two years before the Stonewall Inn riot that launched the gay rights movement and when the psychiatric community classified homosexuality as a sociopathic mental disorder.

Moth's letter with the news of Uncle Bruce's death found me in Peace Corps training in a rain forest in Puerto Rico. I hadn't known Uncle Bruce was gay - another controversial subject our family had never discussed.

Chris, Moth, Uncle Bruce, 1965, Tuckerman Ravine, Mt. Washington, NH

In 2007, after our parents' deaths, I couldn't stop thinking about Uncle Bruce. By then all of Mother's siblings had passed away. Aunt Jean, widow of Moth's older brother Jim, was willing to share memories of Bruce. So was my cousin Rosemary who had lived in Kentucky near Moth's family since emigrating from England in 1956.

I also discovered that Jenny had gone to Bruce's funeral with Mother. Furthermore, shortly before Fath died, Chris had asked him about Bruce.

"Fath told me that Uncle Bruce had been on the phone with the minister who had been counseling him," Chris recalled. "Bruce told his minister that he had a gun in one hand and a martini in the other. I also remember that a number of years earlier, Uncle Bruce had been rescued from a carbon monoxide 'accident' that involved the car running in his closed garage."

Jenny told me, "After the funeral I accompanied Mother and Grandma to his tiny bare apartment in Anderson, Indiana where he had moved to start a new life. There we found the box the gun came in and the sales receipt. He had been on the phone, being counseled by his Evangelical Lutheran pastor when he shot himself."

Rosemary had many stories of Bruce's generosity and kindness. She shared memories of him as a surrogate father when, as a pre-teen, she and her mother Mary, the abandoned war bride of Bruce's older brother Mickey, came to the States. "His death was such a shame. He was a great help to me when we moved here, always taking me places. He got me my first full time job. He even got my mom her first job in America at a restaurant where he worked as a chef."

"He was very tolerant of everyone," Rosemary recalled, "even having black friends when it wasn't considered proper. I remember in the late 50's he took us to Coney Island in Cincinnati where the swimming pool was still a 'private club' (to keep the Blacks out), but they couldn't enforce the rule and Bruce always invited some of his black co-workers to go along. In some small way he fought the system for equality."

"Later, as I got older," she reminisced, "I realized how important his actions were. He would be so proud now of the advances most people have made in their attitudes regarding gays, and that we now have our very first African American President."

Uncle Bruce - a good and honorable man, gone too soon at age 38.

In April of the next year, only a couple days after the Washington, D.C. riots following Martin Luther King's assassination, Mother's father Howard and his friend Rhoda surprised her with an unannounced visit. Rhoda later reported it as a "happy reunion," though I can't imagine it was anything of the kind for my mother.

Meanwhile, in Seoul, Rex worked as a Plans and Policy Officer at the Joint Command Level for the United Nations Joint Command Headquarters. He prepared war plans and conducted studies used in the determination of policies and procedures for the UN Command and the US Forces in Korea. The studies covered a broad spectrum of activities ranging from pure military to those involving the coordinated action of the entire Country Team.

The thirteen months Fath was in Korea were during volatile times. 1968 brought the Tet Offensive in Vietnam, an attempted raid on South Korean President Park's "Blue House" residence by North Korea and North Korea's January capture of the USS Pueblo two days later.

On the home front President Lyndon Johnson announced on March 31, "I shall not seek, and I will not accept, the nomination of my party for another term as your President." Three months later Robert F. Kennedy was shot to death on June 5 during his presidential candidate campaign.

Fath frequently made presentations for and travelled with four-star General Charles H. Bonesteel, III, commander of all U.S. and United Nations forces in Korea. General Bonesteel had direct access to the Joint Chiefs of Staff in Washington.

One of the highlights of Fath's career was being chosen to represent his headquarters at a Joint Chiefs meeting in May, 1968. He was called to D.C. "due to his high degree of competence ... to represent this headquarters and assist in the design of a war game of great importance to this command."

His commanding officer noted under "strengths" in Fath's June 1968 effectiveness report, "He has been able to achieve rapid and smooth coordination when working with either civilian or military associates to include those of the ROK [Republic of Korea]. His strengths are his outstanding professional competence; his appreciation of all elements of a nation's power; his will to accept responsibility and act to fulfill it; his calm manner in discharging his duties. It is suggested that this officer be utilized to represent the Air Force on Joint Staffs at reasonable intervals..."

There were representatives from many countries at the UN Joint Command Headquarters. Fath and his housemate, an Armenian officer, went to work making their assigned house more like home.

"Our house was the best house in the whole area," Fath bragged. "It had been a three-bedroom with no kitchen. I arranged to redefine it as a two-bedroom and made a kitchen out of the tiny third bedroom. The only stipulation was that we had to pay the maid the three-person rate, which was perfectly alright with us.

"I built shelves in the closet. We got a gas stove with four burners and a big oven, a large refrigerator and furniture from family housing." [In the home movies the shelves appear to be well-stocked with bottles of booze, or "hooch," as Fath called it.]

"A civil engineer friend got us paint and found an electrician to put in a 220 power line. We paid him back for his kindness by serving him a dinner I had prepared – meat loaf, baked potatoes, canned vegetables and baked rolls. He couldn't get enough of my rolls! They were just those Pillsbury Parker House ones. I really impressed them with my culinary arts. I even baked a cake! We were pretty proud of our house."

The Pares' year-long separation was rewarded with a coveted three-year tour of duty in Wiesbaden, Germany, as Fath reported in a letter to his mother, written from Korea on September 8, 1968:

Dear Mom,

Guess I'm doomed to forever stay in the dog-house. It's been since 27 August when I got your last letter and my notes say I haven't written since 18 August. Well the truth is I've been a little busy and there's been nothing to report. Now, however, I have news and a break. First the news. I have both a departure date from here and from the states for Germany. I leave here at 11:30 on Friday, 20 Sept. That flight takes me to Seattle. From there I'll go down to Portland where I'll spend an evening and day with Chris at Reed. Then on to Kansas City where I'll be with Jenny at Park for a similar period. Then on to Washington, arriving there sometime late on 22 September. I've enclosed a plan that I sent Bettie today for her approval. As you can see we plan to be in Jeffersonville to see you at about 5 PM on 1 Oct and leave to return to Falls Church at 5 AM on the 7th. We leave McGuire Air Force Base at 1:30 AM on 30 Oct. I think it's about 6 ½ hours flight time to our landing in Germany.

The same day I got all this info I also got a message from the base in Germany that I could expect on-base quarters in about 3 months. Before, it had been 11-12 months. We've been fighting by telegram for over a month. They still haven't recognized Jenny as a legitimate dependent, because of her age, but she is a dependent until she's 23 (that's next August) because she's a full-time student in a qualified school. I'll be able to get this all straightened out when we get there. The thing is, if she's recognized, I get 3 rather than 2 bedrooms and they let her come over next June for free. Otherwise, she has to pay her own way.

Here the weather has been just beautiful except for a couple of days of the hardest and steadiest rain you ever saw. Mom, you've never seen it rain as hard since the 1937 flood, nor as long. This river went over the banks. The shanty towns on the hillsides slid off on a great mud slide. In one night there were over 30 people lost in the wreckage of their homes. But the rest of the time it's been wonderful. Last year at this time it was miserably hot but this whole summer we've had only a couple of weeks that have been really uncomfortable.

Well, Chris and Jenny are both back in school [after having the summer off] and Bettie is alone again. I think she rather enjoys her private apartment. I think I'll be able to get into her club again, tho. We're both getting awfully tired of this letter writing thing. It's good, but a poor substitute for face to face contact.

Just noticed in your letter a question about how long I'd be in Germany. It's a 3 year tour. So I'll come home from there and retire in a couple months. By the time you get this letter it'll be the 11th of September and like me you'll be thinking of Dad. [Rex's father Hall died two years earlier on September 11, 1966.] Goodnight, Mom. God bless and keep you. We'll see you soon. All my love and kisses and some to Judy, too. [Mom's dog] Rex

Before they left the States for Germany, the Pares made it down to Venezuela where I was serving as a Peace Corps Volunteer.

Moth had a long fascination with Latin American geography and was eager to see Angel Falls, the world's tallest water fall.[2] I had researched the details. Roundtrip flight from Caracas to Canaima plus room and board for two days and one night came to about $50.00 per person. Unfortunately, the limited flights and accommodations at Angel Falls were already booked, so we substituted the world's highest cable car for the highest water fall and headed to the Andes mountain range in western Venezuela.

From Merida, Venezuela's highest city at 5,385 feet, we rode the *teleferico* (tram) up to Pico Espejo, the country's second highest mountain at 15,867 feet. It was an 8-mile ride with a 10,300 foot rise in one hour.[3] As one of the guidebooks said, "the most exciting $3.52 you'll ever spend." In the clouds at the summit, the thin air gave Moth and me the giggles. We laughed uncontrollably until tears streamed down our cheeks.

Bettie and Candy
changing trams on way
up to Pico Espejo

The Pares also spent a couple days at my work site near Calabozo (Which means "jail" in Spanish.) in the central plains (called *Llanos*), about five to six hours south of Caracas by car. There they valiantly braved the heat and mosquitoes.

When I was at Antioch, one of my co-op jobs had been to recruit for the new, federally-funded Head Start Program, headed by Sargent Shriver who had also been the first Peace Corps director. My Head Start target population had been children of transplanted Appalachian families living near Wright Patterson Air Force Base in southwestern Ohio. Later, when the program launched, I taught these same 3-5 year-olds.

As a community development volunteer in Venezuela, I launched a similar pre-school program to prepare the children in my community for success in first grade. The Pares enjoyed meeting these children and their parents.

Candy's house in Venezuela

Bettie and Rex began their German adventure on October 30, 1968. In Wiesbaden, Fath worked hard at the office and exercised regularly at the gym. Moth found a job as a substitute teacher. They both studied German and took every opportunity to travel around Europe and the UK. At last Moth was really seeing the world. They visited German wineries and made friends with their favorite vintners.

Each of us three kids tested our parents' rules and expectations in our own ways. No matter what choices we made, they always stood by us, sometimes disagreeing, but always offering unconditional love. Perhaps the best example of this was when Chris resisted being drafted into the Army.

The Pares had been in Germany about eight months when Chris graduated from Reed College in May of 1969. It was at the height of the Vietnam War and students all around the country were protesting. Chris had been one of the thousands of protesting students; he had also turned in his draft card in a public ceremony. Failure to carry one's draft card was a Federal crime.

In August, after visiting the Pares and Jenny in Germany, twenty-year-old Chris started a job in Chicago. A week later he received a notice from his draft board to report for induction in Virginia. The notice had been sent to Fath at his office in Germany. It included a notation that Chris was delinquent. At the time, most draft boards followed the practice of accelerating the induction of young men who turned in or burned their draft cards.

Despite Fath's chosen military career, he supported Chris's position and encouraged him to go to Toronto where Chris had been accepted into a PhD program at the University of Toronto. Instead, Chris went back to Portland and arranged to have his induction transferred there. During the induction ceremony, Chris refused to step forward for the oath, another federal crime. He then left the country for Toronto, started classes and had collected two of his fellowship checks when he decided to voluntarily submit to induction under the original order.

Within a couple weeks after his induction a federal judge ruled that some draft board procedures regarding induction – such as punishing boys who had turned in their draft cards - were not consistent with the law. One month later the Supreme Court agreed.

Around the same time, Chris declared himself a conscientious objector, refused to fire his rifle during training, and was shipped to Fort Sam Houston to attend medic school. In March of 1970 the local American Friends Service Committee helped him find a lawyer. Chris borrowed $1,500 from the Pares and some Army friends. His high school math teacher in Arlington, Virginia volunteered to hand-copy his draft file, and his lawyer tried to time Chris' case so he would get a "good" judge.

While Chris was in Texas, I moved from Vermont, where I had been living since my 1969 return from the Peace Corps, to San Francisco. Mother wrote from Wiesbaden to give me Grandfather Howard's address in the city, assuring me she would understand if I chose not to contact him. I'd never had a relationship with my grandfather and wasn't too keen on starting one. I was still pondering the issue a few weeks later when I heard from Moth again. Howard had died. I was off the hook.

In Germany that fall, while working out on a treadmill at the base gym, Fath noticed a pain below his sternum that radiated to both shoulders and elbows; he felt a bit faint. He was taken to the emergency room, diagnosed with acute myocardial infarction and admitted to the Intensive Care Unit. Without any previous warning, 49-year-old Fath had suffered a major heart attack.

The Army immediately gave Chris emergency leave to go to Germany where he sat with Moth in the waiting room of the Intensive Care Unit at the Wiesbaden Hospital.

During Chris's stay in Germany, a Texas judge wrote an order in his favor and told the Army to act on it immediately. Chris had won his fight. His induction was voided, and Fath had supported him at every step.

Fath, after three months of rest and physical therapy, recovered sufficiently to return to the office. Not long after, in August 1971, he was transferred to Los Angeles for transition to retirement.

Although in his 1968 letter to Mom from Korea, Fath had anticipated retiring after his tour in Germany, he no longer wanted to do so, but he had no choice. I think when he wrote to Mom, he had anticipated being promoted by the end of the Germany assignment, thereby being able to retire at a higher rank with more pay. His immediate superiors did recommend him for promotion to full Colonel, but ultimately his medical condition disqualified him. In May, 1972, after almost 30 years of active duty - 29 years, 7 months and 13 days by Fath's count - he was forced to retire from the Air Force as a Lt. Colonel.

Rex's official retirement photo

Part Four:
Retired Means Always on the Go

Chapter 20

Settling in and Speaking Out, 1972 - 1980

The Pares soon saw the setback of forced retirement as an invitation for more travel and adventure. They purchased a 1966 26-foot Airstream trailer. They named it "Camelot," hitched it to the latest Buick and spent ten months touring the United States, with a side-trip to Europe. They visited friends and family all over the country while investigating potential places to settle down.

Fath, who once said that seeing long hair on a man turned his stomach, grew a beard and let his hair grow down to his collar. After almost 30 years of following strict rules and regulations covering everything from hair length to social activities, Fath –

Mr. Rules himself – realized he could do whatever he wanted. He rebelled. Old friends who opened their front doors to greet Rex and Bettie reported being shocked when they saw him.

Rex's passport photo
1971

Freed from all constraints, they set out from Los Angeles in May 1972. Despite stretches of bad weather, treacherous roads, car and trailer problems, their travel journal is generally upbeat. On their first day on the road, Fath noted, "Last day to shave 'til beard!" and for a couple weeks thereafter, he commented on his beard's progress.

Meandering north up the west coast, they stopped at wineries, factories and other attractions - Almaden and Mirassou, Nestle and Smucker's. They evaluated a couple communities in the Central Coast area, but decided the location was too far from military hospital facilities. They visited me in San Francisco and made arrangements for me to pay their bills and forward their mail for the next 12 months.

Chris came to San Francisco to see the Pares. "He took one look at me," reported Fath, "and reminded me that once when he flew back home from college, I almost didn't take him home from the airport because of his long hair. Now mine is longer than his was!"

The Pares contacted Rhoda Miller, Howard's friend of ten-plus years, while in San Francisco. She lived less than a mile from me. They took her to lunch and invited me along. Rhoda was a handsome woman and a good conversationalist. Later she and I had tea several times and exchanged holiday cards and notes until her death in 2004. She and the Pares also corresponded and they would occasionally visit her in San Francisco.

I never asked Rhoda about my grandfather and I don't recall her talking about him. It was only after my parents' deaths in 2007, when I found an archived article in the Los Angeles Times, that I learned more about Howard's crime. I doubt my parents ever knew the details of his vicious knife attack on his second wife. I would guess Rhoda didn't know he had served eight years in San Quentin. Grandfather Howard was a masterful liar.

The city of Santa Rosa, sixty miles north of San Francisco, was the Pares' next stop. They spent a week there sizing-up the area before continuing north where they celebrated Fath's 51st birthday and their 31st anniversary at a campground on the Rogue River near Grants Pass. Oregon offered an abundance of temptations for factory-focused Moth - a Weyerhaeuser Wood and Paper plant, a salmon hatchery, the Pendleton Woolen Mills. Chris joined the Camelot crew from Portland to Denver, hiking the eastern Oregon mountains with the Pares and baking his famous cardamom bread in Camelot's tiny kitchen.

From Denver, Chris took Amtrak to his job in Chicago and the Pares headed for Kansas City to pick up Jenny for a side-trip to the Ozarks. They never got there. The car's transmission gave out near Branson, Missouri where they spent several "miserably hot and sticky days" before delivering Jenny back home and driving to Tennessee.

They spent the next month visiting relatives in Tennessee, Indiana, Kentucky and southern Ohio. Fath finally got a hair cut. "A barber cut Rex's curls away!" reported Moth, "They'll grow back." She also noted her own visit to a local beauty shop for her weekly shampoo and set. "Progress – my beauty operator was black. There is hope! She – Mary - tells me she was the second black operator in a shop in Cincinnati – a white shop, that is."

A couple days later Mother wrote, "We find people's intolerance to blacks hard to take. We must try to be more tolerant of the intolerant. We will not say 'you-know-what.' Lord, help us to see our own faults." (I assume Moth's "you-know-what" referred to the "N-word," commonly used there at that time.)

In mid-August, after a stop at the Airstream service center for repair and over-hall – only $50, including free parking – the vagabonds arrived in Euclid, Ohio at the home of Norma and Sid Kepets, their friends from camp-following, Air Cadet days. "We always find so much to talk about," Mother enthused. "They are a great couple; we love being with them." This was followed by her moan, "Norma and Sid are so slender. They had been dieting. We are gaining!" The Pares religiously weighed in every morning, recording the results in their journal. Indeed, after months of almost non-stop visiting, both had gained weight.

Continuing east, they toured the Steuben glass factory in New York State and headed for Springfield, Massachusetts. There they parked Camelot in the driveway of Joanne and Bruce Dutton, our former neighbors on Lloyd Avenue. Bruce, a longtime employee of the phone company in Springfield, took them around the communications facility. Joanne, who worked at Friendly Ice Cream's corporate headquarters, also gave them a tour which, no doubt, included generous samples.

They went on to Boston where they toured the Vogue Doll plant, then south to the Hershey plant in Pennsylvania. "Even the air is fattening!" Fath exclaimed in their journal.

October found Bettie and Rex at the home of friends in South Carolina. While there, Fath prepped Camelot for winter, draining tanks and lines while Moth gave the perishable food to their friends with whom they would leave the trailer while touring Europe.

The Pares drove to Charleston Air Force Base, planning to hop on a Space-A flight to any place in Europe. (Retired service personnel could fly for free by standing-by for available space on a military plane.) They rose daily at 3AM to get in cue for a Frankfurt flight, only to be disappointed.

After a week of getting up in the middle of the night and still stuck in 12th and 13th place on the list, they decided to try their luck at a base in Dover, Delaware. The eleven-hour drive back north included time spent repairing a loose drive shaft and being stopped by the Delaware State Police for doing 70 in a 60 mph zone. They got off with a warning. "For shame," Mother wrote, "That'll learn us."

In Dover the next evening they lucked onto a flight to Mildenhall, England - "Old Moldyhole," as Fath called it. For the first time in a week, they enjoyed a good night's sleep.

The flight took off at 7:30 PM on October 11 as planned, only to return 15 minutes later because the landing gear wouldn't go up. Finally, in the wee hours of October 12, they left on the same plane, arriving in England at 1:15 PM on Friday the 13th - their lucky day.

The adventurers crammed the next four days in London with theatre, shops, walking and food. They visited museums and stocked up on English specialties at Fortnum and Mason. They saw three plays including "The Mating Game" and a zany farce called "Move over Mrs. Markham." They "took tea" at Brown's Hotel where waiters astonished patrons by whisking the cloth off their table, leaving the tea service intact.

Back in Mildenhall they waited two days before boarding a troop plane with sling seats for the short flight to Germany. "We felt good to be back," Moth noted. They visited friends who were still stationed there and enjoyed eating at favorite restaurants. "The Wiener schnitzel was sure good, and a good house wine. The wine in this area is so good," Moth confided. "Hate to say it but it's better than California whites." After socializing in Germany for two weeks, they hitched a flight to Spain.

In Madrid, Mother, a hotel stationery addict, was excited to find writing paper and envelopes in their room. She raved about the food, especially the leg of lamb, and expressed concern about thirteen-year-old boys tending tables in the hotel restaurant. The rain in Spain was in high gear and didn't let up until the day they left. "We walked aimlessly until Rex finally found a news stand that had a map for sale," Moth revealed. "With a map he's fine."

After an all-day tour to Escorial and the Valley of the Fallen Heroes of the Spanish Civil War, a rainbow gave the travelers short-lived hope. The next day it poured. The relentless rain caused them to stay longer at restaurants and at the Prado where they waited to make a dash to the next point of interest. While attempting to stay dry they commiserated with other travelers. They met a professor of animal nutrition from New Zealand, a couple from South Africa with whom they exchanged addresses and a young American couple to whom they gifted their books about the Prado.

For the first time, the intrepid explorers seemed a bit tired and discouraged. On November 5 Moth wrote, "Up, up and away from Spain. Wouldn't you know it is a beautiful, warm, sunny day, now that we had five days in the rain!" With Italy their goal, they scored space on a plane to Frankfurt by way of Adana, Turkey where police dogs sniffed them and their baggage "to detect dope."

In foggy Frankfurt Fath signed them up for any Italy destination. After four days of weather delays and flight cancellations, they were bumped off a flight after having already checked their bags and received boarding passes. They were about to call it quits and start working their way back to the States when seats on a flight to Pisa became available.

Tired but happy, Rex and Bettie travelled by train from Pisa to Florence where they found a hotel on the banks of the Arno. They crashed and slept late the following morning. Over the next couple days, they hiked to all the sights in Florence. They raved about the beauty of it all and also about a full meal for two costing the equivalent of $3.06. For snacking in their room, they purchased wine, pears and "pretzels" that turned out to be sweet cookies. According to Fath's pedometer, he and Moth had walked 66.3 miles since their arrival in Europe four weeks earlier.

The next morning brought rain, precipitating their decision to move on to Napoli. Packing quickly, they hurried to the station and boarded a train scheduled to arrive in Naples mid-afternoon. After inspecting a hotel near the station - "Ugh," was Fath's verdict – they taxied to the Hotel Rex. Fortunately – considering the name – Rex declared The Rex "nice and only $8.75 with bath."

Three days of exploring Naples, the surrounding ruins and the Isle of Capri left Fath and even high-energy Moth tuckered out. It was time to plan their return to the States. For the next four days they waited, were bumped, spent a night in the terminal, checked back into the Hotel Rex, visited the National Museum and walked along the sea front park. Finally, on November 22, "Hooray! The Med Evac had room for us," Moth cheered. "We are on the first leg of our journey home." Their route required plane changes and layovers in Germany and Spain. Their layover at the Madrid airbase was long enough for them to take the Metro in for Thanksgiving dinner at La Barraca, their favorite Madrid restaurant, where they feasted on roast lamb, melon and ham.

Days later they were still waiting for a Space-A flight home. They were beat. "We don't recover as quickly," Moth observed. "Rex was up and down all the night before. It's too much, terribly tired. We were both almost sick from fatigue but we have so much to be thankful for."

Every day they got their hopes up, only to have them dashed. "No luck," Moth wrote on Saturday. "Pretty sad situation." While at the terminal on Sunday, they met a couple from South Dakota and a man from Indiana who made casket handles for a living. On Tuesday, "No go. Took the bus and metro to Madrid," Moth noted. "No mail at Amex. Walked to the Plaza del Sol and bought

Christmas cards." On Wednesday morning, Fath's entry sings, "At terminal found a C-5 had added 73 seats!! Roll call & we're on our way – they cleaned the list & the terminal!"

Six hours later, the weary wanderers landed in Charleston, South Carolina. At customs they declared purchases totaling $139.05, including a small oil painting for $6, twenty-two pieces of Toledo Damascene jewelry for $31.75, five dollars worth of Spanish Christmas cards, two boxes of toothpicks for $2 and three bullfight posters totaling $1.95. They had walked 106.3 miles in Europe.

By Monday, December 4, the travelers had retrieved their car in Dover and the trailer in North Carolina. The friends who had stored Camelot for them[1], had decorated it for Christmas. "They are such loving, generous people," Bettie penned. "Gobs of mail to read. So glad to be home in our Camelot."

Not too far down the road, near Valdosta, Georgia, the adventurers decided to alight for a month of dieting and R & R. They settled in at Bailey's Mobile Manor where they wrote Christmas cards, mailed packages and caught up on almost two months of mail. Within a week and a half, Fath's weight was down five pounds and Moth had lost almost four.

In mid-December they left Camelot at Bailey's and drove to Chicago to spend Christmas with Chris and Jenny who had trained from Kansas City. By New Year's Eve they were in Cincinnati with Bettie's mother Lona and a neighbor, watching Guy Lombardo on TV, drinking Cold Duck, and playing cards (Society Crap, Fan Tan and Crazy 8's) for pennies until 1:00 AM. "Bettie lost 45 cents and I won 55," Fath bragged. "Great fun. Got to bed about 2 AM., Bettie on the cot and me on couch."

On the road back to Georgia, they saw two wrecks involving cars pulling trailers. "Whew!" Fath wrote, "Sure glad to get to Camelot. She was waiting as we'd left her. Diets begin again!!"

After resting and re-stocking, they hit the highway, this time headed for Florida to visit Rex's brother Max and his wife Marie, who were also trailering. "Had dinner with M & M," Fath wrote. "Played cards til nearly midnite, for pennies. I won – Bettie lost – but together we ended up a few cents ahead. Fun. We sure enjoyed Max and Marie. Hate to go." .

They drove through days and days of rain after leaving Florida in late January, plagued by one problem after another - car and trailer breakdowns, flat tires and pooped-out oil pump. The furnace in the trailer died and the roof sprung a leak. Temperatures dropped and roads iced up. Moth's birthday on February 10 found them stranded in Slidell, Louisiana. "Happy Birthday, Bettie," Fath wrote at the top of the journal page. "I love you very much." Beneath his note, Moth added, "I'm 50 years old today; that's half a hundred!"

Fath left Moth in the trailer and started hiking in the cold rain. He hitched a ride to the next town where he found a trucker to tow the car and trailer back to an Esso Station in Slidell. The ice storm had knocked out the power in half the town, making it impossible to pump gas or fill Camelot's propane tank.

While they were waiting for the storm to end and the car to be repaired, Fath got busy fixing the trailer's leaking rear skylight. Moth's entry in their journal is titled "Sunday in the Junk Yard – my Rex can fix anything." This must have felt like a déjà vu experience for the Pares, similar to the time in Okinawa when they pulled "El Jeepo" under a motor pool shed for shelter from a sudden tropical storm. Once again, they found themselves surrounded by greasy motor parts, though the temperature was a lot colder than it had been in Okinawa.

Ten months after leaving Los Angeles, 13,230.8 trailer miles and 24,570.7 car miles, the Pares returned to Santa Rosa, the home town they had chosen. They liked the small-town atmosphere, the weather, the proximity to San Francisco and the availability of military hospitals and services.

"Home at last after 10 months of wonderful wandering," Fath penned. They parked the trailer and began intensive house-hunting. Five days later they found their home on the outskirts of town at 5386 Gold Drive, across Melita Road from a horse pasture. "Whew!" Fath wrote, "What a load off."

My parents had an uncanny knack for running into people they knew from a previous context. After settling in Santa Rosa they discovered Mrs. Collingwood, our Topeka neighbor from twenty-plus years earlier, was in a local nursing home. Although Mrs. C. didn't seem to know who they were, they visited her on a regular basis.

One of the most fortunate examples of discovering an old acquaintance happened when shopping for furniture at the local Ethan Allen store. Fath and the salesman quickly discovered they had been together in the 22nd Bomb Wing at March Air Force Base in 1950, the first to fly their B-29s to Korea at the beginning of the War. Wally Donaldson and his wife Margie, whose hobby was making teddy bears, soon became the Pares' close friends.

On May 23, 1973, Bettie and Rex moved into the house that would be home for the rest of their lives. They parked Camelot on a trailer pad in the back and put the well-traveled old red carpet on the floor of their two-car garage, where it stayed for the next 34 years. Bettie and Rex were home at last. As they had done so many times before, they joined a church - the First Baptist Church of

Santa Rosa, got to know their neighbors and became involved in the community.

It was their good fortune to be living next door to the Sullivans, a young family with three children for whom the Pares became another set of grandparents. Moth enjoyed teaching the five-year-old twin girls, Kerry and Michelle, how to make clover necklaces and the proper way to sit in the mesh hammock on the screened-in porch – a *chinchorro* from Venezuela. Fath took the twins' older brother Patrick under his wing, eventually influencing his decision to apply to the Air Force Academy in Colorado Springs.

Both talented handymen, Fath and Tim Sullivan shared tools, equipment and elbow grease, each always ready to help the other with the latest home-improvement project. Tim and Shirley cultivated a large kitchen garden to which they gave the Pares free run. Shirley frequently knocked on their door offering baked goodies, fresh-picked berries or tomatoes. When the Pares' three-variety apple tree was producing, they kept the Sullivan family supplied with fruit. The Pares couldn't have asked for better neighbors.

Rex and Bettie strived for personal relationships with barbers, waitresses, cashiers, paperboys, dentists – just about everyone they came in contact with. Waitresses around town soon knew Fath's preference for oatmeal with brown sugar and cinnamon; one breakfast spot bought a cinnamon shaker just for him. Grocery store cashiers told Mother stories about their husbands and children.

During fresh strawberry season, Dee Dee, a waitress at the Hillside Café, knew Fath would want a waffle with fresh berries and whipped cream. The minute she saw their car pull into the lot on Saturday mornings she would place his order. The amount of whipped cream Fath wanted got to be a joke between them – he could never get enough. One Saturday, after he'd teased DeeDee with his third request for more, she kept squirting whipped cream as she moved from the waffles on his plate to Fath's hand and up his arm to the elbow. A horrified gasp arouse from adjacent booths, but Fath thought the joke was hilarious.

Jennifer, Nicole Rose, Bettie, Rex, March 1977

By February 1977 the Pares were awaiting the arrival of their first grandchild. Camelot was stocked with food and ready to be hitched to the car when the call came from Kansas City that Jennifer had given birth to a six pound, two ounce girl named Nicole Rose. A few days later they parked Camelot at an Army base outside of Kansas City where they stayed for a month, driving into town every day to see Jenny and Nicole.

Moth took over the cooking and cleaning. Handyman Fath, tool box at the ready, started working a list of requests, including cat doors for Alley Cat. Jenny remembers being enormously relieved when they arrived and delighted with how enamored they were with Nicole. "Fath was so taken with her," she wrote in a thank-you note to Aunt Ann, "that I thought he might try to steal her."

On Moth's 56th birthday Fath gave her a little toy bear. She named it Gladly, The Cross-eyed Bear. He soon became a family member, revealing a whimsical, imaginative side of my parents' personalities that I'd never known.

They treated Gladly like a precious pet. He was only four inches tall, but quite mischievous. He liked to play hide-and-seek and he saved shiny pennies. The Pares sent us a snapshot of his first Christmas - Gladly on the hearth with his own little tree, surrounded by presents. Over the years he amassed quite a collection of toys and miniature books.

Gladly often accompanied the Pares on their travels. He enchanted the housekeeping staff at a posada in Spain and he guarded their hotel room when they toured London. When Gladly didn't travel with them, he kept an eye on things at home. He could always count on a postcard from the Pares wherever they were wandering.

Margie Donaldson, whose hand-made bears were the source of Fath's inspiration to buy Gladly, had often heard Moth recite poetry. In 1980 Margie invited her to entertain sorority sisters at a chapter meeting. Always ready to perform, Moth gave a presentation about being a woman, wife and mother. She enhanced her talk with poems and quotes she had collected over the years. These are her notes, titled "Strictly Personal," from the final portion of the presentation.

I'm a dreamer, a romantic. Secret thoughts and dreams fill my heart and head. The great imagination I had as a child has lived on. From the story book worlds of elves and fairies and make-believe, I grew to dreaming of being a tap dancer like Ruby Keeler, a movie star, next a missionary in far away Africa, a nurse. Oh, I could see myself – an angel of mercy in a starched white uniform and cap. Perhaps this was an escape from my burden (or what I thought was my burden) – a normal home where I helped care for my 5 brothers.

I escaped to books and found a home in the library. One day my 5th grade teacher, old "piano-legs Kladelbush," requested each of her pupils memorize a poem to recite in front of the class. I chose "The Highwayman" by Alfred Noyes [about 100 lines], that ballad of the robber and his beautiful love. I was no longer Bettie, with straight, sun-streaked blond hair still in a Dutch bob. I became Bess, the landlord's daughter, a tragic, brave heroine.

Come with me to the 18th century England, for I remember that ballad well. Wasn't I brave? And he was so handsome, so dashing and so very bold. [Here she recited the poem.]

The next year I was fair Ellen of "Young Lockinvar" and galloped away over the moors of Scotland, courtesy of Sir Walter Scott. I soon had quite a repertoire. Poe thrilled me with his rhythms, "The Raven," "Anabel Lee." Whittier's "Barbara Frietchie," "Paul Revere's Ride" by Longfellow, Coleridge's "The Rime of the Ancient Mariner." (At times these came in handy when I baby sat or was on a date. You don't "get into trouble" if you are talking, even if it's a monologue. "The Raven" turns 'em off.

Jobs, marriage, WW II, followed my cadet around the country. Children. When our children were small, while they napped, I dreamed over the ironing board. These were the days before permanent press – starch, dampen, iron days. I liked to iron. In my day dreams I was always taller than my 5'2" real self and oh, so slender, willowy, if you will. I'd be dressed in soft, flowing, pastel chiffon frocks. My hair would be black, naturally wavy. A quiet, rather mysterious woman I'd be, eyes dark and deep-set and a little sad, my movements so graceful. I'd be aloof, standing a little apart – slightly breathless (Can you see me?) – sought-after but unattainable.

I traveled, too – via National Geographic and travelogues I'd go to far away places. I'd hum as I vacuumed, the words on my lips as I dusted: "Going to China or maybe Siam … I look for the day I can get underway to search for those castles in Spain. They call me a dreamer, well maybe I am. But I'm going to see for myself."[2]

To be honest, I didn't think I'd get there. 1968, Rex returns from 16 months in Korea, 'I'll take you to London, Bavaria …' Well, now I've been to Siam; I've seen those castles in Spain. Dreams can and do come true. I'll never be tall and willowy, no more than I'll be quiet and graceful. I tell it all: I'm clumsy.

Who do I want to be now? I want to be no one but me. I like being me. I'm richly blessed – health, husband family, church. God watched over me; I'm so thankful.

I'm never bored; I pity those who are. Don't wait for things to happen. Make them happen. Decide what you want to do or be and try. Assume the "Chorus Line" attitude: "I can do that!"

Try! Nothing ventured, nothing gained. Do your best and should you fail (and we all do at times) forgive yourself, right away. Forgive and forget. Dust yourself off and get on with living. Jesus is so forgiving of us. We should be more forgiving of ourselves and one another.

There have been many "me's." You have surely gone from one role to another. I've seen many of you change in the seven years I've been here. Sometimes it's easier to change if you move to another town like I have done so many times. Perhaps it's not so easy if you've always lived in the same town.

I've been a wife, mother, homemaker. I taught Sunday school, was active in the PTA and the Officers Wives Club. I was a college student in Massachusetts, taught junior high in Virginia, travelled and entertained in Germany and now I've settled down in Santa Rosa.

Earlier this year when I turned 57, I was looking for a new challenge and decided to find a job as a bank teller, training with girls one third my age. A friend told me, "Men retire and soon the wife goes to work." This bothered me; then it came to me (and this was added to my reasons for working): I need to retire from my routine – just as a man does.

I need to prove myself in yet another way. And give my husband the opportunity to be a house husband. We are both learning new skills. We treasure our time together – our new relationship. Yes, we sacrifice some freedom, but I can look forward to retiring.

Chapter 21

Crisis in Paradise

Did Mother really "tell it all" in her presentation to Margie's sorority sisters? True, in March of 1980 at age 57, she started working as a teller at Exchange Bank in Santa Rosa. This decision, as my Father explained it, was so she could accumulate enough Social Security credits to qualify for her own payments.

Moth's taking a job came as quite a surprise to my two sibs and me. Now I think there's another possible explanation. It turns out that Fath had been binge drinking on the sly.

I have childhood memories of Fath having a cocktail – usually a Manhattan or a Martini – when he got home from work, but I don't remember ever seeing him drink too much. Moth, who mentioned her low capacity for booze in her Okinawa letters, usually accompanied him, but nursed one Manhattan or Whiskey Sour for literally two or three days, storing what remained of her cocktail in the freezer until the next evening.

Chris recalls that when Fath left for Korea in 1967, Rex's mother asked Bettie if she was concerned Rex might stray while he was away. According to Chris, Moth replied that she wasn't nearly as concerned about Fath having a mistress as she was about his having a weakness for liquor.

As we were trying to piece together this part of our parents' history, Jenny pointed out that when Fath was working at the Pentagon in D.C., our parents' social life changed considerably. They were expected to attend more office events where drinking was a key component of the evening.[1]

I began to wonder whether Mother started working again *because* of Fath's drinking or if he started it because he was suddenly alone all day. It's also possible that his drinking and her decision to work were entirely unrelated.

Yet another possibility is that memories of war, pushed down in his consciousness for over 36 years, were now bubbling up. "Lots of what you do and see in war are much better forgotten. I'd rather just let it die in the back of my mind," Fath had written to his mother in 1944. Was he using the alcohol as an anesthesia to numb emotional pain?

Moth must have been aware of the drinking problem when she spoke to the women's group. Understandably, she chose not to talk about this painful personal detail.

As I struggled with the questions of whether and how to write about this aspect of my practically perfect father - the man who could do anything, the man who quit smoking cold-turkey - Jenny came across a forgotten July 1978 letter from Moth. When Moth wrote the letter, Jenny was living in Kansas City with one-and-a-half year old Nicole.

After sending a "woof" to Jenny's dog Hannibal, and a "meow" to Alley Cat, Moth went on with an account of the Pares' activities and news of other family members.

On page five she writes, "I want to tell you something. Fath may or may not tell you so don't comment if he does – that is, to say that you've heard. We no longer have anything alcoholic in the house and we do not drink any alcoholic beverages anywhere else.

This decision was made 12 or so days ago. It was necessary. We'll both miss wines and champagnes. Since the decision, we've been to restaurants and friends' homes and all is fine. So, you see, we too have problems at times. Thank God for our decision (a very private one)."

Moth relays a few more insignificant news items and closes with, "We love you both so very much. Fath and I are very much in love and we are so thankful for our family, our church, home, and friends."

The letter Jenny found caused me to recall an incident that took place three months before her letter, when the Pares were visiting me and my husband Neil in New Jersey. The men had enjoyed a cocktail or two before dinner and we had served a cabernet with the meal. At some point toward the end of the meal, Neil was telling a story about his own mother, known for getting butter on her thumb every time she buttered a dinner roll. Amused, Fath reached for Moth's hand and buttered her arm. I distinctly remember that Moth was not amused.

A few weeks after Moth wrote the letter to Jenny, the Pares announced to all three of us that they were no longer drinking and they had given the contents of their garage "wine cellar" to Chris.

Despite a few clues, my first realization that Fath's drinking was a major problem came in early 1980 when I visited them from my new home in Chicago. This was shortly after Moth had started her job at the bank. I planned to spend the night in San Francisco on my return trip in order to catch an early morning flight home. That afternoon, after arriving in San Francisco, I called the Pares' house for another good-bye. On the other end of the line I heard a slurry voice. It was Fath; he sounded like he was drunk. I asked him if he was okay and he assured me he was. True to family form, I didn't ask any more questions.

What I now know is that one night in mid-June 1980, as Fath - drunk - slept it off out back in Camelot, Mother picked up a yellow lined pad and wrote him a letter in four installments from 7:30 PM to 5:30 AM the following day. He saved the letter in a file labeled "Special Things," the month and year written in his hand. I came upon it after my parents' deaths.

7:30 PM

"Dear Rex, and you are very dear to me, I write out of fear for what is to come. A very wonderful true love, unbelievable, sweet and rare is in danger.

We have a great problem, we have a triangle and the other third is alcohol. The three of us can't make it. It will destroy our love and both of us. Gradually these times will come more often; now I have a fear each night when I come home [from work]. There will be a time when I won't want to come home; I'll know that I've lost you. If I continue then to live with you our great love for one another will change to dislike, disgust, then hate for one another. I don't want it to go that far; I hope you don't.

I'm weak. I'd run out, I can't watch my idol, my perfect guy, change to a drunk. I'd run far; I'd have to.

Pray – oh how we need God's help. You've put up with my faults and been very dear and oh so good to me. If you helped make me what I am, I too have helped make you what you are.

My heart is breaking. Your lies and deceit crush me. What can we do?

9:30 PM. I was concerned about you – decided to look in the trailer. You were asleep. I'll lock up now. It provokes me – you sleep it off and I am upset and miserable.

Thank you. The house looks clean and is clean. I appreciate that. Do I ask too much of you?

11:45 PM. Can't sleep. I love you. I try to remember that you have an illness; I try to understand; I write this – that it's all up to you – and God.

Two images haunt me. One is that old man across the street from us on Edison [in Virginia]. When I see you walking when you're drunk I see him. The other is [XXX]. I pitied that old man; but I loathed [XXX]. I wonder who I remind you of at time like this.

5:30 AM. Look back over the week past – the times – special times – we had together. Friday you shopped for just the right pearls [for their 39th anniversary]. Sat. we shopped together and then went together to our friends' 50th, Saturday evening relaxed at home.

Your birthday and our anniversary – just us. The earrings were a surprise; they are so beautiful. Life for us is so good. I'd like to erase from my mind times like last night but like paper that's been erased – a scar is left."

My parents worked together on this challenge. Fath swore off liquor – again - but slipped back more than once. They kept the issue pretty much to themselves. Fath's December 31st, 1981 letter to Moth is upbeat and doesn't mention the elephant in the room:

"Dear Bettie, 1981 has been one of the best of our years together! Although we have had some sadness [the death of Bettie's mother in June], most of my memories are happy ones." Fath then lists 10 high points of the year, among them: Chris's

January wedding to Ellen Huberman, Jennifer and Nicole's move from Kansas City to Santa Rosa, the October birth of Chris's first son Benjamin, and "you terminating work at the bank."

Moth with Ben

We know very little about what else transpired with regard to our father's drinking between 1980 and September 1984 when he publicly confessed to the congregation of their church that he was an alcoholic.

We do know that at least once Mother packed a suitcase and spent the night alone in a motel. We also know that a few days before Fath's confession, she had called an ambulance after he passed out at home. The emergency room doctor reported his blood alcohol level was life-threatening.

After Fath went public at church, Moth confided to me that, for her, the most difficult part of the ordeal was coming to terms with Fath's deceit over the previous four years. To cover his tracks he must have lied almost nightly when they recorded their cash expenditures in the household log.

Fath never talked to me about his announcement at church. When I questioned whether he was truly an alcoholic, he only offered, "If I'm not an alcoholic, then I'm just a drunk." After several years of abstention, he did begin to drink wine again in moderation, and seemed to have it under control.

Fath's "Special Things" file held a stack of cards and letters of support from church members and other friends he had informed about his challenge. As far as I know, he never again hid bottles of booze in the garage, nor fudged his nightly report of cash expenditures to hide his vodka purchases. Nor was he ever again carted off to the hospital in an ambulance because of excessive drinking.

Chapter 22

Grandsons, Sweepstakes and Travel

Life was good for Bettie and Rex. Jennifer married Don Norris in 1985 and Chris and Ellie gave them a second grandson, Alexander.

Ben, Moth with Alex

The Pares enjoyed spending time with the boys, occasionally staying with them in San Francisco. They were doing just that in October, 1989, while Chris and Ellie were on an east coast mini-vacation and business trip - their first since Alex's birth. Late afternoon on October 17, while Fath was running errands and Moth was alone with the boys, the house began to shake. Eight-year-old Ben, well-versed in earthquake procedures, directed his grandmother and baby brother to get under the dining room table where they remained until Fath's return.

The 6.9 magnitude Loma Prieta earthquake rumbled through the Bay Area knocking out power and shutting down MUNI, the San Francisco Municipal Railway. On the east coast, the boys' parents heard news of the quake and spent the next three hours frantically attempting to call home, but phone service was intermittent. They finally connected just before the Pares and the boys departed for Santa Rosa where they hoped to find power and working telephones.

Ben, recalling the incident shortly after his thirtieth birthday, reported, "Although I'm a little fuzzy on the details, I remember both of the Pares did a good job of keeping their composure and calming us, and that the power was out right after the quake."

Chris and Ellie were unable to fly back from the East Coast until Bay area airports reopened. They soon began to plan their move out of quake-prone California.

The Pares continued to travel, touring the Far East, Bali, Thailand and New Zealand, making friends and re-discovering acquaintances wherever they went.

In 1988 Fath had double by-pass surgery. It barely slowed them down. In April 1990 they went to a 448th Bomb Group reunion where Rex and the other members of Crew #74 saw each other for what may have been the first time since their last war mission together in 1944. The Pares also began to attend high school reunions in Jeffersonville, Indiana.

One of the things they liked best about traveling was meeting people - from tour companions on a Netherlands trip to students on the plaza in Oaxaca, Mexico. For years afterwards, Moth maintained a correspondence with many of these travel acquaintances and she and Fath even visited some of them.

Our parents' talent for discovering a common link with strangers surfaced in the most unlikely places. While chatting with a couple across the aisle on a train through Mexico's Copper Canyon, they realized Fath and the man had worked together in 1942 at the B.F. Goodrich plant in Louisville before Fath enlisted. Another time, on a trip to Scandinavia, Fath and a woman on the tour thought they knew each other. They finally figured out he had offered her a ride one time when she was stranded with a broken-down car at a service station near Santa Rosa.

Gladly continued to be a part of the Pares' lives. "Gladly is ten years old! (He doesn't look it.)" Moth wrote in early 1990. "Margie Donaldson was just here & she was impressed with his toys – the skate board, his Legos, and his computer. The Donaldsons have hundreds of bears. They're everywhere; they're everywhere."

The following Easter Moth set out her china and silver and served broiled leg of lamb with avgolemono sauce for six guests, including the Donaldsons. She noted in her guest book that Margie brought Gladly a stuffed rabbit.

Moth ratcheted up her contest activity. Between 1978 and 1991 she won trips to London and Holland, a cruise to Mexico, a weekend in Washington, DC, a microwave oven, three clothes dryers in the same year, and over 70 additional prizes ranging from a Malibu Barbie Doll to ballet tickets, luggage and a beach towel. Bettie's success in such contests was legendary.[1]

When she won the Schweppes Sweepstakes Grand Prize in 1981, with a declared value of $2,122, she had to start keeping track of her contest expenses to decrease the tax on her prizes. From 1982 to 1984 she spent more on stamps, envelopes, pens and contest newsletters than she won. Some years she barely broke even, but in 1990 and 1991 she did well, winning prizes worth $4,420.45 against expenses of $435.80.

The Schweppes prize was an all-expense-paid trip to London, the grandest of all of Moth's winnings. It was made even more memorable by a young British couple - Martine and Richard Bernhard - who had volunteered to host the winner. The Pares were charmed by the Bernhards who took them to Rules Restaurant – the longest continuously operating restaurant in London.

Moth corresponded with the Bernhards for years, and the Pares visited them in their home ten years later during a 1991 vacation to the UK. Richard and Martine, by then parents of two sons, again entertained the Pares royally. Fath filled a page and a half of his journal describing the sumptuous dinner they served in their home.

On the same 1991 trip, Fath went seeking Roke Manor, "if it still stands." Roke Manor was a mansion on a large estate near Ramsey which was given over to the US Army Air Corps in 1943 for use as a rest and recreation facility for officers of war-weary bomber crews. "Our crew," Fath wrote, "had a tough mission in late July '44 and as a result we were sent on 'flak leave' to the 'Flak House' – Roke Manor." [The "tough mission" probably was the July 29 Bremen mission for which Fath was awarded the Distinguished Flying Cross.]

"So today after 47 years I returned to see it... now a defense electronic warfare research center managed by Siemens. ... At 12:30 I went to the gate house and talked to the security guard/gate keeper who explained that no one without official business was allowed on the grounds. He called his supervisor, however, and next thing we knew, the supervisor came in, popped me a snappy salute and welcomed Colonel and Mrs. George to Roke Manor.

"What feelings rush back when you see things that you experienced so long ago."

Chapter 23

Déjà Vu and Machu Picchu

I recall a few incidents in the late 1980s or early 1990s, that caused me to suspect something was wrong with my mother. After Fath's 1988 bypass surgery, Moth and I were walking around their yard when she pointed out a couple things that needed to be done – chores Fath would normally do. She made a disapproving remark about his not keeping up. She didn't seem to have any sense of the seriousness of his operation.

I started noticing other disturbing changes in her behavior. She began to have what appeared to be sudden anxiety attacks; she would get shaky, upset, anxious, confused. Fath would whisk her off to their bedroom, put her to bed, hold her hand and talk softly to her until she fell asleep.

Three years after my parents' 2007 deaths, I was reading their travel journals, and came upon another clue about the timing of the onset of Mother's memory problems. On their 1990 trip to Spain they went to the Valley of the Fallen Heroes, their third visit to the site since 1970. Fath noted in their journal that Moth didn't recall ever having been there. Also in the early 1990s, Jennifer recalls incidents when Mother became confused and disoriented while driving.

By the mid-1990s I was encouraging Fath to have Moth evaluated for Alzheimer's; he repeatedly refused. He argued that because there was no cure, there was no point in a diagnosis. Their doctor, he claimed, said Moth's symptoms were normal aging.

Despite Fath's refusal to consider that Moth might have Alzheimer's, he did recognize that her ability to remember recent events was deteriorating. In 1996 he gave her a desk diary and encouraged her make daily notes. Most of these related to what they ate, where they took their morning walk, the people they called, visited or corresponded with, movies and doctor appointments. It appears that, as time went on, Fath often dictated the details of the day's events to Moth in the evening.

Always a stickler for precision, Fath would get upset when Mother incorrectly reported some minor detail – such as the color of their first Volkswagen - and would correct her harshly. His constant criticism and apparent inability or unwillingness to recognize Mother's struggle finally lead me to address my concerns in a letter.

April 27, 1996

Dear Fath,

This is a very difficult letter. I've thought about writing for a long time. It's been very difficult to do so. There's a problem I need to tell you about – something I – and other members of the family – have been very concerned about for a long time.

It has to do with how you talk to Moth. You often seem upset when you talk to her. Your voice is harsh and your tone is critical. You interrupt her frequently to add or correct seemingly insignificant details. You look and sound angry with her. It seems she can never do anything right, whether it's serving the right cookies or putting the pots and pans away. You sound as though you're disciplining an unruly child. You do it a lot, Fath, and you've been doing it for several years.

Believe me when I say that it makes all of us very uncomfortable to witness. It's embarrassing and demeaning to Moth, and I'm sure it's upsetting for her, although she never says anything about it. We (Neil and I) believe it is damaging to her self-esteem and self-confidence. And frankly, Daddy, it doesn't make you look very good. Those who don't know you would see you as a mean, nasty bully. Those who do know and love you have a hard time reconciling this behavior with the good, kind, understanding man we know and love.

I know you truly love Moth and you don't intend to hurt her, but you are. And I just felt I had to address it, however belatedly.

This is very important, Daddy. Please think about it. We are willing to talk about it with you if you want to. And always be sure of this – that we love you very much.

Love, Candy

On our next visit a couple months later, Fath thanked me for the letter. He didn't discuss it. He never mentioned it again. I could, however, tell he was trying and that it was extremely hard for him.

In 1997 the Pares embarked on a grand tour of South America - Moth's dream since Latin American geography class in college. Fath wrote the journal on that trip. He began with this preface:

"Tuesday 28 Jan 97. This South American Adventure really began in 1962 when Bettie was in college at Westfield State

College in Westfield, MA. Mrs. Lillian Wallace was her faculty advisor and taught Bettie's course in South American Geography. Someday seeing Iguassu Falls and the Machu Picchu Inca ruins became her lifetime goal."

Their trip started in Buenos Aires, followed by Iguassu and Rio de Janeiro. Fath meticulously recorded details of baggage weight, flight time, rolls of film, and the meals on each flight. They spent two days in Santiago, Chile and celebrated Moth's 74th birthday in Lima, Peru.

From Lima they flew to Cusco where they boarded the train for Machu Picchu. When their tour group got off the train below the ruins, Mother refused to get in the van that transports tourists to the site. She insisted she had already been there. Fath cajoled, pleaded and reasoned with her, to no avail. Mother never went up the hill to the ruins of Machu Picchu.

My father sobbed when he related the Machu Picchu incident to me. I had never seen him cry. He could no longer fool himself. Something definitely was wrong with Mother.

Moth continued to have déjà vu experiences. Going out to dinner on a visit to Chicago, for instance, she would claim to have been to the restaurant before, when none of us had ever been there.

In July, 1997, when the Pares ten-year-old grandson Alex was visiting from Boston, they went to a first-run movie in downtown Santa Rosa. Part way through the show, Moth announced she had already seen the movie and wanted to go home. Fath replied that he and Alex wanted to see the show; Moth could wait for them in the theatre lobby. A few minutes later when he went to check on her, Moth was gone. He had the theatre searched, then he and Alex started walking the streets nearby, looking for Moth. Finally,

Fath called the police. He and Alex eventually found Moth in the public library several blocks from the theatre.

Moth made note of this incident in her diary, still convinced she had previously seen the movie. "I got confused – We went to a movie and I had seen it so left & walked around town & got lost! Rex was worried & reported to the police who put out an alarm for me. Right after that Rex and Alex saw me & picked me up & reported to police. I've got to do better!!!"

Moth got lost more than once driving to nearby familiar places and had to call Fath to direct her home. Eventually, the Pares announced Moth was giving up her drivers' license. I had assumed it was because of her disorientation, but now, having read her diaries, I wonder if there was an additional reason. Did she believe she wouldn't be able to pass the written drivers' test?

"January 7, 1998, I'm tired and rather troubled … Jan 29, Studied for drivers' license … Feb 2, Did not go for renewal of driving license & don't want to drive any more! So there!"

Despite Moth's decline, Fath managed to maintain an outwardly upbeat attitude. In an August 1998 letter he reported on the weather, a trip east to visit relatives, Moth's weekly visit to the hair-dresser, and "Chris reports that author Ed McBain ("87th Precinct" series) has a new paperback out – 'Gladly, the Cross-Eyed Bear.' Should we sue?" Fath still had his playful sense of humor.

I began to suspect Fath, under the guise of maintaining Moth's dignity, was glossing over her problems when he talked with their doctor. I decided I needed to intervene and faxed a letter to the doctor on July 27, 1998, describing Mother's failing memory, confusion and inability to follow directions. I asked him about prescribing Aricept. He faxed a typed reply the same day:

"I think the best course of action that will enable your mother to either improve or at least slow down the progression of her symptoms is the warm supportive environment that Rex is providing her. Keeping her as active and involved in their shared activities is probably the best course of action to slow down the progression of her symptoms. Also, establishing a consistent routine for her to adhere to."

Their doctor agreed to discuss the use of Aricept with my father at his next appointment. Fath faxed me his report of the visit:

11/05/98

"We saw the doctor on 20 October and had a productive session. Moth is extremely healthy for her age (or even someone 20 years younger). All her tests have come back either normal, within acceptable range, or negative. He gave her an oral test to establish a baseline for future exams. It included about 20 questions relating to date, time, place, birthday, social security number, repeating names of objects (later asked to recall). She scored 70 out of 90.[1]

"He (I think reluctantly), prescribed Aricept 5 mg once daily at bedtime. The drug is specific for Alzheimer's disease and not especially for memory problems. I checked the Air Base pharmacy but they don't stock the drug. So we went to Longs' here in Santa Rosa where they would fill it. Our HMO declined to approve because no background had been established. When our doctor provided justification they approved. Moth began taking it on 2 Nov 98. I'll be observing and keeping notes on results & side effects. She's behaving well and seems normal in every way except for the memory which is often normal and at other times (especially when she's tired) she has significant problems recalling things."

The Aricept did seem to help. A little less than two months after Moth started taking it, Neil and I were in Santa Rosa over the Christmas holidays. Mother seemed to be calmer than she had been for several years. She was more involved in conversations and seemed to be tracking better. We were all encouraged and optimistic that this might buy her some time.

On the other hand, there still were times when her frustration at not being able to carry out a task caused a teary meltdown. We witnessed one of these incidents on another visit. The Pares had planned one of our favorite meals – grilled leg of lamb with avgolemono sauce. Fath had boned and marinated the lamb and was in charge of the grill. Moth was to make the sauce. Fath arranged the ingredients and required utensils in chronological order on the kitchen counter. Despite his set-up, the task was too much for Moth. She fell apart. Fath put her to bed and I made the sauce.

After dinner, I invited Moth to take a stroll and tried to get her to talk about her frustration and fears but she refused to even acknowledge there was anything wrong. I never tried again. To this day I'm sorry I didn't. Maybe she talked about her fears with Fath, but knowing her approach to life – "Look on the sunny side, always on the sunny side" - it's quite possible she never did. It seemed clear that although both she and Fath were aware something was wrong, they each seemed to be pretending otherwise.

The Pares continued to be active at the First Baptist Church. Moth was on the counting committee that met on Monday mornings to count and bank the offerings from the previous Sunday. She reported the counting activities in her dairy, always followed with details of where the group went afterward for pastry and coffee. The group seemed to have fun doing their weekly task and Moth always looked forward to it.

The church's minister resigned in May of 1998; Fath was on the search committee to find a new one. After six months of interviews and invitations to preach, the committee recommended a candidate who was installed as the new pastor in December.

Angina sent Fath to the hospital in September 1999. Another bypass was considered too risky, so his cardiologist opted for angioplasty. The operation was difficult – three failed attempts, three burst angioplasty balloons before a stent was successfully installed. His condition was so serious that I flew out to Santa Rosa. He remained hospitalized for five days.

Throughout 1999 and the first half of 2000, Moth periodically noted on Sundays, "good sermon" or "We like him." By summer 2000, she was no longer mentioning Sunday church or Monday counting. In September, her Sunday entries start mentioning attending services at other churches and at year end my parents stopped tithing to the church that had been their spiritual home for the past twenty-seven years.

This was a troubling and sad period for Fath. He had invested so much time and energy in the church community, calling on homebound and elderly members, volunteering his handyman skills and serving in leadership positions. In 1990 he had been honored with a plaque "… for your conscientious, devoted and dedicated service as a leader. Your contributions have been an inspiration to us all." Now, besides seeing Mother beginning to slip away, he had lost the very foundation he had expected would be there to support him through difficult times ahead.

When I pressed Fath to explain why they had resigned their membership, he complained the minister was focused on making the service more attractive to young people – even had a cappuccino bar installed in the vestibule. It didn't seem like a church anymore. Furthermore, they no longer sang the old familiar hymns and had thrown out the old hymnals. With a little more prodding, he revealed that the minister no longer counseled or visited ill members. Not only that - he didn't accept such duties as part of his responsibilities.

Aha! There it was. The pastor hadn't called on Fath when he was hospitalized for the angioplasty. Visiting sick people, the pastor had told him, was not his priority. Fath had often said he didn't need a church to be able to have a relationship with God. He joined a church for community and, from Fath's perspective, the pastor's position was untenable; it didn't support the church community.

Moth had been limping and wincing for some time, although she seldom complained of pain and usually brushed off inquiries when asked about it. She identified the pain as being in her left knee and eventually began to avoid walking. When her knee was finally x-rayed in late 2000, the doctor discovered the problem wasn't her knee at all, but her left hip; there was no lining left between the ball and socket.

It was only in preparation for hip surgery in February 2001 that Moth was finally evaluated by a neurologist who confirmed her Alzheimer's diagnosis. The discussion then was about whether she had the mental capacity to participate in the rehabilitation process and comply with the post-surgery cautions. We were also concerned about reported incidents of troubling side-effects of anesthesia on Alzheimer's patients. Fath insisted he could manage Moth's rehabilitation, and procedures were put into place to avoid post-anesthesia delirium and hallucination.

Jenny, Fath and I alternated staying in the hospital with Mother after her surgery. I was shocked by how little the well-meaning staff knew about Alzheimer's. A nurse lectured me about Moth's self-administered morphine drip. Only the patient was allowed to activate it; I was forbidden to do so. The patient, however, couldn't follow the simplest instructions even when she wasn't under sedation. Whenever Mother appeared to be in pain, I gave her a dose of morphine – it was regulated so that it wasn't possible to over-dose.

Moth would wake up and want to get out of bed to urinate. She didn't understand why we wouldn't let her leave the bed, nor could she comprehend that she was catheterized. Another illustration of her diminished capacity: She kept insisting I "move the ironing board" because she "didn't like to leave it up in the living room." I finally realized she was referring to the wheeled serving/vanity apparatus and moved it out of her sightline. At one point she asked me, "Is Rex George your father?" "I sure hope so," I replied, "Do you have something to confess to me?" Her response was a flirty smile and one of her conspiratorial winks.

Moth in hospital after hip surgery, February 2001

On the day before she was discharged, Jenny and I brought the family poetry tome to her room. We were showing off, competing to see which one of us could recite William Wordsworth's "Daffodils" from memory. (Jenny won.) Mother joined in and the three of us entertained the nurses peeking in the door. Moth could still recite many poems.

Around this same time Moth started losing things – a raincoat, an umbrella, jewelry. Twice in as many days she left her amethyst ring in a public restroom. On the first occasion the ring was still there when she returned to look for it. She never found it the second time. On another morning, she put on her antique aquamarine drop earrings – the ones Fath had bought for her in wartime London. When she and Fath returned home after their morning walk, she was missing one of the earrings. Most likely she had failed to put the back on the post to secure the dangly earrings I had coveted since childhood. She also twisted and broke gold chains, chewed on pendants and bent clasps on brooches. Reluctantly, Fath started buying her inexpensive jewelry.

Misspellings become more frequent in Moth's diaries. She mentions a community meeting about a proposed housing development that would "emproch on our road." She notes "Rex made friend frided toast for lunch," and "Left my unbrals in Greta's car." She reports a "bressy, windy day," and in 2001 writes the date as "Teusday May 20second." August 23, 2001 is the first example of her writing the first letter of her name with what looked like a shaky "M" instead of a "B".

If it rhymed or was put to music, there was a good chance Moth could remember it. One day she started chanting an old advertising jingle, probably from her teen years. We had never heard her sing it before. "Hi, ho, whadaya know? I drink Falls City 'cause I love it so!" Fath confirmed it was an old radio ad for a Louisville beer.

Pretty soon Moth gave us all rhyming nicknames, some of which we had heard before, others not. She started calling Fath "Rexy-by-Hexy", and herself "Bettie-Spaghetti" with the tag line "… and don't you forgetti." Jenny had often been referred to as "Jenny-Penny" - the Okinawa housemaid had called her that. Chris became "Mistopher-Christopher" and I was "Candy-Dandy."

There were many "song cues" that would start Moth reciting or singing. At one point Neil distributed a list of forbidden words, with accompanying fines for the person who slipped and caused another chorus of "My Darling Clementine" or "Did you ever go a-fishin' on a hot summer day?"

Relatively early in the progress of her disease, Mother could be quick, sassy and mischievous. One day she was belting out the Air Force song, "Off we go into the wild blue yonder, flying high into the sky." Fath was quick to correct her, "It's not the *sky*, Bettie, it's the *sun*." "Well," hands on hips, she huffed indignant and shot back, "You have to get to the sky before you get to the sun!" She stuck her tongue out at him and stomped off .

Chapter 24

My Father Can Do Anything

We grew up believing our father could do just about anything and were almost never disappointed. His first grandchild, Nicole, bragged about his talents at school. He welcomed the most challenging household repairs. Relatives and friends around the country made to-do lists in anticipation of the Pares' visits. Dripping faucet? Running toilet? Need an oil change? Got a problem with that electric outlet? Not to worry, Rex was your man.

He was also our doctor. Whenever one of us kids had a sore throat, he would get out the tongue depressor, a long swab and the Merthiolate and paint our throats as we choked and squirmed. Susie McGough, our playmate in Okinawa and Sacramento, recalls Fath curing her with the nasty orange liquid and grinding aspirin to use as a poultice on her scraped knees. Years later Jenny called him into service again when Nicole had a scratchy throat.[1]

Fath loved splinters and welcomed any opportunity to use his perfected extraction technique. He liked to work on us and was always itching for a chance to do so. When I was in the 5th grade in Topeka, I fell on the school playground, lodging a piece of gravel in my right knee. After the school nurse failed to extract it, she called our house. Mother took me to the emergency room at Forbes Air Force Base where we were met by Fath. He watched the doctor's unsuccessful attempts at prying out the gravel, then asked if he could give it a try. Instead of squeezing, he pulled the surrounding skin away from the gravel and out shot the stubborn stone.

Fath had been acting out his dream of being a doctor since his Boy Scout days. When he talked about his World War II Market Garden mission, his doctoring of the two men in the bomb-bay who had been hit by machine gun fire seemed to be his most vivid memory of the mission, more important than his own injuries.

Moth once wrote to her mother from Okinawa about having cut herself so badly she had to be taken to the emergency room for stitches. She reported that Fath was hoping for bad weather so he could remove the stitches himself. She wasn't kidding. He had lots of practice working on Moth – she tended to cut herself on a regular basis.

Fath pierced Moth's ears. He numbed each lobe with an ice cube, put a wine cork behind and stabbed her ear with a sterilized needle. Having perfected his technique on Moth, Fath offered to pierce Nicole's ears.

"When I was nine Grandad pierced my ears in our kitchen," Nicole recalled in an 2010 email. "It was during a visit they made to our house in southern California. I always knew he had pierced my mom's ears and my grandma's as well. First we went and picked out some pretty little 14k gold earrings. I was nervous, but I REALLY wanted pierced ears, so I was willing to do it. I had been attended to by 'Dr. George' many times before. Somehow I was less scared because HE was doing it. LOL! [laughing out loud]

"After soaking the earrings in alcohol, we were ready. He made marks on my lobes, then I held ice on my ears for what seemed like forever! Next he cut a potato and took the needle out of the alcohol. He put the potato behind my ear, and quickly poked the needle thru! It was the MOST PAIN I HAD EVER

FELT!!!!! I cried and begged him not to do the other side! After I had calmed down, he finished the job and I was happy! Now I know that a piercing gun is a virtually painless way to do it! Live and learn. LOL!"

Fath was a dentist, too - fortunately not until after we three kids left home. He considered himself an expert at repairing Moth's dentures and as time went on, he had plenty of opportunities to do so. In his travelogue from their 1990 Iberian adventure, Fath noted on one of their first days in Spain, "Saw Super Glue in shop window on way back from dinner. Next day returned to buy glue to repair Bettie's teeth; one popped out at dinner a few days ago."

Jenny told a story about Doctor Rex at our parents' memorial service in 2007. "Several years ago now, Moth said to me, 'If you don't hear from me for some time, I want you to come over and check in the garage. I may have died and Fath has got me on that workbench, trying to get me fixed up so I'll work again.'"

Fath valued precision and detail; he prided himself on his resourcefulness and ingenuity. He was systematic and organized. Sometimes his solutions were more complex than necessary and sometimes they solved problems most of us didn't even know existed.

He invented a toothpaste transfer device for re-filling expensive travel-size tubes with paste from less expensive large ones. I still use the toothpaste gadget he gave me. He could easily construct a box of perfect proportions for whatever item he planned to ship.

He spent hours driving Mother all over town, searching for the perfect replacement buttons for her green-checked shirtwaist dress because the daisy-shaped originals were difficult for her arthritic fingers to manipulate. After finally finding the new buttons, he toiled for two evenings securing all fifteen down the front of her frock with heavy-duty thread.

The man could work under the hood of the car, change the oil - you name the job - in white jeans and never get dirty.

There was a correct way to do just about everything and it was his way. I was reminded of this one time when I was helping with the laundry and folded his undershirts the wrong way.

Fath's belief that he could do a better job than a professional – plumber, electrician, carpenter – caused problems from time to time. The air conditioning system he had installed shortly after moving into the house in 1973 coughed its last cool gasp in 2004. He refused to call an electrician, probably because he knew his self-installed wiring in the crawl-space attic was not up to code.

While the air conditioner was on the blink, Fath went through an elaborate routine to keep the house "cool" during the day. He kept all the drapes closed, and he and Moth sat around in the dark. At night he opened the windows and positioned fans to capture cooler evening air.

Having lived through Chicago's record-setting heat wave in summer of 1995 – when 739 heat-related deaths were recorded over a five-day period - I was concerned about my parents' health and safety without air conditioning. Santa Rosa summer temperatures could easily top 100 degrees. Fath wouldn't bend or budge.

Finally, Neil and I played the trump card and refused to stay with the Pares when we visited in June of 2005, choosing an air-conditioned hotel instead. That did the trick. In early August Fath emailed, "This just in!!! Confirming recent rumors of cooling relations with Chicago relatives. A complete overhaul of the air handling system at 5386 Gold Drive has been completed. Ice cubes are piling up in the computer/guest room. I'm sure the changes will insure continuing cool relations with our favorite guests. Outside right now it's 91 degrees; here at the keyboard it's a comfortable 72 degrees. We're loving it!!"

One day while visiting the Pares in 2006, I walked by their bedroom and saw Fath repeatedly dragging Moth's panty hose over the bedroom carpet. "The poor man's finally lost it," I thought to myself. But no. He explained that this technique was the best way to remove wrinkles after taking hosiery from the dryer. I had never realized panty hose could wrinkle, much less that it would be a problem if they did.

The Pares' clothes dryer had been on my nag list for a long time. The exhaust duct from the dryer in the garage to the outside wall was so badly clogged with lint that it took forever to dry even the lightest load. I discovered Fath often hauled wet laundry to a laundromat to dry it. We offered to pay to have the blocked duct cleaned out. "No, they don't do a thorough job. I can do it myself," said the man who by then was stretched to the limits taking care of his almost completely dependent Alzheimer's-stricken wife. I sent him an article about the danger of fire. Still no action.

On another visit in October 2006, I begged him to allow us to call a professional. He countered with, "I'll work on it tomorrow if you take care of Moth." No problem. We entertained Mother, took her for long rides in the car, visited Jenny across town, came back six hours later and found 85-year-old Fath sitting on the cold, hard concrete garage floor, surrounded by dryer parts.

He had disassembled the entire dryer to give the motor a thorough cleaning and had yet to put it back together.

The duct was still blocked. His solution? He disconnected the duct and used a pair of Moth's de-wrinkled panty hose as a lint filter.

Chapter 25

Bettie's Decline

By 2002, Moth's mental state had deteriorated dramatically. She became confused with the simplest tasks, such as setting the table for four people. She repeatedly asked, "How many forks?" Tasks with more than one step were impossible for her to accomplish. Fath struggled to tone down his instinctive behavior – giving detailed, navigator-type, step-by-step instructions.

One time when they were visiting us in Chicago, we were all in the living room, dressed to go to dinner. Moth asked Fath, "Should I take my purse?" "Yes, Bettie," he replied. "Where is it?" she asked. Fath: "It's back in the studio where we sleep." Moth: "Where's that?" Fath: "Turn around and head for the kitchen. When you get to the hall, turn left, then turn right at the front door. Walk diagonally through the den, turn left toward our bathroom and right into the studio. It's in the far left corner on the little library steps." Moth, with a puzzled look on her face: "What is?"

Moth wandered and got lost a few times. Sometimes Fath went out looking for her; when he was desperate he called the police. One time a young couple spotted her about two miles away along busy, two-lane Highway 12. Suspecting something was wrong, they stopped, convinced her to get into their car and brought her home. Fath's constant drilling to "train" Moth on their address had worked this time. But even he recognized the need for a back-up plan. He ordered a "safe home" bracelet for her from the Alzheimer's Association.

Relieved of all household chores, Moth spent much of her time singing along to old MGM musicals. Her favorites included "Oklahoma," "Meet Me in St. Louis" and especially "Singing in the Rain." She was happy to sit and watch "Singing in the Rain" almost every day. She would sway to "Fit as a fiddle, and ready for love; I could jump over the moon up above." She greeted each day with "Oh, What a Beautiful Morning" from "Oklahoma" as she sashayed down the hall to breakfast.

It was the Pares' custom to read a Bible chapter in the morning after breakfast - a comforting ritual for Fath. We questioned Moth's comprehension, but every once in a while, we would see a flash of understanding - as we did the morning they were reading about the trials of Job. Moth listened intently to the long list of Job's woes, then said, "So what? Did he have Alzheimers'?"

As time went on, Moth's reading capability deteriorated; she showed no sign of recognition when she skipped or mispronounced a word. (I have since learned that Alzheimer's patients maintain understanding of the written word long after they can no longer speak or understand the spoken word.[1] How I wish I had been aware of this when communicating with Mother became more difficult.)

By 2003, Fath was showing signs of stress and fatigue. In addition to doing all the household chores - cleaning, shopping, cooking, laundry, yard work, bill-paying, correspondence - he was doing everything for Moth. After we noticed she'd used lipstick on her eyebrows, he started applying her makeup for her. He styled her hair each morning.

He spoke for her. I'm sure this was a well-meaning attempt to reduce her anxiety when she was asked a question, but often I wished he wouldn't be so quick to jump in. One night after dinner we were talking on their screened patio as the evening darkened. Neil, who had a talent for getting Moth to talk, asked her about her biggest regrets.

Before she had a chance to speak, Fath said to her, "I know what they are. One is that you never got to hold our baby Susan before she was buried and the other is my drinking." These seemed more like Fath's regrets, still haunting him after all those years - the two things he could never forgive himself for. Moth listened to his confession and vigorously nodded her head in agreement.

After the Machu Picchu incident in 1997, the Pares never traveled overseas again. In 2003 they made their last annual Thanksgiving trip to Boston. Air travel was much too complicated and confusing. Eventually they stopped attending the monthly National Geographic Society programs they had enjoyed for years. By the mid-2000s their adventures were limited to riding around Santa Rosa, Moth choosing the direction to go at each stop sign or traffic light. Sometimes they would meander out to Lucas Wharf in Bodega Bay, enjoy a fish and chips lunch while overlooking the ocean and drive home again. Fath, ever the navigator, reported the outbound trip took 40 minutes, the drive home 41.

Each time we visited Santa Rosa, Moth seemed a little less connected. At breakfast she poured orange juice on her cereal and tried to eat it with a fork. One day I asked her for a pair of tweezers, causing near panic as she offered up brushes, Q-tips, and lipstick out of the vanity drawer in the guest bath. She no longer knew what tweezers were.

Worn out from being the sole caretaker, Fath seemed physically and mentally slower. It took him longer to make decisions. He was easily distracted when driving and his reflexes were slowing.

In the fall of 2003, I made an appointment to meet with a local Alzheimer's Association representative and was pleased when Fath agreed to join me. We brought Moth along. I had anticipated a ten to fifteen-minute meeting, an opportunity for my father to make a connection and learn about available resources. We were there an hour and fifteen minutes with Family Care Associate Noelle Thill. She immediately established rapport with Fath, putting him at ease and neutralizing his defensiveness. She addressed many of his concerns and objections even before he expressed them and quickly gained his respect and confidence.

Despite the successful meeting and Ms. Thill's follow-up home visit, Fath wasn't ready to consider day care or a home companion for Mother. Ms. Thill didn't mince words. She told him that a very high percentage of caretakers wore themselves out and died before the person they were caring for.

Fath nods off

We had read about Namenda, the new Alzheimer's drug already available in Europe. As soon as it was approved by the Federal Drug Administration, we lobbied the Pares' doctor for a prescription. Moth started taking it mid-January, 2004. Fath confessed, "I'm more excited about this than I should be, but we have faith in the reported experiences where the drug has been used."

Moth seemed a little more engaged after taking Namenda for a couple months, but her lack of judgment and social inhibitions continued to get worse. She frequently removed her dentures or played with them while eating. She passed gas with abandon and held her hands across her crotch to announce the need to urinate.

She gave come-hither smiles to her sons-in-law and grabbed Neil's behind on more than one occasion. She flirted with a flustered young waiter, playing peek-a-boo with a paper doily and whisking it away to reveal one of her signature mischievous winks.

Moth no longer had an internal monitor to regulate her eating. Five minutes after breakfast she might ask if it was time to eat. She would rummage through the refrigerator and kitchen cabinets, eating whatever she could find, be it cookies, prunes or ice cream. Her weight was going up as Fath's was decreasing. Mother, who weighed 115 pounds when Fath retired in 1972 and 123 when she had her hip replaced, now weighed in at 156. Fath, who had retired at 169 pounds, was down to 145 by year-end 2005.

Fath persisted in the belief that he could "train" Moth, reason with her, or motivate her with lectures and admonishments. He believed it was okay for her to walk by herself in the neighborhood because "she knows she's supposed to stay on our cul-de-sac and that I expect her to be back in 15-20 minutes." This drove us crazy. She had no concept of time. Furthermore, I had walked with Moth, and it was clear she was accustomed to hiking along - and even crossing - Melita Road, a winding two-lane, heavily-trafficked country road with no sidewalks.

To deal with Mother's nighttime wandering, Fath started keeping the house locked from the inside with a key he carried at all times, even in his pajama pocket at night. Moth frequently woke and attempted to go outside. We were relieved she could no longer wander out, but were concerned about her being trapped if something should happen to Fath.

Whenever I anticipated seeing the Pares after a two or three month absence, I was anxious that Moth might not recognize me. She usually did, but didn't always get my name right. Often she asked me if I was Greta, a friend she went to breakfast with on Wednesday mornings.

When Moth went out to breakfast with Greta Soso, Fath sent her with a credit card to pay her share, which was never more than $7-$8. He knew she could no longer do arithmetic. He stocked her purse with $30.02 "in case she needs it" – exactly $29.00 in currency and $1.02 in coin. I have no idea how he arrived at that particular amount.

Mother and Greta had two traditions. They passed the same birthday card back and forth for years, adding a new note each time, and they went to the Hillside Café for mid-week breakfast. Faithful to the end, Greta continued their twenty-year breakfast tradition. The waitresses knew Moth would have "Bettie's breakfast" - one fried egg with toast and a packet of boysenberry jam.

"We would always sing at breakfast," Greta recalled at the Pares' memorial service, "and the waitresses would say 'just keep it down a little.' I wanted to keep going to breakfast with Bettie until she didn't know me anymore, and it was getting close to that time. I now know eleven verses of 'Darling Clementine.'" (This was a bit of an exaggeration on Greta's part, unless Moth had made-up new verses in addition to the seven in our "Treasury of the Familiar.")

C. and Moth singing Clementine – "ruby lips above the water"

Toward the end of 2004, Fath finally agreed to hire a bi-weekly housekeeper. He also engaged a yardman to handle the outdoor chores. He still insisted on doing his own laundry and ironing, even though he reported having twenty-five shirts waiting to be ironed. Despite the extra help, six months later in mid-2005 Fath was showing more signs of chronic fatigue. He would nod off during the 5:30 evening news before the lead story was over. On more than one occasion I saw him fall asleep in the middle of a conversation. He stayed up after putting Moth to bed at night so he could catch up on paperwork, but usually fell asleep before he could accomplish anything.

Fath got less and less sleep. He reported that Moth "overflowed" five nights out of seven. He bragged he had reduced to half an hour the turn-around time between discovering Moth was wet, changing her night clothes and the bed linens, putting the soiled sheets in the washer and returning to bed. He had a catalogue on his desk offering a variety of more-absorbent protective undergarments, but hadn't gotten around to ordering.

Later that year he announced his solution to the nighttime wetting problem: He was setting the alarm to go off every two hours during the night in an attempt to wake Moth *before* she wet the bed. Now, instead of getting up once – maybe twice – during the night, he was awakened three to four times by the alarm. He seemed so enamored with his ingenuity that he couldn't see the benefit of more obvious solutions.

Moth's nighttime wandering also disrupted Fath's sleep. She would awake and begin repeating she wanted to go home. He would reason with her, explaining that she *was* home. He often took her outside in the middle of the night to verify the house number and street sign for her. Sometimes this exercise would happen more than once during the night.

In early January 2006, Fath announced during one of our increasingly frequent phone calls, "I recently determined I don't have to get up at 6AM everyday!" Having been an up-and-at-'em man all his life, he was reveling in this simple discovery. (I don't recall ever being allowed to sleep late as a teenager. When Fath was up, we were all up.) Six months shy of his 85th birthday, he had come to the realization that it was OK to sleep in.

He seemed more upbeat over the next few months. He even started talking about driving to Southern California to visit Argie Torres' widow Betty – a three day trip each way. I shuddered at the thought of him driving. "I'm fine, Moth is fine and we're still having fun," he insisted.

During a phone call one Saturday night in August, Fath reported he had shut off all the water in the house. He'd been working on leaky faucets in both bathrooms and had discovered - after all the hardware stores in town had closed - that he needed new packing nuts. The water was still off when Monday night came around. I cautiously suggested he call a plumber. "I am a plumber," he snapped back.

Lucky for the Pares, their neighbor Shirley Sullivan brought dinner over for them that weekend. She seemed to be doing so more frequently. I would hear reports of a chicken dish, cedar-planked salmon with all the fixings, a tomato tart, zucchini bread, veggie soup, and Thunder Cake with its secret ingredient – tomatoes.

The Cheneys, their across-the-street neighbors, would often show up with cookies. Jim Cheney even cleaned the leaves out of the gutters on my parents' roof. Both the Cheneys and the Sullivans checked to see if the Pares' morning newspaper had been picked up from the driveway or whether Rex had taken the flag down at night or put it back up in the morning. We couldn't have asked for better watch dogs.

After a 2006 visit to Santa Rosa, Chris reported Fath had scared him half to death by nodding off for a brief moment and drifting into another lane while driving on multi-lane, high-speed

Highway 101. On his next visit Chris told Fath he would no longer ride in the car if Fath was driving.

Not long after, I sent Fath an article about the dangers of "mini-naps" while driving. In a follow-up phone call he refused to acknowledge the possibility that this could happen to him. He attempted to reassure me with, "Sometimes I do doze off when we're stopped at a light, but Moth, my co-pilot, watches the light and tells me when it's time to go." (He thought this would inspire confidence?)

When we were in Santa Rosa for the Christmas holidays, I came to regret I hadn't had the guts to refuse to ride with Fath as Chris had done. In the back seat of the car on a return trip from picking up prescriptions at Travis Air Force Base, Neil and I screamed "Stop!" in unison as Fath was about to rear-end the truck braking in front of him. He had been distracted giving Moth instructions about where to dispose of a candy wrapper. A little farther along, he nodded off and wandered into a left-turn lane on Highway 12. When he jerked his head up and veered back into the northbound lane, we almost hit another car.

Every night Gladly, the Pares' cross-eyed bear, would join them in the den for the evening news. He watched "Singing in the Rain" over and over again with Mother as she slipped deeper into Alzheimer's. He forgave her for chewing on him when she thought he was food.

Moth went through a phase when she chewed on everything from cardboard coasters to jewelry. One afternoon Jenny and I were chatting in the living room while Mother napped in the bedroom. A crackling sound caught our attention. We raced down the hall to the bedroom where we found Moth with a mouthful of hearing aide bits. We never found all the pieces; she must have swallowed some, including the battery.

Moth takes a snooze

Throughout it all, Mother remained chipper and clueless, chanting her rhyming report, "We had fun and no harm done," frequently followed by "We both have wonderful husbands; they have lovely wives. We'll all be happy for the rest of our lives."

Chapter 26

Fit as a Fiddle, May 2007

Whenever he was asked how he was holding up, Fath would reply, "We're still having fun." He once told Neil, "I was born to do this." My father's eventual downfall was the belief that no one but he could take care of Mother.

As Doctor Rex, he wouldn't take himself to the hospital in January, 2007. He was sure the pain behind his shoulder blade - the severe pain that had kept him bedridden for days - was a pulled muscle. He didn't want to bother any of the friends or relatives who would have been happy to help on a short term basis. The very weakness that had been noted in his 1958 performance evaluation – not willing to delegate, believing so strongly in his own abilities that he wasn't open to help from others – caused the beginning of the end of his grasp on life.

In February Fath was hospitalized for a severely abscessed lung caused not by a pulled muscle, but by undiagnosed pneumonia. Over the next few months he was in and out of the hospital with a variety of other ailments. Jenny and I soon had to admit we couldn't take care of Mother on a long-term basis. With Fath's agreement, we negotiated a short-term respite for her at Primrose Alzheimer's Living, a highly-regarded local facility that specialized in full service care for people with impaired memory.

We all feared a difficult transition, but Moth had so lost touch with reality that she hadn't even asked for Fath during the time he was hospitalized. As we filled out paperwork on her first day there, she went off arm-in-arm with two aides, merrily serenading them with "Meet Me in Saint Louis, Louis. Meet me at the fair."

Ben and Chris visit Fath in hospital. March 2007

Eventually, after Fath was released from a skilled nursing facility, he agreed to consider assisted living. Jenny, Chris and I let out a big sigh of relief when he contracted for a small studio apartment in a facility that also had an Alzheimer's wing where he hoped Moth could eventually move.

He and Chris were shopping for a twin bed for the new apartment when Fath had a heart attack. Back to the hospital he went.

At one point, Moth and Fath were in the same hospital. She had been admitted from Primrose with a diagnosis of pneumonia; he was in for a MRSA-infected wound from the angioplasty following his heart attack.[1]

279

Mother, now without hearing aides or dentures, was known by the hospital staff as Bettie Spaghetti. In late stage Alzheimer's, she was entirely dependent on others and often completely out of it. Even when I held her hand and talked to her, I seldom got any response. But one time when handsome nurse David McCullough entered the room and greeted her with, "Good morning, Bettie Spaghetti, looks like another bad hair day," she flashed a big toothless grin and winked at him. The flirtatious Bettie of old was still alive somewhere in that tangled brain.

When Mother was moved down the hall to the Transitional Care Unit, she had the good fortune of being attended by a young woman named Leti. Leti could calm Bettie Spaghetti with her warm smile and soft voice. She was quick to respond when Mother was agitated or needed to be changed. She was a special angel, worth her weight in gold.

And then there was the Lift Team - what a wonderful concept - young men with the unlikely combination of brute strength and sincere tenderness. Luis Gamino, Sal and the other team members took care of Moth with the devotion and dedication one might expect of sons or grandsons. They always treated her with dignity and respect, even as they were changing her diapers and bedclothes for the third time that day.

When Fath's nurses learned Moth was on another ward, they delivered him - in protective garb and gloves to avoid spreading the MRSA bacteria - upstairs to see her. He sat in his wheelchair, holding Mother's hand in his gloved ones, using her full name as he repeated, "I love you Bettie Jane Gibson George. Rex Hall George loves you."

Mother hadn't opened her eyes or spoken during his visit. Visibly disappointed, Fath called for the nurse to wheel him back to his room. Suddenly Moth opened her eyes, looked straight into his and said in a clear voice, "Fit as a fiddle and ready for love."

That was the last time they saw each other. The day after Fath was released to the assisted-living facility, he fell in his apartment and broke his hip. Thirteen days later, he died in the hospital on May 17, 2007. Moth, in hospice at Primrose, followed her cadet a week later on May 24. They were just a couple weeks short of their 66th wedding anniversary.

Epilogue

The Memorial Service

Rex and Bettie's memorial service two months after their deaths drew old friends and new, relatives from near and far, and acquaintances whose lives they had touched – all eager to tell their Bettie and Rex stories.

The Bethel Baptist senior prayer group, who had visited and prayed for them over the three months they were in and out of hospitals, was there in force, as were several members of the First Baptist Church.

Longtime friend Betty Torres made the trip from Southern California accompanied by her three daughters.

Greta Soso talked about the fun she and Moth always had at the Hillside Café and claimed "Bettie could do the Charleston better than anyone I know." Her husband Mitch, a respected educator, told rambling humorous tales about his friendship with Rex.

Joan Friesen, whom Fath had hired as associate pastor of the First Baptist Church twenty-one years before, when he was the church moderator, happened to be in town from Oregon. She reminisced about his leadership skills and Moth's hospitality.

Margie Donaldson recalled Moth reciting poetry to her sorority group and Sharon Adams, who considered herself an adopted daughter of the Georges, praised them as encouraging and supporting mentors, always available to those in need.

Tim Pelton, their paper boy during the Pares' first four years in Santa Rosa, expressed fond memories of "wonderful, kind, upbeat people who gave generous tips and invited me in for lemonade on a hot day."

One of the next-door twins, Kerry Sullivan Friend, now with a daughter of her own, recalled swinging in the Georges' hammock. Her mother Shirley thanked Rex for having rescued her from a mouse one night when her husband Tim was away.

From the back of the room, a woman stood and identified herself as Susan McGough, our Okinawa playmate from 1947! She said she came representing her family in Ohio and the Williams family – also from Okinawa times – now in Southern California and Washington State. Susan lauded the brave women who took their children to post-war Okinawa where Japanese soldiers were still coming down from the mountains, unaware the war was over. She marveled at the serendipity of three couples from such different backgrounds meeting and becoming lifelong friends. Rex and Bettie were Baptists from Kentucky, Willie and Doris Williams, "nominal Protestants" from Washington and her own parents were Irish Catholics from Brooklyn.

Rex's barber, Laurel Barnett, who had visited him in the hospital to trim his hair, came to the service, as did Noelle Thill from the Alzheimer's Association and Ann Swan, who knew Bettie when they both worked at Exchange Bank in 1980.

Rex's deceased brother's son, Max Jr., his wife Laura and daughter Zhi drove down from Chico, California to pay their respects. And one of Rex's cousins from Kentucky, Bob George and his wife Charmon described Rex and Bettie as "brilliant, witty, wonderful people who taught us how to live and love life."

Gladly

One of the many decisions we had to make after our parents' deaths was what to do with Gladly, the faithful bear who had been with them for 28 years. What a relief when the Pares' younger grandson Alex, a junior in college, said he wanted to adopt the cross-eyed bear. Gladly has now been to college, is in grad school and recently participated in Alex's wedding.

Gladly on the dance floor
at wedding

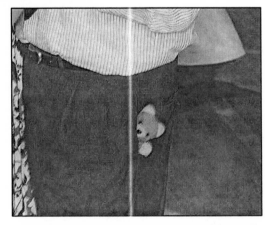

Strange - nobody wanted the "antique" 57-year-old, well-traveled red carpet.

Jenny's Dream

Several months after the memorial service Jenny dreamed she saw the Pares, dressed in everyday house-clothes, carrying boxes of possessions into a very large church - a church as big as a city block. They were both laughing as they approached the entrance. Moth walked through the doors of the church first.

There were many children inside, all laughing hilariously. Moth started laughing too. Then Fath, coming along behind, began to laugh. He laughed so hard he collapsed and was rolling around on the ground outside the church, laughing out of control.

The children then reached for him, took him by his arms and gently pulled him across the threshold into the big church.

Bettie and Rex were still having fun.

Acknowledgements

I am blessed and forever grateful to my parents, Rex and Bettie George, for their contagious love of life and for documenting their adventures. My mother's desire to publish her letters from Okinawa was the initial inspiration for this project.

I could never have done this without the encouragement and contributions of my siblings, Jennifer George Norris and Christopher A. George. They both enriched the story with their own recollections about our home life. Chris, the detail main with an amazing memory, checked facts and provided invaluable technical information about our father's work. Jennifer shared her vivid and frequent dreams.

About a year after my parents' deaths, I attended a workshop on writing family stories. In only four hours, Carol LaChapelle, the instructor and author of "Finding Your Voice, Telling Your Stories," had given me the confidence that I needed to tackle the job of publishing Mother's Okinawa letters, my initial view of this project.

In another writing class sponsored by the Pritzker Military Library, I met Cyndee Schaffer who had just finished a book ("Mollie's War") based on her mother's letters about her WW II experience as a WAC in Europe. Cyndee's success gave me the energy to carry on. Pritzker librarian Teri Embrey and her able assistant Amanda Catanio tracked down several rare books for me.

At another point, when the idea of having to type Mother's letters seemed an insurmountable task, historian Dr. Laura McEnaney, professor at Whittier College, gave me invaluable advice. "Hire a typist, Candace!" She also prodded me to include more historical context.

My Aunt Jean Gibson, widow of Mother's oldest brother, shared her perspective on some touchy family topics. My father's sister (Edyth Annetta Mackey) filled in some holes in the story and shipped me a box of memorabilia that included my father's yearbook from his Basic Training class.

George family niece Nicole George Hill and nephews Ben and Alex George offered memories about their grandparents. Cousins Rosemary Gibson Casey, Mary/Kathy Sturk and Max George, Jr. also had tidbits to add.

Family friends from my parents' early years contributed stories and photographs. Many thanks to Norma and Sid Kepets, Doris Williams Tessier, Betty Torres and Jean Weber Wallace. (Jean passed away in 2011.)

Friends from my past reappeared and offered advice, information and encouragement. They include Susan McGough whom I first encountered in 1947 on the ship to Okinawa and Jim Dunlap from my 9th grade Latin class in Springfield, Massachusetts. Jim even got his wife and their dentist involved.

"Call-it-like-you-see-it" editor extraordinaire, Jill Dearman of Bang the Keys, read an early draft and gave me valuable criticism and warm encouragement. Thanks, Jill, I needed that.

Family, friends and neighbors - too many to name – continually expressed interest and encouragement.

I'm grateful to generous colleagues in the Off-Campus Writers Workshop, the Puerto Vallarta Writers Group and the

ACKNOWLEDGMENTS

Military Writers Society of America. Fellow authors who had never met me in person willingly shared their publishing experiences and advice. Thanks to all of you. You know who you are.

Finally and most important, I want to thank my husband, Neil, for his unfailing support, encouragement, patience, respectful critique and professional editing. If there are any typos or grammatical errors, I can blame them on him.

Bibliography

Alt, Betty Sowers and Bonnie Domrose Stone, *Campfollowing: a history of the military wife*, New York: Praeger, 1991.

Ambrose, Stephen E., *The Wild Blue – The Men and Boys who Flew the B-24s over Germany*, New York: Simon & Schuster, 2001.

A Pocket Guide to Okinawa, Office of Armed Forces Information and Education, Department of Defense, 1961.

Boyne, Walter J., *Beyond the Wild Blue – A History of the U.S. Air Force*, New York: St. Martin's Griffin, 1997.

Bradley, Omar N. and Clay Blair, *A General's Life, an Autobiography by General of the Army Omar N. Bradley*, New York: Simon and Schuster, 1983.

Brett, Jeffrey E., *The 448th Bomb Group (H), Liberators over Germany in World War II*, Atglen, PA: Schiffer Publishing, 2002.

Fussell, Paul, *Wartime – Understanding and Behavior in the Second World War*, New York: Oxford University Press, 1989.

Jenkins, William E., *Okinawa: Isle of Smiles*, New York, Bookman Associates, 1951

Klaw, Barbara, *Camp Follower: The trip out*, TheAtlantic.com, October, 1943.

Klaw, Barbara, *Camp Follower: Job hunt*, TheAtlantic.com, November, 1943.

Klaw, Barbara, *Camp Follower: We girls; sometimes life was wonderful*, TheAtlantic.com, December, 1943.

Keyso, Ruth Ann, *Women of Okinawa – Nine Voices from a Garrison Island*, Cornell Univ. Press, 2000.

Madison, James H., *The Indiana Way – A State History*, Indiana University Press, 1990.

May, Elaine Tyler, *Homeward Bound: American Families in the Cold War Era*, New York: Basic Books, Inc., 1998.

Merritt, Marian Chapple, *Is Like Typhoon: Okinawa and the Far East*, Tokyo, The World News and Publishing Company, circa 1955-56.

Merritt, Captain Robert F., *1ˢᵗ Air Division, Okinawa*, Okinawa, Japan: Staff Public Information Office, 1947.

Okinawa, Pacific Outpost, Washington, D.C.: The National Geographic Society, April 1950: 538-552.

Shacklady, Edward, *Consolidated B-24 Liberator*, Bristol, UK: Cerberus Publishing Limited, 2002.

Shea, Nancy, *The Army Wife*, New York: Harper, 1954.

Shea, Nancy, revised by Anna Perle Smith, *The Air Force Wife*, New York: Harper, 1960.

Steinbeck, John, *Bombs Away – the Story of a Bomber Team*, New York: The Viking Press, 1942.

Wertsch, Mary Edwards, *Military Brats – Legacies of Childhood Inside the Fortress*, New York: Harmony Books of Crown Publishers, 1991.

Yellin, Emily, *Our Mothers' War: American Women at home and at the Front During World War II*, New York: Simon & Schuster, 2004.

Endnotes

Chapter 2

[1] In January 1937 the Ohio River flooded; it was the worst flood in American history. The rains started the second week of the New Year and persisted for over two weeks, depositing and estimated 165 billion tons of rain and occasional snow. On January 18 the river passed flood stage from West Virginia to Cairo, Illinois. There were mass evacuations all along the Ohio and hundreds died.

Water was rationed and many areas were without heat in 20 degree weather; most river-front cities lost electricity. In Cincinnati gas tanks ruptured, and a snapped streetcar wire started a fire. The river was an inferno. Three and a half square miles of the city burned.

As the water continued to rise, martial law was declared in Louisville and the largest relief effort in peacetime history was launched. The Federal government supplied over 7,000 boats for rescue efforts in the 12,721 square miles that were under water.

The Cincinnati suspension bridge was the only bridge that was still open across the Ohio River. In normal times it was 30 feet above the river, but at the height of the flood the bridge was only a couple feet above the water. In Louisville empty whiskey barrels were used to construct an emergency pontoon bridge.

The Red Cross delivered food by boat to people stranded in attics and helped evacuate hundreds of thousands of people. Almost the entire town of Jeffersonville was evacuated and transported by train to higher ground away from the river. The Red Cross also conducted mass inoculations for typhoid.

The flood affected 22 states along the Ohio and Mississippi Rivers, left over 200 dead, 800,000 homeless and more than 8,500 buildings destroyed. (citation: 1993 video tape by Tim Young Productions, Inc.)

Chapter 3

[1] In those days it was common practice to "whisk stillborn babies away from their families to morgues; doctors and nurses pretended nothing happened, mothers were sedated and parents suffered alone." ("A Vast and Sudden Sadness" by Claudia Kalb, Newsweek, February 9, 2009.)

[2] As the war went on, the draft age range expanded. In the beginning, the low end of the age range was 21; later it was lowered to accept boys as young as 18. Boys even younger than 18 – including Rex's brother Max who enlisted in September of 1940 at age 17 ½ before finishing high school - either lied about their age or got their parents' permission in order to join the war effort. The high end of the age range changed also. Rex's 47-year-old, First World War veteran father had to register for the World War Two draft, but was never called up.

[3] "Dinner" was the main meal of the day, eaten mid-day. Evening "supper" was a lighter meal.

Chapter 4

[1] Ironically, the U.S. tolerated anti-Semitism even as we were sending almost 500,000 Jewish American men and women to help fight Nazism in Europe. (B'nai B'rith Magazine, Fall 2011.) And we continued to condone racial discrimination, despite the 2.5 million African Americans who had registered for the draft. (National Archives, African Americans in World War II.)

[2] Madison, James H., *The Indiana Way – A State History*, Indiana University Press, 1990.

[3] From 24-page mimeographed booklet, "Aviation Cadet Manual" 317th AAFFTD, June 1943, Curtis Field, Brady, Texas. The manual contains regulations on everything from laundry to automobiles, local customs, churches and pay.

[4] "The navigator candidate will have a different temperament from pilot and bombardier. He is rather more studious and more a perfectionist ... there is no 'fairly close' in navigation. The duration of the course is fifteen weeks. ... The basic instruments are stars and time to which man-made instruments are applied by the prime instrument of all, the

navigator. ... Of the whole bomber crew, the work of the navigator is the most intellectual. He does not handle any control of the plane. ... He will learn dead-reckoning, instruments, maps and charts, radio navigation. In celestial navigation he will learn the general theory, time and hour angle, instruments, star identification, and astronomical triangles. In meteorology he will learn the theory and principles of weather analysis, the interpretation of weather maps and forecasts. He will learn the meteorology of the ocean, of thunderstorms, tornados, and icing conditions." John Steinbeck, "Bombs Away – the Story of a Bomber Team," (New York: The Viking Press, 1942), pp. 92-109.

[5] "Departure Point Class Book of 44-2," Army Air Force Navigation School, San Marcos, Texas

[6] DO-BUNNY "fell prey to German jet fighters on 25 March 1945", Palm Sunday, on a mission to bomb an underground oil storage depot at Buchen. Jeffrey E. Brett, "The 448th Bomb Group (H), Liberators over Germany in World War II," (Atglen, PA: Schiffer Publishing, 2002), pp. 212-214.

Chapter 5
[1] What the "D" in D-Day means: In Stephen Ambrose's "D-Day, June 6, 1944: The Climatic Battle of World War II," Time magazine reported on June 12 [1944] that "as far as the U.S. Army can determine, the first use of D for Day, H for Hour was in Field Order No. 8, of the First Army, A.E.F., issued on Sept. 20, 1918."

In Paul Dickson's "War Slang," he quotes Robert Hendrickson's "Encyclopedia of Word and Phrase Origins": "When someone wrote to General Eisenhower in 1964 asking for an explanation, his executive assistant Brigadier General Robert Schultz answered: 'General Eisenhower asked me to respond to your letter. Be advised that any amphibious operation has a departed date; therefore the shortened term D-Day is used. ... The invasion of Normandy was not the only D-Day of World War II. Every amphibious assault – including those in the Pacific, in North Africa, and in Sicily and Italy – had its own D-Day."

(*Citations from the web site of the National WWII Museum in New Orleans, www.nationalww2museum.org.)

[2] "The largest [organizational] unit in the Air Force is the Wing and it would correspond roughly to a brigade in the land Army. It is the largest air fighting unit which one commander can efficiently control and directly supervise. The Wing Commander supervises the training and tactical operations of his groups. The next unit under the Wing is the Air Force Group which is usually composed of three squadrons of the same tactical type, that is, fighter or bombardment. Its commander is generally of the rank of Colonel or Lieutenant Colonel and is always an experienced flying officer. A bombardment group is composed of 60 officers and 800 men.

The squadron is the air unit corresponding to the battalion in ground arms. It is commanded by a Major and is the basic flying combat unit. A fighter squadron is composed of 28 officers, 150 men and 28 planes. A bomber squadron has 21 officers, 180 men and 13 planes. ... There are six types of combat squadrons with slightly different organization and personnel strength, dependent upon the type of aircraft they fly – fighter; light, medium and heavy bombers and reconnaissance." John Steinbeck ibid, pp. 172-174.

[3] Norma returned to Cleveland to live with her parents when Sid left for the China-Burma-India theatre with the First Combat Cargo Group. He and his crew supplied British troops in Burma, brought out wounded troops and prisoners, hauled aviation fuel and evacuated American troops who were being overrun by the Japanese. Sid separated from the service in 1946 and returned to Cleveland.

[4] Lee Connor (1921 – 1996), the pilot, was also awarded the DFC for this flight.

[5] Military Regulations: "The Distinguished Flying Cross is awarded for heroism or extraordinary achievement in aerial flight. The act of heroism must be evidenced by voluntary action above and beyond the call of duty. The extraordinary achievement must be so exceptional and outstanding as to clearly set the individual apart from his comrades."

Chapter 6

[1] As troops returned to the States after WW II, the number of polio cases in the U.S. increased dramatically and the early 1950s brought epidemics, with 58,000 cases reported in 1952. Researchers theorized

that troops stationed in locations with primitive sanitation may have carried the virus back with them.

In April 1955 the news of successful trials using a vaccine developed by Jonas Salk caused nationwide celebration, and mass immunization started in 1957. By 1996 there were fewer than 10 polio cases a year reported in the U.S.

The virus still exists in poorer parts of the world such as Africa and Asia, and in 2000 there was an outbreak reported in Haiti and the Dominican Republic. (Sources: Wikipedia and Edmund Sass, Ed.D. at www.cloudnet.com/~edrbsass/poliohistory.htm .)

[2] Rex's father Hall George was a government war goods procurement inspector. His territory was the Midwest and the South; he was away from home for weeks - even months - at a time. Rex's younger brother, Max, was stationed in the Marshall Islands in the Pacific during the war.

[3] Rex had been taking pictures and developing his own film since early high school days. Good quality photographic paper was scarce during the war.

[4] General of the Army, Omar N. Bradley and Clay Blair, "A General's Life, An Autobiography," (New York: Simon and Schuster, 1983), p.276.

[5] General Bradley had specified that no bombs larger than 100 pounds be used in order to avoid heavy cratering where American ground troops would be advancing. Bradley, ibid, p.277.

[6] Bradley, ibid, p.282.

[7] This mission on September 18, 1944 was known as "Market Garden" and was the subject of the movie "A Bridge Too Far" and a segment in the television series "Band of Brothers".

Chapter 7
[1] Sugar was the longest war-time rationed food item. It was the first to be rationed in May 1942 and sugar rationing didn't end until June, 1947.

Chapter 8

[1] Rex had more than enough service points to have taken his family to Okinawa immediately, had Jennifer been at least 6 months old when he was transferred. Points were awarded for months of service, overseas service, number of war missions, awards such as the Distinguished Flying Cross and number of children.

Chapter 9

[1] The ship was built in Richmond, California and launched in late 1944. It had been used during the war to move troops around the Pacific, Australia and India.

[2] The B-4 bag was a hanging bag that folded to 16 X 15 X 25 inches. It was designed for Army Air Corps flyers in WW II and held a fresh uniform and storage pockets for a complete change of clothes.

[3] Jimmy, Bettie's oldest brother who fought in the South Pacific during the war. (Howard James Gibson (1921 – 1987)

Chapter 10

[1] Okinawan housemaids earned approximately $5-$10 per month. Overseas military families were expected to employ local workers, not only to help the economy of the host country, but also to expose them to the American way of life. Military dependents were considered "unofficial" ambassadors for the U.S.

[2] Quonsets, named after Quonset Point, Rhode Island where they were first manufactured, were used extensively during WW II because they could be shipped and assembled easily. After the war they were used as inexpensive shelter for college students, families, farms and small businesses.

[3] Bettie's dependent allotment checks were sent directly to her mother to manage and to use for purchases that Bettie requested. Bettie and Rex also sent home money orders from what they were able to save from Rex's paycheck.

[4] "Lady in the Dark", 1941 Broadway musical, book by Moss Hart, music by Kurt Weill, and lyrics by Ira Gershwin. Bettie often sang a

somewhat altered version of the song, "The Saga of Jenny", to Jennifer: "Poor Jenny, bright as a penny, her equal would be hard to find. Deserved a bed of roses, but history discloses that she couldn't make up her mind."

[5] Opera Creams are an incredibly rich chocolate-coated vanilla fondant made in the greater Cincinnati area.

Chapter 11

[1] These beaches are opposite each other on the narrowest part of the island. Most of the island north of here was off limits due to unexploded ordnance and the possibility that there still might be hostiles hiding in the rugged terrain.

[2] At this point Germany was the only other country where the military allowed dependents. Rex was stationed in Germany twenty-one years later in 1968.

Chapter 12

[1] A typhoon is a tropical cyclone over the northwest Pacific Ocean, west of the International Date Line. During WW II, Pacific tropical cyclones were informally given women's names by US Army Air Corps and Navy meteorologists; they often named the storms for their girlfriends or wives back home. In 1953 the US Weather Bureau began using women's names for hurricanes and in 1979 started using both female and male names.

[2] Bananas and other imports had been scarce during the war when commercial ships were re-purposed for transporting war-related goods.

[3] A relocation camp was located in Ishikawa; many of the Okinawans who worked on base lived there.

Chapter 13

[1] The leper colony was approximately 50 miles north on a small island off Okinawa. The more mountainous northern part of the island was "off limits," access forbidden to military personnel for security reasons. "Off limits" was only a few miles north of our housing area.

[2] Bettie spells the name of her second maid several ways. The correct spelling is most likely Tomiko or Tomoko. "Ko" means child; "Tomi" is wealthy/abundance and "Tomo" is wisdom or friend. Ironically, the name of the maid fired for stealing was Nobuko which means faithful or trustworthy.

Chapter 14

[1] In 1942 the United States stopped production on all cars as automobile manufacturers retooled to produce airplanes and other war-related equipment. On October 26, 1945 Ford was the first to introduce new cars to the pent-up American market. Within days, almost half a million orders were placed.

[2] Roy still recalled this dinner in 1991 when he wrote, "I remember once very shortly after I arrived on Okinawa in early 1948, Rex invited me over to their quarters for dinner. This was a thrill for me to get a home cooked meal! And it was a bit of a burden for Rex because he had to provide me with transportation from my BOQ - a Quonset hut at the head of Habu Holler - to his quarters and back again after dinner. Bettie had ham for dinner that night – one of my favorites."

Chapter 15

[1] Smokey Hill Air Force Base was re-named Schilling Air Force Base in 1957.

[2] Lona later said that Pillsbury had changed the name of her recipe from its original "Lona Belleman Gibson's Black Walnut Spice Cake." "The recipe is strictly Pennsylvania Dutch – not Dixie," she said. "My ancestors – great, great grandparents – came from Berks County, Pennsylvania and settled on Mad River Road south of Dayton, Ohio."

[3] For the 60th Bake-Off in 2010, eight of the 100 finalists were men; the grand prize was $1,000,000.

Chapter 16

[1] In my attempts to verify this event, I learned that The Alley had been producing plays since 1947. When we attended in 1952 it was a 230-seat theatre in the round, located on Berry Avenue in an abandoned fan factory. That was a breakthrough year for The Alley. The New York

Times theatre critic Brooks Atkinson had ventured out from Broadway and given a big round of applause to this community theatre, where tickets sold for $1.80. Atkinson concluded his March 9 article with "… the future of the theatre in America is in the hands of small, local institutions like those discussed here today. They are close to the people who go to the theatre."

My phone call to gracious Tom O'Dell, "the only person who might know," confirmed that The Alley did have a children's program in 1952. Mr. O'Dell, however, couldn't identify the play we might have seen because programs weren't usually printed for children's productions.

To learn more about The Alley Theatre's history and its visionary founder Nina Vance go to www.alleytheatre.org.

Chapter 17
[1] I haven't been able to identify the source of that reference, although a George Adolphus appears in a rhyme from one of our favorite books, "Goops and How to Be Them" by Gelett Burgess, 1900.

[2] Some 40 years later, my husband Neil tracked down the source of Center Alley and bought me a copy of Harold L. Chase's "Anguish Languish," published by Prentice-Hall in 1956. Apparently, months before publication of the book, Arthur Godfrey had read another one of the fairy tales, "Ladle Rat Rotten Hut" (Little Red Riding Hood) to his radio audience, eliciting thousands of fan letters. The stories must be read aloud to be fully appreciated.

Chapter 18
[1] "A Treasury of the Familiar, Volumes I and II", edited by Ralph L. Woods, MacMillan Company, New York, 1942.

[2] "Walt Disney's Surprise Package, A Giant Golden Book," Simon and Schuster, New York, 1944.

[3] The MTA was the Metropolitan Transit Authority which offered above ground trains and buses as well as the nation's oldest subway system. It was the predecessor of the current MBTA, Massachusetts Bay Transit Authority. Known as the "T", it is the nation's oldest mass transit system, serving 78 communities in Eastern Massachusetts.

Chapter 19

[1] Ann Polumbus, letter dated June 4, 2007, upon learning of Bettie's death.

[2] Angel Falls' main perpendicular drop is 2,648 feet in free fall; coupled with a lower drop of 564 feet, the official total height is 3,212 feet. The falls is two and a half times higher than the Empire State Building and well over 15 times higher than Niagara Falls.

[3] Glacier-covered Pico Bolivar is the highest at 16,423 feet above sea level.

Chapter 20

[1] Flak and Frances McDuffie, retired Air force friends.

[2] "Far Away Places" written by Canadian Alex Charles Kramer and recorded by several bands and singers, including Ray Conniff and his orchestra, Perry Como and Margaret Whiting. It was the number two hit for Bing Crosby in 1949. Kramer and his wife/professional partner were inducted into the Songwriters Hall of Fame in 1982.

Chapter 21

[1] Several studies cited in "Military Brats" by Mary Edwards Wertsch point to a high incidence of alcoholism in the military. A 1975 report suggested "the rate of alcoholism in the military was three times that of the civilian population," and a May 1989 study concluded that "the percentage of heavy drinkers in the military is nearly twice that of the comparable civilian population." Wertsch's interviews with military brats revealed that "just over half had at least one alcoholic parent."

Wertsch places much of the blame for this "shockingly high" rate of alcohol abuse on the Department of Defense (DOD) for selling tax-free alcohol on base at heavily discounted prices and for ignoring – sometimes even promoting – heavy drinking. She writes that "drinking is so much a part of the culture that it has almost been a requirement."

Women interviewed for her book "recalled being told by their husbands and by other wives that during social functions they should hold a drink in their hands, even if they never touched it." Adult children told stories of their fathers coming home drunk from the "dreaded Friday night Happy Hour at the Officers Club." Mary

---

Edwards Wertsch, "Military Brats – Legacies of Childhood Inside the Fortress," (New York: Harmony Books of Crown Publishers, 1991)

Chapter 22

[1] One of Moth's contest strategies was to focus on locally sponsored sweepstake drawings that allowed multiple entries. She spent hours collecting and filling out entry blanks, and folding them in intricate ways so that they took up more space in the collection box. Fath then drove her to all the local shops that were sponsoring the contest, waiting in the car while she raced in to deposit a fistful of folded entries. I think she had as much fun entering the contests as she did winning them.

Chapter 23

[1] The MMSE – Mini-Mental State Exam – is a quick diagnostic tool for dementia that tests the individual's ability to understand, remember, communicate and think. It includes questions about day, date, season and location. The patient is asked to spell a word backwards, repeat the phrase "no ifs, ands, or buts," identify a common object such as a ballpoint pen, and remember and repeat at the end of the interview a string of three unrelated words, such as "apple, penny, table."

Chapter 24

[1] While verifying the spelling of Merthiolate (Microsoft Word didn't recognize any of my attempts.) I discovered that Merthiolate contains mercury which kills many disease-causing microbes but can be poisonous and is no longer recommended as a topical antiseptic.

Chapter 25

[1] Research by speech pathology professor Michelle S. Bourgeois of Ohio State University.

Chapter 26

[1] Methicillin-Resistant Staphylococcus Aureus – MRSA –requires that the patient be quarantined to avoid the spread of the bacteria to other patients.

CPSIA information can be obtained at www.ICGtesting.com
Printed in the USA
LVOW121709270912

300607LV00007B/113/P

9 781937 763626